Praise for *The Equality Machine*

"A timely book on how we can create technologies that fight bias instead of intensifying it. Orly Lobel offers a compelling vision for a digital future that's fairer to all of us."

—ADAM GRANT, #1 *New York Times*–bestselling author
of *Think Again* and host of the TED podcast *WorkLife*

"What if technology could help? Two decades ago, that idea seemed obvious. Today, it seems impossible. But in this beautifully written and wide-ranging work, Lobel shows how a smart architecting of our technical environment can make us better humans, in a healthier environment. This is critical thinking and insight when—and where—we need it most."

—LAWRENCE LESSIG, Roy L. Furman Professor of Law
and Leadership, Harvard University

"With great computing power comes great responsibility. *The Equality Machine* shows how we can direct AI for good and create a society in which our lives are not limited by gender, race, sexuality, age, geography, or ability. As always, Lobel gives us a crystal-clear, front-row seat to our evolving digital realities. A must-read!"

—JONAH BERGER, Wharton School, University of Pennsylvania,
and author of *The Catalyst* and *Contagious*

"Artificial intelligence in particular and technology in general are changing almost every aspect of the human experience. Can smarter and smarter machines make life better and better—and not just for the few and the privileged, but for everyone? Lobel offers a compelling, inspiring, and actionable argument that the answer is yes."

—ANGELA DUCKWORTH, University of Pennsylvania,
chief scientist, the Character Labor, and author of *Grit*

"Who should we believe? The glass-half-full people who tell us that AI is going to bring about the next stage of human development, or the glass-half-empty people who tell us that this will be the end of all that is good about humanity? What Lobel shows in *The Equality Machine* is that the answer is up to us. We can implement AI in ways that deepen our challenges, and we can implement this technology in ways that both fix some of our existing problems and promote our human agenda."

—DAN ARIELY, author of *Predictably Irrational*

"*The Equality Machine* offers a hard-headed yet hopeful analysis of how digitization and artificial intelligence can reduce discrimination and promote opportunity. By rejecting both utopian dreams and dystopian nightmares, Lobel shows that it's up to us to enlist these new technologies as forces for good and engines for progressive values. One of our sharpest legal minds has produced an utterly compelling book."

—DANIEL H. PINK, #1 *New York Times*–bestselling author
of *The Power of Regret*, *When*, and *Drive*

"With rich and engaging examples, Lobel brings together the too-often siloed debates over fears and hopes about artificial intelligence. With real, human intelligence, she identifies workable guards against gender and racial biases. She also highlights profound moral, political, and technical challenges worth both immediate and long-term attention."

—MARTHA MINOW, 300th Anniversary University Professor,
dean emeritus, and director, Berkman Klein Center
for Internet and Society, Harvard University

"*The Equality Machine* is beautifully written, brimming with enthusiasm and can-do spirit. Lobel makes a compelling argument that AI can help solve some of our most important social problems, ranging from discrimination to human trafficking. Deeply aware of technology's virtues and limits, Lobel offers singular insights for anyone interested in technology and safety."

—FRANK PASQUALE, law professor
and author of *The Black Box Society*

"Most discussions of AI and equality today focus on the negative: how AI systems pose risks of algorithmic bias and discrimination. Without being a tech apologist, Lobel gives us a much-needed dose of the positive: how AI can advance our aspirations for greater equality at work, in healthcare, at home, in our language and imagery, and in our relationships. *The Equality Machine* will take you on a tour of what people can build when aspiring to use the power of AI to make the world a more equal place. Read it and get inspired to join them."

—GILLIAN HADFIELD, director,
Schwartz Reisman Institute for Technologyand Society,
University of Toronto, and senior policy adviser, OpenAI

"Lobel offers a contrarian and original view: that technology can be a foundation for equality and inclusion rather than a source of bias and inequality. Read this book to find out why and how."

—OREN ETZIONI, CEO, Allen Institute for Artificial Intelligence

"With this incisive and engaging book, Lobel invites academics, nonprofit leaders, investors, business leaders, and policymakers to use data to solve the world's most pressing problems, being neither cavalier nor afraid."

—JONATHAN ZITTRAIN, faculty director,
Berkman Klein Center for Internet and Society,
Harvard University, and author of *The Future of the Internet*

"Finally, a bold, positive, and forward-thinking approach to the challenges we face with automated technology."

—KATE DARLING, MIT Media Lab and
author of *The New Breed: What Our History
with Animals Reveals About Our Future with Robots*

THE
EQUALITY
MACHINE

THE EQUALITY MACHINE

Harnessing Digital Technology
for a Brighter, More Inclusive Future

ORLY LOBEL

PUBLICAFFAIRS
New York

PublicAffairs
Hachette Book Group
1290 Avenue of the Americas, New York, NY 10104
www.publicaffairsbooks.com
@Public_Affairs

Printed in the United States of America

First Edition: October 2022

Published by PublicAffairs, an imprint of Perseus Books, LLC, a subsidiary of Hachette Book Group, Inc. The PublicAffairs name and logo is a trademark of the Hachette Book Group.

The Hachette Speakers Bureau provides a wide range of authors for speaking events. To find out more, go to www.hachettespeakersbureau.com or call (866) 376-6591.

The publisher is not responsible for websites (or their content) that are not owned by the publisher.

Print book interior design by Jeff Williams.

Library of Congress Cataloging-in-Publication Data

Names: Lobel, Orly, author.
Title: The equality machine : harnessing digital technology for a brighter, more inclusive future / Orly Lobel.
Description: New York : PublicAffairs, 2022. | Includes bibliographical references and index. | Identifiers: LCCN 2022013119 | ISBN 9781541774759 (hardcover) | ISBN 9781541774735 (ebook)
Subjects: LCSH: Diversity in the workplace. | Equality. | Multiculturalism. | Information society.
Classification: LCC HF5549.5.M5 L59 2022 | DDC 658.3008—dc23/eng/20220728
LC record available at https://lccn.loc.gov/2022013119

ISBNs: 9781541774759 (hardcover), 9781541774735 (ebook)

LSC-C

Printing 1, 2022

To Danielle, Elinor, and Natalie—
keep challenging, changing, and charting better worlds

And to On,
love of my life and fellow traveler—keep flying high

Yet, in spite of these spectacular strides in science and technology, and still unlimited ones to come, something basic is missing. There is a sort of poverty of the spirit which stands in glaring contrast to our scientific and technological abundance. The richer we have become materially, the poorer we have become morally and spiritually. We have learned to fly the air like birds and swim the sea like fish, but we have not learned the simple art of living together as brothers.

—MARTIN LUTHER KING JR.

I was taught that the way of progress was neither swift nor easy.

—MARIE CURIE

Contents

Contents

V. HEART

VI. SOUL

Introduction

I have three girls; the middle one is bionic. When she was thirteen, Elinor was diagnosed with type 1 diabetes. Today she wears the first-ever smart insulin pump. The pump is a smart machine because it makes autonomous decisions and learns and improves based on the information it receives from a glucose sensor also connected to her body. These wearable digital devices—the pump and the sensor—communicate with each other and help keep Elinor healthy. She, her older sister Danielle, her school nurse, my husband, and I all have an app on our smartphones that tracks the digital signals on Elinor's blood sugar levels in real time. Whether you—like my bionic daughter—wear a smart device that keeps you alive, or, like most of us, simply use your smartphone, and perhaps your smart watch, as vital accessories, we are all moving toward an ever more digital coexistence with machines that shapes every aspect of our lives.

Technology can be lifesaving; it can help us be healthier, safer, and more equal. And yet, technology also brings peril. Artificial intelligence (AI), automation, and big data can replicate and exacerbate ongoing injustices. The examples of technology failures are numerous. From screening job candidates to deciding whom to release on bail, automated decisions have too often caused harm, making decisions that mirror long-standing societal prejudices. Robotics design frequently reflects culture-specific values and gendered norms. Big

Tech controls data and uses it in ways that are opaque yet impactful on our behaviors. And Silicon Valley, the epicenter of innovation, is notoriously dominated by homogeneous leaders who do not reflect our global community. These problems are real and immense.

The reality is that the train has left the station. AI is here to stay. AI is here to expand. Now we find ourselves at a critical junction. Do we reject technology that has failed us, or do we direct tomorrow's technologies for the good of our society? Do we merely continue pointing out the risks and flaws, or do we envision a brighter path forward? The idea behind this book is to ignite a deeply informed and constructive conversation about the path toward equality and empowerment in the digital era. I hope to move the debates forward, beyond the often-futile rifts of recent years. We need to boost technology's potential as a positive force—a purpose that is profoundly personal to me. I am quite certain that you will find it personal to you too.

Before I became an attorney and law professor, I served as an intelligence commander in the Israeli military. Those were the early days of *intranets*, before the internet became part of civilian life. My job was to strategically evaluate data pertaining to national security risks, putting together a fuller picture of current and future threats, relying on an increasingly dense digital network of knowledge. I learned to anticipate the ways that data can be misleading. I witnessed firsthand technology's potential for harm. But I also saw its ability to level unequal playing fields and deliver swift justice. Internally, within my unit, I saw how the network of computers became a great democratizer for my fellow female soldiers and me. With a focus on equitable assessment of female and male soldiers, we developed a system of transparency using the intranet to keep a digital record of the contributions of different analysts such that female commanders began to receive more credit for our insights and hard work. This was in the mid-nineties, and many women from my unit went on to become technology and policy leaders in academia, government, and industry. I studied law and economics first at Tel Aviv University and then at Harvard, and now, as a professor and policy expert, I research how law and technology can be directed to tackle our most difficult social challenges.

When I was my eldest daughter's age and planning for my upcoming military service, women were excluded from combat positions. I ended up marrying an F-16 pilot rather than becoming a fighter pilot myself. After my military service, I clerked on the Israeli Supreme Court, drafting court decisions that ultimately held such gender restrictions unconstitutional. My fighter pilot husband, University of California San Diego professor On Amir, who is now a behavioral economist, became my frequent co-author. Together, we research human bias and the potential of design and policy to bring about change. We each consult major tech platforms and public regulators on how to make technology ethical, safer, and more equitable. We also rely on technology to help us raise our three daughters and to support our work-life balance. Tracing the arc of our lives, we see how machines have transformed who we are and how we live in a fundamental way. How we work and learn, how we interact and play, how we relate to others and to ourselves—all are being shaped and reshaped by technology. Every day, we interact with machines that are getting smarter, faster, and more intimately familiar with us.

When Tech Gives Us Lemons

Equality is today's foremost moral imperative. Unfortunately, in our quest to innovate rapidly, technology has too often contributed to greater inequalities. But technological advances can be—and often are—in service of inclusion and empowerment; it's all about making deliberate choices. We constantly hear horror stories about technology gone wrong, biased AI, and a looming dystopian human-machine future. Bestsellers with titles like *Weapons of Math Destruction, Algorithms of Oppression, Automating Inequality, Technically Wrong, Surveillance Capitalism*, and *Invisible Women: Data Bias in a World Designed for Men* all sound the alarm about how new technology can diminish, exclude, and perpetuate inequality. And they aren't wrong. As we shall see, the reasons for technological inequities are varied, ranging from bad data fed into systems by engineers to autonomous learning and replication by machines of our existing societal disparities to unethical corporate decisions and biased design choices.

Certainly, technology failures do present imminent dangers and must be addressed. Yet problems precede progress—and progress supersedes perfection. How can we integrate AI into our social systems in ways that promote fairness and equal access? Can we design robots that challenge gender and racial stereotypes? Can we use machines in decision-making processes where we humans have been notoriously flawed and discriminatory? Can we automate traditional "women's work," including domestic and caregiving work? Can we direct automation for greater inclusion and more diverse participation in our labor markets and political lives? And how can we make our human energies and labor more valuable as automated production increasingly becomes our reality?

I believe that every aspect of our lives—work, family, school, sex, art, and play—can be improved by confronting rather than shying away from the challenges of new technologies and by identifying and promoting the best choices for a new era of machine-human coexistence. My two decades of research have taught me the importance of being critical but constructive. We are rebuilding our home structures and economies, schooling, healthcare, and employment systems, romantic and familial relationships, and marketplaces and political forums. As we move metaphorically in these pages through the body parts of machines—mind, body, senses, heart, and soul—my hope is that you too will become cautiously optimistic and smartly constructive about where we are heading.

Our starting point: despite its risks and flaws, digitization can and must become a powerful force for societal good—for fairness, inclusion, economic growth, expanded opportunities, innovation, and, above all else, equality. AI can be a force for debiasing, and it can provide early detection of discrimination and abuse. AI, robotics, and digital platforms can forge a path toward a better, more diverse, and empowering future in innumerable ways: from closing pay gaps to exposing and correcting biases in hiring and marketing; from keeping a digital record of workplace harassment to diversifying the cultural images we see online; from increasing privacy and safety to upending traditional gender roles and rejecting racial stereotypes; from subverting closed-minded "marriage markets" to broadening our sexual experiences; from supporting eldercare to opening up spaces and opportunities no matter one's ability or geography. Through the wise and forward-looking implementation of tomorrow's technologies, we can envision a society in which our lives are not limited by gender, race, sexuality, age, geography, or ability. But equality will not come without deliberate choices, oversight, and direction. The time is now to put skin in the game and develop a robust vision of what we can achieve.

A Blueprint for Building an Equality Machine

We've always had an ambivalent relationship with machines, and in particular with robots, seeing them as both subservient and supreme, facilitative and fearsome. In reality, with any technological advancement, equality must be prioritized, claimed, and ensured. My goal throughout this book is to develop practical tools and rules alongside broad principles for an inspiring vision of our digital future that moves the needle on equality. In itself, technology is value neutral. And yet, depending on its function and purpose, technology can either eradicate or perpetuate inequalities. Let's identify here at the outset several guiding principles:

To embrace digitization as a force for societal good, we don't need to find it perfect. We only need to be convinced of its potential and ability to do better than our current systems. Human decision-making is inherently limited, flawed, and biased. We should strive to grasp AI's comparative advantages as well as its comparative limits. A progressive system is one that takes the best qualities of our respective decision-making capabilities—human and machine—and presents them as a better-than-before hybrid model. Moreover, we need to compare the net gains and losses from imperfect systems. The inquiry should be comparative and relative, not absolute. The goal should be progress, not perfection.

We should see mistakes as opportunities to learn and redouble our efforts to correct them. Rather than sensationalize stories about technology failures, we should focus on how technology can do better. Leaders in the fields of AI, robotics, and digitization are making amazing leaps in research and technological innovation all the time, but wins are never without losses, and glitches and missteps will always cause alarm. Yet even during some of our darkest times (and perhaps especially so)—recently, the Covid-19 pandemic and the social upheavals of 2020, with so many confined to their homes or protesting in the streets against brutality and discrimination—we saw how technological advancements served as a positive force. Technology connected us during isolation, provided care and interaction for the elderly and the sick, assisted the transition to remote work, helped mobilize civil rights activism, kept live records of systemic abuse by law enforcement and private corporations, and made those records known. The mobile capture and widespread social media dissemination of the video of George Floyd's murder at the hands of a Minnesota police officer are but one example. Data mining also helped policymakers and scientists assess risks, monitor compliance with shelter-in-place ordinances, and accelerate the race for mass Covid-19 vaccination and herd immunity. When the *application* of technology fails—as with racially biased facial recognition algorithms, for instance—these failures can be better exposed than past wrongs that were hidden from sight and not recorded. And failures can often be better corrected than our human fallibilities.

We can scale success and learn from experimentation. Throughout the book, we will uncover so much to celebrate: tech communities—in research, business, and the public sector—developing algorithms that detect bias and discrimination in everyday workplace and social settings; software designed to help employers close pay gaps; bots that detect early signs of a propensity to harass and allow victims to report harassment anonymously; digital platforms transforming the images used in media, politics, and marketing to foster more diverse and empowering representations of women and people of color; a lively feminist debate on whether and how sex bots can mitigate trafficking and sex crimes and liberate desire and difference; digital health data collection and analysis that can reverse thousands of years of biased research; and so much more. Even oft-maligned social media platforms and mass digital media offer opportunities for broader communication and greater inclusiveness. Now more than ever before, our society needs meaningful, systemic change. The way forward is to incentivize experimentation, deploy technological advancements for societal goals, selectively keep humans in the loop, continuously audit, and scale successes through deliberate—and often public—choices.

__The goal of equality should be embedded in every digital advancement.__ Inherent in the world of machine learning is the ability to learn and improve, but we need to be clear-eyed and articulate about what improvement means. We need to consider the feedback loops between technology and society. Algorithms will replicate past wrongs unless we explicitly direct them not to. This also means we need to separate technological *capability* from its *function* and actively envision redirecting the original purposes of innovations. We can learn to flip the scripts of what technology represents and who it serves, and instead imagine uses and capabilities that serve the greater good and the goals of equality and inclusion. We can also identify how competing goals—such as accuracy and fairness, equality and privacy, and efficiency and inclusion—become win-win goals, overall gains rather than zero-sum choices, when enhanced by technology and ongoing learning. As new digital technologies are introduced in every aspect of our lives, rather than simply bemoaning past wrongs and decrying the risks of replicating them, we need to actively select uses of technology that empower and build a better society.

__We should count what matters.__ We can leverage digital technology to collect the right data, missing data, alternative data, and complete data, and shed new light on age-old problems. We measure what we care about. We collect data about what is important to us. Far more than our human capacities, the computing power of machines today can mine through unprecedented amounts of data and extract patterns about our world. Big data, the massive data sets that we now have computing capabilities to store and analyze—and in particular, information about us humans that can identify and quantify social, psychological, economic, and health trends—can offer highly granular information about the sources of discrimination and disparity along with solutions and avenues to progress. The capacity to sort and mine through immense amounts of data enables algorithms to educate us about inequality. But addressing inequality starts with better data. Empowerment relies on tracking information that matters.

For example, the Bread for the World Institute recently issued a report showing that 92 percent of gender-specific economic data is missing from Africa. We are not measuring the struggles of those who are most in need. Millions remain in the shadows. But we can tackle the problem today thanks to technology, and the institute is working with volunteer coders, data scientists, statisticians, and graphic designers to begin to systematically collect what matters—to materialize the missing data and bring problems like these to light. Supreme Court Justice Louis Brandeis famously said that sunlight is the best of disinfectants, and electric light the most efficient policeman. To prevent discrimination, we need to shed light on it. To debias, we need bias detection. To make sure history is not repeated, we need to study it. If Justice Brandeis were alive today, he might say that data done right is the best of disinfectants, and digital illumination the most powerful social equalizer.

We must understand technology as a public good. The immense amounts of data we are now collecting, as well as the technological leaps that are enabled by this data, should be understood as a public good. AI is improving all the time by gobbling up endless information tied to our autonomous selves, from health and genetics to images, voice, and cognition—every aspect of our behavior. This also means that we should challenge the reality of just a few corporations dominating and controlling the data extracted and the algorithms fed by that data. In my work on intellectual property and human capital, I have shown that knowledge and innovation are shared resources, developed through shared multigenerational contributions, and their benefits should also be shared rather than monopolized. The free spread of ideas, to paraphrase Thomas Jefferson, like the air we breathe, has been the moral and natural way humanity has seen progress over the globe. When it comes to patents, copyright, and trade secrets, there are fierce battles and vibrant debates about the right lines we should draw in what is owned and what is part of the public domain. These fundamental questions about the costs and benefits of controlling knowledge and the distributional effects of intellectual property and antitrust regimes must now be worked out with regard to big data and AI capabilities. Just like information, knowledge, innovation, and our talent pools more generally, AI and data should be understood as a *commons*—a shared resource capable of addressing some of the world's toughest problems: global health and pandemics, world hunger, environmental sustainability and climate change, and poverty and inequality. We should move toward more open-source big data as well as public initiatives to crowdsource data collection for public goals. And we need to incentivize more competition and less concentration in the development and use of new technologies. Competition lowers costs and fuels choice, customizable options, and user-driven preferences.

We can create AI that challenges stereotypes. We need to build machines and design robots that subvert long-standing constructions of identity. Robots, digital assistants, chatbots, GPS systems, apps, and many more of the machines we build are receiving human names, voices, personalities, and shapes—and also quite frequently gender and ethnicity. The word *robot* comes from the Czech word for "slave"; Czech playwright Karel Čapek coined it from the word *robota*, which means slave or forced labor. His play *Rossumovi Univerzální Roboti* (Rossum's Universal Robots), which premiered in Prague in 1921, described a factory of robots, or artificial slaves, that were mass-produced for global export. In 1924, the play was produced in Tokyo for Japanese audiences with the new title *Jinzo Ningen* (Artificial Human). From slaves to artificial humans, robots designed to look and behave like humans—*androids*—are still in their infancy, and popular culture is seduced by a fantasy of robots that are just like us. We need to examine the reasons for designing robots that look human and sentient—appearing to be able to sense, perceive, and mimic human behavior and emotions. Developers can and should create more neutral virtual assistants. But we can also experiment with the design of robots—care robots, sex robots, machines that perform work at home and at the office—with the specific goals of challenging stereotypes and conventional assumptions. We can adopt an active approach to design that challenges the status quo and questions traditional scripts. We need to examine when and why robots should convey human characteristics, when they can receive more fluid and ambiguous forms, and how they can be carefully integrated into the fabric of the family and society to foster connectivity, space, and equality.

Policy can incentivize, leverage, and oversee technology. Especially when communities are unequal and rifts pervasive, shifting the focus from traditional anti-discrimination litigation and legislation to improved technology presents strategic advantages. For example, alerting a company to the existence of pay inequities discovered through software analysis is less accusatory than uncovering intentional discrimination by a single decision-maker. Technology can also ensure that corrections are systemic rather than a patchwork of one-shot fixes. For example, a policy reform that requires dynamic, up-to-date electronic pay scale transparency can create far more systemic, forward-looking, and sustainable change than a class-action lawsuit, which merely examines and corrects past wrongs. Likewise, using bots to protect online sexual privacy and autonomy is faster and more proactive than waiting for platform users to file a complaint. AI can detect discrimination in cheaper, more accurate, more quantifiable, and more fine-tuned ways than broad-brush rules, complaints, and after-the-fact litigation. But in concert, law and policy have a key role to play in regulating technology in ways that leverage these comparative advantages and maintain an ongoing public oversight role. Policy can require built-in monitoring, reporting, and accountability across the development, design, and deployment stages of new technology.

We must make choices in a deliberate and inclusive way. Beyond the cultures of all-boy networks, hackers, geeks, nerd-kings, and bros—exclusive homogenous clubs that hitherto have spearheaded AI's development—lie the stories of diverse leaders who are changing the face of the technology communities. Throughout the book, we will celebrate diversity at the forefront of AI research, business, and policy, with the hope that celebration will inspire more to join the ranks. We need to encourage diverse talent to enter the field early and deliberately. We need better policies that create inclusive tech environments. And diversity is intertwined with multidisciplinary inquiry: technology should be thought of not as the narrow job of computer scientists and engineers, but rather as the work of psychologists, ethicists, policymakers, economists, historians, artists, anthropologists, sociologists, life scientists, and more. In the following chapters, we'll travel from California to Tokyo, New York to London, Seoul to Amsterdam, and beyond, meeting roboticists, ethicists, activists, policymakers, parents, educators, and business leaders. We will uncover a clear, hopeful, and progressive message on how to harness tomorrow's technologies to untangle and counterbalance centuries of inequality.

My aim is not to provide an exhaustive list of technologies or principles for building an equality machine. We are delving into fields so rich and dynamic that we need to pace ourselves while also racing ahead with our collective imagination. As we attempt to make machines more like humans, we are learning more and more about what it is that makes us *us*. This book is about psychology as much as it is about technology, about morality as much as about policy; it's about history and the future, about what humanity teaches us about machines, and what machines teach us about ourselves. As we uncover the inequitable dimensions of digital existence, we are also learning about our most fundamental principles, beliefs, values, and desires—broadly as a society and more narrowly as individual human beings.

Technology has for centuries reconfigured identities and societies, but never has this reconfiguration been so rapid and acute as in our times. The idea of smart machines being introduced into every aspect of our lives is both seductive and terrifying. With great computing power comes great responsibility. At stake is no less than our humanity. Each chapter of this book is a window to reveal life as it is and as it can be. Through the lenses of fairness and equality, gender and identity, power and progress, let us envision the human-bot revolution in the coming years in a way that challenges us to look at ourselves anew. Digitization and automation are here to stay, and engaging with all they entail by proposing positive uses, progressive improvements, creative solutions, and systemic safeguards is the way forward.

I
A FORCE FOR GOOD

CHAPTER 1

Why We Need an Equality Machine

There is always a light, if only we're brave enough to see it. If only we're brave enough to be it.

—AMANDA GORMAN,
National Youth Poet Laureate, 2021

The quest for equality is a microcosm of all the struggles of humanity. We care about fairness, welfare, justice, democracy, safety, well-being, happiness, freedom, our planet. Each of these profound values itself engenders internal tensions and sustains multiple meanings, as does the notion of equality. Yet, unequivocally, the single most important thing that we can do to bring progress on all of these fronts is to tackle the inequities that pervade our worlds, and in so doing empower the more vulnerable. It is a moral imperative—lifesaving, planet saving, and dignity saving all at once. Karl Marx wrote that the power relations between men and women are a window into "the entire level of development of mankind." In 1846, together with his frequent collaborator Friedrich Engels, Marx reasoned that the first division of labor is that between man and woman, and the first class oppression is that of the female sex by the male. Improving gender equality goes hand in hand with tackling racial, social, and economic inequities, and it liberates all to truly choose and shape their identities. In many of the social problems we tackle today, it is virtually impossible to separate gender from race, sexuality, nationality, and class, just as it is near impossible to separate notions of liberty, justice, and the pursuit of happiness from providing these fundamental values to all.

Around the world, movements toward gender and racial equality are literally saving lives. Nicholas Kristof's writings about gendercide—detailing the hundreds of millions of missing women, gender selection in abortion, violence against girls and women, and unequal access to healthcare, education, and parenting—reveal a tragedy that exceeds all the male deaths in the wars of the past century.[1] Moving toward equality is a virtuous cycle. In places like rural India and Africa, for example, when villages begin sending girls to school just as they do with boys, the girls' health and well-being improve and the overall economic and physical well-being of their communities rises. Diversity, too, is fundamental to survival—of organizations, societies, and species. Many of the problems we will explore in this book have varying manifestations and responses as we cross borders and cultures. Many of the problems that women and minorities face—discrimination and exclusion in markets, physical and verbal abuse, unequal access to medical care and health benefits, objectification, sexism and racism in the media and political life, disproportionate burdens of childcare and domestic work, and infringement on autonomy and freedoms—are faced by other disadvantaged groups as well. Most issues are far, far worse for those who have the least digital access, cannot afford new technologies, and experience the challenges of intersectional exclusion (i.e., those with multiple vulnerable identities, such as being an immigrant woman of color). The devil, often, is in the details. But the devil is also in the bigger picture: in the fundamental principles of equality, dignity, and human flourishing. Our fates are tied together.

Builders and Blockers

News headlines often warn that new technologies—from artificial intelligence to robots to big data—have a gender or race problem. Such problems have been pervasive: automated advertisement bots that show different types of job openings to men and women and to younger and older workers; credit or lending algorithms that prefer men to women and white applicants to Black applicants; facial recognition systems that fail when presented with non-white faces; social media algorithms that prioritize profit at the expense of teenage girls' well-being; popular digital personal assistants (like Alexa, Siri, and others) designed as subservient female bots. The list goes on and on. Technology indeed often embeds inequality. But what if we flipped the script and instead adopted a mindset that *inequality faces a tech challenge*? What if we considered challenges as opportunities to do better—opportunities not only to address technology failures but to use technology to tackle societal failures?

Over a decade ago, early in my research on innovation and technology, I noticed a split in the debates. There were the insiders, who hailed technological innovation, automation, and the rise of the internet and big data as a utopian new era that would foster efficiency, growth, and opportunity. Disruption was both goal and means, regardless of distribution. Man would become God. Yes, I said *man*, because these insiders were almost universally white men in a particular corner of the world—my corner, in fact, here in California. There were also outsiders with a rising voice: women and people of color, people from outside Silicon Valley, and people from other parts of the world—many of them from developing countries and rural areas—who warned against exclusion and inequality propelled by new technologies. What struck me the most about this landscape was how dichotomous it was. In my professional and private lives, at conferences and in the classroom, in the political sphere, in the media and the literature, I found conversations about technology's potential to *empower* lacking. The two sides were talking past each other, one group of haves from the inside, one group representing the have-nots from the outside. There was little attempt to complicate, engage, and envision inclusive and empowered paths forward.

A particularly acute version of the utopia/dystopia split is between bias-fixers, who believe that we can address problems in the system, and bias-blockers, who want to abolish technology when it has proved harmful. Progress requires overcoming the twin specters of denying risk and denying promise, of uncritical embrace and critical paralysis. Bias fixing is too narrow—there is certainly a need in our inquiry to ask about whether certain applications of technology are viable or legitimate. For example, civil liberties activists have questioned whether we ought to disallow algorithms that identify a person's sexuality or ethnicity; we'll discuss this question of algorithmic blindness/awareness later in the chapter. But technological advancement is rarely something that can be readily blocked, nor should it necessarily be. Instead, technology needs to be built and put to use responsibly.

Within this jagged landscape between utopia and dystopia, the technology field itself is fast-moving, and each year we learn more about its risks as well as its potential to address the things we most care about. To employ technology for good, something must change in the way we debate new advancements and developments. We need to change the story of "technology = power = evil." We need a more comprehensive portrayal of what is currently under way and what the future can hold. We need to reject the black-and-white story of diametrically opposed futures—a robopocalypse at one end of the spectrum and a robotopia at the other—and have a richer conversation about the transformations occurring in every sphere of our lives.

The Equality Moneyball

In *Moneyball: The Art of Winning an Unfair Game*, Michael Lewis recounts the story of Billy Beane, the Oakland Athletics general manager who built a winning baseball team on the cheap. Beane used statistical analysis while others were still using human judgment and perceptions, hunches and gut instincts. Remember our guiding principles: we cannot correct what we don't measure. We cannot improve what we don't study. Today, statistical analysis is a major tool in every aspect of our lives—from job matching to dating, from politics to media, from consumer marketing to law enforcement. In many contexts, even simple mathematical models outperform human experts. As computing power increases, computers can access ever-larger data sets and apply sophisticated algorithms to predictive modeling, dramatically increasing accuracy. An algorithm is simply a set of instructions; basically, it's a formula that takes you step by step through a decision-making process. Today's algorithms can gobble up and find patterns in huge amounts of information, and this capacity is rapidly increasing. Imagine an equality moneyball.

eBay offers a potent illustration of disparity detection through digital data analysis—and how we can learn from what we find. The company is a pioneer in its willingness to open its under-the-surface data for researchers to mine. Usually this kind of data is kept secret, a practice that needs to change. When eBay recently released a vast data set spanning more than a decade and billions of data points about online auctions, two researchers—law professor Tamar Kricheli-Katz and economist Tali Regev—were among the first to study it. On eBay, as on many online marketplaces, sellers can specify personal information when they register, and even when gender is not specified, buyers can often guess the seller's gender by their name or by their selling histories. Kricheli-Katz and Regev looked at more than 1 million auctions on eBay and found that women consistently receive less money than men when selling the very same products. These disparities held true even when controlling for sellers' reputation scores, initial minimum prices, and "buy it now" prices. The study found that when men and women offer the exact same new products, such as iPods in original, sealed packaging, sellers identifiable as women receive fewer bids and lower final prices—receiving on average only 80 cents for every dollar that male sellers receive.[2] Even greater gaps exist when women sell products that are perceived to be typically owned by men, such as electronics. Astonishingly, gift card sale prices are subject to the same gap as new products: women who sell a $100 Amazon gift card receive less than men selling the same $100 Amazon gift card.

As we will see in Chapter 3, 80 cents to the dollar is a figure all too familiar to anyone aware of the gender pay gap in the job marketplace. There it was—that same gap—when selling identical items online. Interestingly, the gender penalty was smaller in the sale of used items: women only received 3 percent less than men. Kricheli-Katz and Regev surmised that this smaller gap could be because buyers subconsciously trust women more regarding the quality of the used products they list. So we see two competing stereotypes at work: women should earn less, but they also lie less—or to flip this, they are humbler in their demands, but they are also humbler and more truthful in their presentations. Another of the study's findings was that men and women use different terms to describe their products, with men using stronger, more flattering depictions. But even when controlling for these differences in descriptions, the money gap between bids for identical new products was 19 percent.

Unhidden Figures

Whether it's businesses or governments using algorithms, we don't have to settle for their opacity and proprietary status. When we see patterns of discrimination clearly, we are much more likely to do something about them. Armed with findings like those on eBay, platforms could design their user interfaces to alert sellers about comparable sales. eBay could redesign the bidding process such that gender as well as race—as we will see later, other studies show similar inequities when it comes to race and ethnicity in online exchanges—would be hidden until after pricing and initial offers. Platforms could also suggest stronger words and descriptions of products to equalize the selling side of the auction. The digital space lends itself to corrections in other ways as well. For example, eBay offers automated sniping agents that bid at the last possible second; it could also tackle irrational inequities by introducing software to assist both sides in presenting offers and making competitive bids. And if companies like eBay don't proactively move to address these inequities, policymakers can play a role in requiring the detection, reporting, and correction of inequities.

The first step, always, before seeking reform is to identify and understand the problem. In the digital space, analyzing data can expose inequities. By contrast, it is largely impossible to conduct such accurate, robust, ongoing, and granular detection of disparities when it comes to the very real price discrimination that exists offline. In one famous field experiment from the early 1990s, participants posed as buyers at used car dealerships. It's not difficult to guess the results: the sellers gave women and people of color higher initial prices than they gave to white men. But how often and at how many dealerships can one run such an experiment? And how easily can we as consumers and regulators address these market disparities, which have pervaded the marketplace for centuries? The elegance of the eBay study helps us imagine the power of digital data both in shedding light on age-old patterns of discrimination and in envisioning solutions moving forward. Algorithms can mine through massive digital records to engender our quest for equality. And better yet, imagine if—rather than researchers tackling the challenge of mining through data like eBay's years after events take place—algorithms *constantly* looked for discriminatory patterns. In this way, bots could effectively become 24/7 watchdogs, detecting real-time patterns that exclude or disadvantage women and minorities in the marketplace.

We are at a critical juncture. Like eBay, online platforms such as Facebook-turned-Meta, Amazon, Google, LinkedIn, Uber, Airbnb, Fiverr, Etsy, and more possess a wealth of information about our behavior and relationships. Facebook rebranded itself as Meta in response to widespread public discontent with the secrecy surrounding the immense amounts of data the company has accumulated and its reluctance to explain how it chooses between profit and the well-being of its users. Some revelations about corporate practices, as in the case of Facebook, come through insiders-turned-whistleblowers. Some, like with eBay, are aided by a company providing access to its data. Other disparities come to light through direct experimentation by researchers studying digital behavior. For example, Harvard Business School researchers designed an experimental field study, creating fake Airbnb profiles of guests looking to book vacation homes; some were white and some Black. Disturbingly, the researchers found that requests from guests with distinctively Black names were 16 percent less likely to be accepted than identical guests with typically white names. These differences persisted whether the host was male or female, white or minority.

Another study compared the ratings of vacation rentals cross-listed on Airbnb and its competitor HomeAway. Airbnb visibly shows hosts' identity; HomeAway does not. And sure enough, the researchers found users' ratings on Airbnb to be racially biased: Black hosts often receive lower rating scores and, in turn, earn less for comparable accommodations. And while the platform's mutual rating and review systems have positive implications for trust and credibility—what I have called in my research "systems of stranger trust"—they are also affected by our biases. Recent studies such as these illustrate ways to detect discrimination: to actively experiment with what happens in controlled settings when gender or race alone—or together—are switched. But we need to conduct these studies in more systemic and ongoing ways, leveraging public policy to incentivize such research.

Digital companies can respond swiftly and strongly to incidents of discrimination. When discrimination is detected, the next step is to find solutions. Services often contain photos and names of users, such that race and gender are often visible. Airbnb could, like traditional hotel chains, require hosts to accept guests without revealing the guests' identities. Like HomeAway, it could hide hosts' identities until later in the exchange. I talked with Airbnb about its solutions, and it prides itself on responding quickly—far more quickly than any administrative agency could when a complaint of discrimination is filed—to any concerns raised by hosts or guests. Airbnb describes the company as having "a zero-tolerance policy for discrimination on the platform." For example, when a gay couple arrived at a Texas bed-and-breakfast and were refused accommodation, Airbnb removed the host from its listings, refunded the money paid for the booking, and paid for a night at the hotel that the couple ultimately stayed in. The company condemned the incident: "Airbnb has clear guidelines that a host or a guest may not promote hate or bigotry." After the Harvard experiment became public, the hashtag #AirBnBWhileBlack went viral on Twitter. Airbnb responded to the findings and outcry by creating stronger anti-discrimination policies, requiring users to actively sign a commitment to anti-discrimination, and changing the way profile photos are displayed. Now profile photos are displayed to hosts only after a booking is confirmed. The company also introduced an "Instant Book" function, which allows guests to book a listing immediately without approval from the host, ensuring a more objective, unbiased deal. Airbnb has removed 1.5 million people from the platform who failed to comply with the platform's anti-discrimination policy. And in 2020 it launched Project Lighthouse to continue to monitor for discrimination on the platform in collaboration with civil rights organizations including Color of Change, Asian Americans Advancing Justice, the Center for Democracy and Technology, the Leadership Conference on Civil and Human Rights, the League of United Latin American Citizens, the NAACP, the National Action Network, and Upturn. Basically, this project continues the initial studies about discrimination on the platform on a far larger scale. Airbnb sends pictures and names of hosts and guests, without other identifying information, to these civil rights partners to receive their perceptions on the identity of the users; in turn, Airbnb uses the partners' perceptions to study whether reservations made by those seen as belonging to a certain race are declined more often than others, which then helps the platform create new features and policies to address biases found.

The discrimination detected on Airbnb and eBay was human-driven, but the digital "paper" trail facilitated its discovery, and digital design allows for its correction. Access to large-scale data can help inform both companies and policymakers about patterns of discrimination more effectively than case-by-case discrimination litigation with its inevitable arbitrariness. AI can help parse the underlying reasons for inequality, ranging from pure bias to disparities in opportunities and behavioral differences. For example, if some of the differences in bidding, contracting, negotiating, or selecting are completely attributable to variances in the ways different groups describe their products, services, or skills, or in how they negotiate or contract, then the solution would be different than if the gap remains even when behavior is identical. AI provides us with unprecedented, invaluable insights that we can harness to create change with more precision—and intention.

We Can Teach a Bot New Tricks

Emily Dickinson wrote, "Let us dwell in possibility." In itself, technology is neutral. Data can be employed for good and for bad. Technology can help and harm. Innovation can empower and exclude. The eBay and Airbnb examples demonstrate how technology allows us to mine through immense quantities of data and uncover patterns. But new technologies are doing more than that: algorithms are increasingly making decisions based on the information they mine and the patterns they detect. A *learning algorithm* is a program that takes information, or what we call *training data*, as input and creates decision paths, or *classifiers*, that use this data for future tasks. For example, an algorithm may be instructed to create the best new Italian recipes. The algorithm will be fed many existing recipes from cooking websites, including ratings and reviews that people have offered, and it will learn what makes top-rated recipes tasty—and popular.

Machines that learn are an entirely new concept. Throughout history, machines were static inventions. If they were defective, we replaced them. Their purposes were set and their life cycles finite: machines would invariably continue to function as they were originally designed to do, and eventually, inevitably, they became obsolete. But the AI revolution changes everything. Machine learning is an application of AI that allows computers to autonomously improve through data and experience without being explicitly programmed on how to do so.

One way that machine learning happens is through *word embedding*, a common research framework that represents text data as vectors used in many machine learning and natural language processing tasks. The machine teaches itself associations from all the text input it receives, and the algorithm learns about pairings. When presented with associations like "wheel: car, wing: ____," a word-embedding algorithm learns to predict "plane." Taking it a step further, "flowers" and "musical instruments," for example, are far more likely to be associated with pleasant words than "insects" and "weapons" are.[3] Just like our minds develop associations, an algorithm learns these connections from processing natural language fed to it. In this way, a computer can learn to solve puzzles, such as "man is to X as woman is to Y." For example:

$$\overrightarrow{man} - \overrightarrow{woman} \approx \overrightarrow{king} - \overrightarrow{queen}$$

But word embeddings are notoriously problematic, and the problem lies in the nature of the beast: machines learn from the data they are fed. That data is what we humans have produced over time. If a machine is fed partial, inaccurate, or skewed data, it will mirror those limitations or biases. For example, when an algorithm is fed mainstream books and news articles as input, the vectors that represent the data are rampant with stereotypes: the word "daughters" is embedded with "sewing," whereas "sons" is embedded with "school." An example of a biased embedding would be:[4]

$$\overrightarrow{man} - \overrightarrow{woman} \approx \overrightarrow{computer\ programmer} - \overrightarrow{homemaker}$$

Word embeddings demonstrate how AI learns language, speech, and thought. Millions of text inputs teach the algorithms which words are closer to others or are positioned similarly in sentences.[5] The following are examples of machine-learned word associations:[6]

Extreme *she* occupations: 1. homemaker 2. nurse 3. receptionist 4. librarian 5. socialite 6. hairdresser 7. nanny 8. bookkeeper 9. stylist 10. housekeeper 11. interior designer 12. guidance counselor

Extreme *he* occupations: 1. maestro 2. skipper 3. protégé 4. philosopher 5. captain 6. architect 7. financier 8. warrior 9. broadcaster 10. magician 11. fighter pilot 12. boss

Language Creeps

Researchers working on these studies assert that these findings underscore the importance of how people interact with others in real life. In other words, words matter not only immediately, but also in how they become part of humanity's digital histories through which machines learn. While some of the academics studying these questions previously dismissed claims about potentially hurtful or discriminatory language as overly sensitive "political correctness," they are now seeing how impactful the language we use is. The words we use not only affect our relationships in the present, but creep their way into what machines learn about us as well, potentially coloring human interactions long after and far beyond when and where they are spoken. As we will see in the coming chapters, biased systems operate in feedback loops: algorithms' predictions can become self-fulfilling prophecies. For example, biased associations may direct an algorithm to show different kinds of advertisements or job openings to men and to women. The algorithm might decide, due to the proximity of vectors, to present women with a stereotypical set of choices when using a search browser—say, ads about shopping and spas—while showing men ads about jobs and tech gadgets. In turn, women will continue to have less information about professional opportunities, continuing and even deepening our reality of occupational segregation and financial disparities.

Research substantiates the prevalence of these biased associations in our written and spoken language. In a study published in *Science*, a machine trained to read through Google News articles learned to make associations between words. Without being guided in any way, the program came to associate male and female names with different types of careers and different kinds of emotions.[7] Bias creeps into algorithms in this way because bias is baked into the language of our culture—because our societies are unequal. Once a machine is trained—namely, once it has read through thousands of news articles—it will exhibit stereotypes to a troubling degree. It will complete the sentences it's fed in a discriminatory way, stereotypically predicting professions, behaviors, and treatment.

To paraphrase the study co-author Joanna Bryson, AI is no fairy godmother—it's just an extension of our culture.[8] So, in the absence of fairy godmothers, researchers are taking the lead in addressing these problems to build better machines. A growing number of computer scientists have committed to making machine learning fairer and more equal and are developing algorithms that would mitigate bias. One type of debiasing algorithm sorts out words that are inherently gendered (such as "daughter," "mother," "king," or "brother") from those that are not (say, "computer programmer," "nurse," "doctor," or "homemaker"). The algorithm can thereby extract the bias from the data, reducing analogies that create stereotypical connections about traits, abilities, and activities. The programmer can thus constrain the algorithm's learning process. In Chapter 2, we will see these advancements being deployed in screening contexts such as employment interviews and résumé parsing.

As we shall learn, however, monitoring the outcomes of algorithmic patterns is a further crucial—and often more effective—step toward debiasing. Research teams around the world are developing new and promising debiasing software. The scientific community has been making great strides in understanding algorithmic bias and discrimination and in teaching algorithms how to detect, measure, and mitigate these biases. One group of computer scientists, for example, recently created software that specifically tests for disparate outcomes. The software pairs algorithms that work together toward parity: one algorithm looks at whether a data set can distinguish between male and female, and a second one attempts to remedy bias by modifying the actual data set so that any algorithm making selections would deliver fair results. This second algorithm goes into the data and blurs attributes that may be correlated to gender or race.[9] In this way, algorithms can be employed to directly override biased decision-making—they can be designed with an additional layer of judgment as to how to respond to biases affirmatively, such as flagging gendered patterns in data or creating a positive presumption for underrepresented groups.

To this effect, Stanford University researchers developed an algorithm named the Multiaccuracy Boost, which is programmed to maximize not only overall accuracy, but also the highest accuracy for each subpopulation.[10] The algorithm breaks the data down into different identity categories and subpopulations and performs an audit on the functioning of other algorithms to determine whether the outcomes satisfy a strong notion of subgroup fairness. The multiaccuracy principle at the heart of the algorithm looks for bias not just with regard to each protected identity, such as race and gender, but also populations defined by the intersections of race, gender, and other identity markers. In initial experiments, this audit algorithm has been successful in also improving the overall accuracy, by identifying subpopulations where the initial models systematically erred. The Multiaccuracy Boost algorithm demonstrates how data science is moving to automate decision-making that can be simultaneously tasked with achieving competing goals: accuracy and equality. It's not an easy task—tensions persist and these advancements are still nascent—but the direction is promising.

Our brains work in schemas too. Associations like those connected with different types of names mirror the biases we have in daily life. Perhaps you've heard of or have taken the Implicit Association Test (IAT). Every year, I ask my law students to take that test, and every year, they are shocked to discover their own implicit biases. The IAT demonstrates differences in response times when subjects are asked to pair certain words. Our human brains are machines limited in speed; whether we are Black or white Americans, the test finds that our small human brain machines are faster at associating names like Greg and Emily with words like "happy" and "good," for example, and names like Jamal and Lakisha with words like "hate" and "bad" than vice versa. Compared with male names, female names are more often associated with family words than with career words. Female words are also more often associated with the arts than with the sciences. Younger people are associated with more pleasant words than old people.

For us humans, decision-making is not only prone to these kinds of identity-based stereotypes, but also muddled by our limited computing capacities, limited information, and all sorts of cognitive biases, such as discounting future or unlikely risks, overconfidence, and overreliance on one type of information. Machines are not prone to such irrationalities. In many contexts, computer models are already consistently superior to human decision-making. Machines are increasingly outperforming people even in situations where they are given limited information. Algorithms have so much information about us—and the power to process all this information together— that they stand poised to supersede much of what we humans do.

These differences between machines and humans are equal parts promising and concerning. Yet often, we're all too quick to discount the promise of technology and amplify the fear. It's understandable: most of us cannot understand the inner workings of an algorithm. Even an algorithm's programmers are often unable to decipher its internal processes. Researchers at the University of Pennsylvania's Wharton School have documented what they call *algorithm aversion*. They find that people become more skeptical of algorithms after they see them outperform humans. In controlled experiments, people were *less* likely to prefer using an algorithm after they witnessed it being *more* accurate than humans. Ironically, it's a very human reaction to a very human limitation.

Against Blindness

Just as debiasing with humans is unlikely to occur simply by blinding us to color or gender, simply removing associations between certain words in word embedding ("homemaker" and "female," for example) is unlikely to do more than scratch the surface of algorithmic bias. Part of the reason we don't want to remove associations or identity markers is that we usually want *more* rather than less information in order to fight long-standing disparities. A consensus is emerging among computer scientists that if the goal is to promote equality and fairness, then it is better to direct an algorithm's outputs than to restrict its inputs. This shift away from restricting input to examining output is termed by computer scientists the principle of *fairness through awareness*: in order to make fair predictions, a (trustworthy) algorithm should be given protected data, such as race and gender markers.[11] This shift is important both because of the difficulty of effectively restricting inputs and because of the benefits—for both accuracy and equality—of having full information, including identity markers, inputted into the system. Indeed, even if explicit references to identity markers are removed—for example, an algorithm sorting through financial data is instructed not to input each individual's gender—the algorithm is likely to be able to identify those markers. In other words, cleaning a data set of direct identity markers—gender, race, religion, sexual orientation, national origin, age, and so on—does not mean that the algorithm will be free of these identities. Identity is pervasive within data in numerous indirect ways. Algorithms learn about our identities through proxies, connections, and patterns in the data. For example, Facebook's algorithm can easily ascertain your gender just by your "likes"; associations are meaningful to the algorithms in ways that humans would not necessarily be able to detect.

Even how we write and speak has gender differences. For instance, when psychologists analyze large bodies of text by male and female authors, they find that women use "I" words ("I," "me," and "my") more often than men. Men use more nouns and women use more verbs. A zip code by itself is often a predictor of race. And if someone owns a specific kind of car, subscribes to a particular app or set of apps, owns a particular type of dog, and lives in a certain neighborhood, the algorithm can—with near certainty—identify that this individual is gay. So even when identity markers don't appear as part of the data, if they are encoded in other attributes, aligning with occupation, geography, lifestyle choices, or social class, then the computer will detect them. As Harvard University computer scientist Cynthia Dwork described it to me, you simply cannot hide the identity of a person because our identities are "holographically embedded" in the data. The fact that I am a woman ripples throughout the millions of data points in any and all information collected about me. AI sees patterns in vast amounts of data.

By their very nature, algorithms are opaque, in the sense that even if you know how to read code, you still wouldn't be able to know what an algorithm will do without putting it into action—the oft-cited black box problem. Alan Turing, the father of modern computer science, said that a key feature of a learning machine is that the human "teacher" is largely ignorant of what is going on inside the "pupil"—the machine. This feature is becoming more and more true about algorithms. Even their designers cannot fully comprehend the processes that happen in the more sophisticated algorithms. Once an algorithm has begun to learn, it's very difficult to completely remove information from its "memory."

But there's another reason we don't want to be identity blind, one that runs deeper than the challenge of achieving said blindness itself. To identify and counter inequities, algorithms—and humans—need to actively consider identities. Restricting inputs makes it more difficult to detect and correct biases. For example, if an algorithm is not allowed to learn that society gives men higher rewards for equal work, it will be difficult to correct those biases in practice. The newer approach preferred by experts in the field, therefore, is to define fairness in relation to outcomes, not inputs.

Here, it is worth pausing for a moment and asking what we mean when we talk about equality, which in and of itself is a far more complicated concept than first meets the eye. Do we mean identity blindness—as in rejecting any consideration of one's gender, race, or other social identity markers? Do we mean statistical parity—that different identities will be proportionately represented in various outcomes, such as being selected for jobs, ads, or credit? Do we mean that the algorithm will be equally accurate (or inaccurate) in its predictions about any identity group? Do we mean that we take into account differences and accommodate people's diverging preferences, backgrounds, and abilities? What happens if there is a tension between equality and accuracy? What if an algorithm could achieve perfect accuracy in predicting success in school or at work, and this prediction showed that certain groups were more apt for a given task? To achieve meaningful equality, is it enough to treat everyone equally or should we do more to promote more vulnerable groups or groups that have been historically discriminated against? These are tough questions, and they aren't new; we've been debating the meaning of equality for a long time. As we shall see, these questions will be answered differently in different contexts. Technology challenges us to articulate what we are really trying to achieve as we search for the answers. We can uncover and learn more about the sources of disparity using new computing power, but we can also direct algorithms in more fine-tuned ways to determine what we want an equality machine to look like.

The Learning Environment

Take the example of using risk assessment software in the criminal justice system, a subject that has been heatedly debated. Algorithms are regularly used in decisions about bail, bond amounts, sentencing, and early release from prison. The controversy around one leading software tool, Correctional Offender Management Profiling for Alternative Sanctions (COMPAS), centers on the algorithms' ability to make these life-altering decisions generally. There are particular concerns about algorithmic bias against people of color. Earlier studies on the software found that certain algorithms charged with flagging who is likely to reoffend are inherently flawed, labeling Black defendants as future criminals twice as often as white defendants and frequently mislabeling white defendants as "low risk." One high-profile, much-cited study from 2018 found that COMPAS is no more accurate than predictions by people with no criminal justice expertise. The study looked at 400 online participants on Amazon's Mechanical Turk who crowdsourced short descriptions of real defendants from a publicly available COMPAS data set. The participants were asked to predict whether the defendants were likely to commit a crime in the future. The study found that the overall accuracy of the lay humans was 62 percent, compared to the 65 percent accuracy of algorithmic COMPAS predictions.[12] More recent studies do question these findings, however: one from 2020 argues that the first research wasn't a good reflection of human judgment in the real world, and that the first study's experimental setting focused participants' attention on the most predictive factors and gave them feedback along the way, artificially boosting their results.[13] In each of the fifty rounds, participants made a prediction, were informed whether the prediction was correct—that is, received immediate feedback—and then received the next scenario.

The researchers explain why, in the lab setting, humans seem to do as well as the computer: "This created a 'kind' environment, one shown to be ideal for humans to intuitively learn the probabilities of specific outcomes, even when the rules are not transparent. Kind environments can promote accuracy, unlike the 'wicked' learning environments that characterize most justice settings, where outcomes cannot be observed immediately or are never observed at all." In other words, humans perform relatively well when information is limited and streamlined, but the more abundant or contextualized the information, the less humans are able to process it in the way that algorithms can. Similar conclusions are now being shown in a myriad of contexts, from hiring decisions to salary setting, to credit and loans, to sentencing and bail.

In the 2020 study, researchers created conditions that are more reflective of the information presented to judges in their decision-making process: pre-sentencing investigation reports, attorney and victim impact statements, and an individual's demeanor, which all add complex, inconsistent, risk-irrelevant, and potentially biasing information (for example, someone who "has a serious drinking problem that interferes with work"). The study showed that when both humans and the algorithm are provided with more complex or otherwise "noisy" risk information, the algorithm fares far better. Or, to put it conversely, participants performed consistently worse than the algorithmic model.

The potential for (in)accuracy in this context, of course, has major equality implications. Another study shows that if we program algorithms to release from pretrial detention all but the highest-risk people, Black and Hispanic people would benefit the most by far because of the vast inequities in the criminal justice system. Again, when we think about how to increase equality in historically unequal systems, we don't necessarily *want* to be identity blind. For example, women generally have lower rates of recidivism. So when we are predicting the risk of reoffending, if we blind the algorithm to gender and merely feed it all the other risk factors, women end up penalized: female defendants would be released at the same rates as male defendants even though they in fact present less future risk. That's why criminal law scholars now believe that risk assessment algorithms used in the criminal justice system should explicitly take gender into account, because otherwise women would be penalized by the algorithms' overestimation of their recidivism rates.[14] The Wisconsin Supreme Court recently held that the use of gender within the COMPAS risk assessment tool does not violate due process because using gender improves accuracy. The court reasoned that "if the inclusion of gender promotes accuracy, it serves the interests of institutions and defendants, rather than a discriminatory purpose."[15]

If current technologies' accuracy can be improved and racial bias reduced through technology, the tragic use of needless and uneven police force and incarceration could be reduced. As racial bias in our criminal justice system becomes all the more apparent, we should focus on comparative advantage and more consistent, reliable, and accurate ways to tackle systemic injustices. In connection with automating bail, sentencing, and early release, legal scholar Colleen Chien has shown the immense potential of automating "clean slate" initiatives—using digitization and algorithms to automatically clear eligible criminal records in accordance with second-chance laws designed to help Americans who were arrested or convicted to expunge their records and regain their footing in the labor market and society. Chien analyzed around 60,000 criminal histories of persons seeking work and concluded that at least 20 to 30 million American adults, or 30–40 percent of those with criminal records, suffer from what she terms "second chance expungement gap"—in part because of overburdened agencies, in part because of "dirty data" (missing criminal justice information) and costly processes. Automation can significantly improve the current inefficient and unfair system, which affects millions of (disproportionately poor and vulnerable) Americans.

Despite all the sensationalized negative publicity on automation and its potential for bias, California has been leading the way in introducing AI in its criminal justice system. In 2019, the San Francisco district attorney, in collaboration with the Stanford Computational Policy Lab, introduced software that scrubs to neutral any wording in police reports that has a racial connotation. The prosecutor then sees the case in a blinded way: the algorithm not only removes the mention of race but also removes physical descriptions, names of witnesses, names of police officers, and geographical signals that could give clues about race.

In some ways, nothing about using statistical correlations and making predictions based on these patterns is new. Scientific inquiry, medicine, marketing, and policy have all been grounded in forecasting the future based on the past. What we are learning about introducing automation into processes is that when we increase the capabilities of predictive systems, some people may be harmed, be it through inaccuracy or accuracy. Algorithms should not perpetuate historical discrimination, but also we cannot expect them to solve all our past wrongs with a wave of a magic wand. Technology is not a silver bullet, but it does move the needle. It can elevate fair outcomes. It shifts dynamics. It takes long-standing, sticky problems out of the mud. And it can lower costs, increase the size of the pie, and accelerate the pace of progress.

Malice or Competence: What We Fear

For all the talk about the possibilities of AI and robotics, we're really only at the embryonic stage of our grand machine-human integration. And AI means different things in different conversations. The most common use refers to *machine learning*—using statistical models to analyze large quantities of data. The next step from basic machine learning, referred to as *deep learning*, uses a multilayered architecture of networks, making connections and modeling patterns across data sets. AI can be understood as any machine—defined for our purposes as hardware running digital software—that mimics human behavior (i.e., human reactions). It makes decisions and judgments based on learning derived from data inputs and can mimic our senses, such as vision. The attempt to create more and more advanced AI is the attempt to mimic our human brain and human cognitive abilities—as well as our human emotional and instinctive powers. Robotics, in the mechanical sense, is trying to simulate our physical bodies; put together, the software and hardware of tomorrow's technologies aspire to offer the complete package: mind, body, senses, and perhaps even heart and soul.

Today, there are computer programs that simulate human decision-making and algorithms that dynamically learn from data to perform specific tasks once performed exclusively by people. Algorithms mine data about the past to predict outcomes in the future. But at this point, there is not yet a general AI—that is, a hypothetical (or future) machine that can do any intellectual task humans can. Maybe one day there will be an artificial intelligence explosion, a tipping point when a powerful superintelligence will surpass human intelligence to the point that humans lose control over technological advancements. This possibility is known as the *singularity hypothesis*. Whether or not this comes to pass and whatever it may look like, it is highly likely that the human-machine entanglement will only become deeper, that the integration of robots will only become greater. We can already say that automation is reshaping how we work and live. At the same time, we are just beginning to create truly smart machines. Our algorithms are good at pattern recognition, but they do not yet think for themselves; we are nowhere close to that point. As Stanford University professor Fei-Fei Li said in her testimony to the U.S. Congress about the state of AI, "There's nothing artificial about AI. It's inspired by people, and most importantly it impacts people."[16]

In 1950, Alan Turing asked whether it would be possible one day to create a computer with consciousness. To describe consciousness, Turing listed what he believed to capture the essence of humans: "Be kind, resourceful, beautiful, friendly, have initiative, have a sense of humour, tell right from wrong, make mistakes, fall in love, enjoy strawberries and cream, make someone fall in love with it, learn from experience."[17] Turing didn't quite answer his own question. Rather, he said that what matters is what we will perceive the machine to be able to do. Hence, he suggested the famous Turing test: Is a machine capable of exhibiting intelligence in a way such that we are unable to distinguish it from a human being? As of yet, what we call "artificial intelligence" is not sentient, and in a basic sense it is not yet artificial nor intelligent. AI tools are human-made tools that help us humans understand and direct the complexity of our world.

The fears surrounding AI oscillate between its nascent reality and its omnipotent future. Thought leaders and industry moguls from Stephen Hawking to Elon Musk have warned that at a critical moment when AI becomes independent, the human race should be quite concerned about its own survival. Hawking wrote, "The real risk with AI isn't malice but competence. A superintelligent AI will be extremely good at accomplishing its goals, and if those goals aren't aligned with ours, we're in trouble." He worried that once humans develop full AI, it will take off on its own and redesign itself without human control. Elon Musk has warned that AI may become a "fundamental risk to the existence of human civilization."[18] The thought experiment goes like this: What if we told a robot to maximize the number of paper clips it produces or the number of strawberry fields it plants? You can imagine how humans could quickly become an obstacle for the robot to overcome in its quest for more paper clips or strawberries: ingenious and singularly focused on the task at hand, the robot will appropriate any and all resources to maximize its paper clip production or strawberry growing bar none, removing any obstacle (read: humans) in its way.[19]

The fear of robots gone rogue is ingrained throughout our collective imaginations of automation and machines: that superintelligent creatures will thwart humanity just as humans have thwarted many a species before. In reality, we are just at the beginning of directing our technology toward real autonomy. At the moment, what we fear is incompetence more than competence, and to that end, we need to focus on improving our systems. This also means that now is the time for a call to action to consider the direction in which our technologies are moving. It means that we have to be proactive in identifying opportunities and goals. In his book *The Master Algorithm*, machine learning expert Pedro Domingos put it bluntly: "People worry that computers will get too smart and take over the world, but the real problem is that they're too stupid and they've already taken over the world."[20] Being at a nascent stage of the technology—while at the same time knowing that we are heading to a future shaped by increasingly complex digital processes—means that we can act mindfully today to shape tomorrow's equality machine.

From Countess to Algorithm

Once upon a time, women were pioneers of programming. In the mid-1800s, British mathematician Ada, Countess of Lovelace, created what is now considered the first algorithm for a computer. Ada Lovelace was the daughter of famed poet Lord Byron and mathematician Lady Byron (née Anne Isabella Milbanke, nicknamed Annabella), also known as the "Princess of Parallelograms." The mathematician mom left the poet dad and set out to teach her daughter rigorously. Annabella instilled a love of math in her daughter, and in her studies Ada came across the work of the famed engineer Charles Babbage, who had invented a giant, gear-filled calculator. In 1833, when she was only seventeen, Ada met Babbage and tried to convince him to collaborate. For a long while Babbage ignored Ada, yet she persisted. Ada took the initiative to translate a scholarly publication about his work from French to English, annotating it to make it twice as long. Babbage was finally impressed. They became collaborators, creating punch cards that would become the basis of machine-automated computation of problem sets.

Ada's fame as the first programmer has led to some recent tributes. The U.S. Department of Defense named a computer language Ada. Hillary Clinton's election simulation algorithm was also named Ada. (The polling algorithm proved detrimental to Clinton's campaign, predicting wins in Wisconsin and Michigan and leading Clinton to put her efforts elsewhere, ultimately losing both states.) But beyond Ada's lifetime successes and token posthumous eponyms, women and minority programmers have been largely marginalized, and their contributions to the field have too often been rendered invisible. In a secret military project during World War II, six women programmed the first electronic computer. As in so much of history, when the project was revealed to the public in 1946, the women remained unnamed, receiving no credit for their work. Similarly, as depicted in Margot Lee Shetterly's book *Hidden Figures* and the Hollywood movie based on it, three Black NASA mathematicians and programmers, Katherine Johnson, Dorothy Vaughan, and Mary Jackson, were pioneers during the space race, only later receiving credit for their contributions. Indeed, software was born a feminine profession, but once the industry boomed, women were sidelined.

Today, as few as 13.5 percent of workers in the machine learning field are female.[21] In fact, this imbalance has been getting worse over the past few decades. Men dominate the tech industry as a whole, but even more profoundly and with greater imbalance in the AI field. For example, at Google, men make up 90 percent of the AI research department, and women of color constitute less than 2 percent of the department. Similar imbalances exist at Twitter, Facebook, and Yahoo. In academia, the number of women receiving computer science degrees and pursuing careers in AI is staggeringly low and declining. In 2016, the National Science and Technology Council described the shortage of women and minorities as "one of the most critical and high-priority challenges for computer science and AI."[22] Without people from all backgrounds and identities participating in the field of AI, the field's trajectory and all that arises from it cannot and will not reflect society as a whole and certainly won't embody the interests of the more vulnerable.

The digital divide is sourced in power. Women and minorities are underrepresented, yet the technologies that are being produced have universal aspirations. Technology is designed and data is gathered by a concentrated few, but the data is derived from—and the tech is consumed by—people all over the world. Technology can build knowledge and construct reality in a way that appears objective and neutral, all the while concealing underlying exclusions. But being underrepresented and focusing on exclusion can be a vicious cycle.

Inspiration Finds Us Working

As we have seen, the public conversation is replete with stories of algorithms running amok and statistics about the dire imbalance in the fields that are advancing these technologies. But behind the scenes, in research labs, non-profit organizations, and government offices, a robust research community dedicated to ethical technologies has emerged. These are the heroes of the next generation of algorithmic fairness and robotics ethics—AI scientists and activists, researchers and business leaders, many of them women and people of color. This is happening around the globe, and we should celebrate the people on these frontiers. We need to scale their efforts and recognize victories. We need to showcase the emerging fields of algorithmic fairness, ethical robotics, and computational social science. To address problems, it is not enough to flag them without offering solutions. To correct and attack disparities, it is not enough to point them out. It is not enough to advocate for more women and people of color to enter the field without addressing the potential of the field itself to do good and to bring change. These problems—the lack of participation and the lack of celebration of opportunity—are endogenous. We can create virtuous—or, alas, vicious—cycles. As Picasso said, "Inspiration exists, but it must find you working."

We find ourselves at a crossroads, poised on the precipice of a profound paradigm shift. Let us be inspired by all the positive potential to embrace AI to create a brighter future. Storytelling matters: if all the stories we hear about technology focus on the harm technology poses to the vulnerable, why would anyone want to enter the field to make it better? Storytelling allows us to challenge the problems of the past and imagine a better future. After all, so many technological advances of the past have been foretold by science fiction writers like Isaac Asimov and Ursula K. Le Guin. Asimov and Le Guin both dreamed of a future that is now looking more and more possible. But both worried about the human tendency to limit the imagination to foregone scenarios. Asimov wrote that "it became very common . . . to picture robots as dangerous devices that invariably destroyed their creators." He explained his own belief that we need to confront risks constructively: "I could not bring myself to believe that if knowledge presented danger, the solution was ignorance. To me, it always seemed that the solution had to be wisdom. You did not refuse to look at danger, rather you learned how to handle it safely."[23] Shifting the narrative to the opportunities for change can inspire us to rethink technology's role in promoting equality and equality's role in technological developments.

So we need to both dissect and dream—to expose the ways that social realities have been unequal and envision an equal existence fueled by an equality machine. Critical discourse should converge around the goal of building avenues for constructive change, not erecting roadblocks. As builders, not blockers, we should strive to develop technologies that enhance our lives and open possibilities. We need to look at what brings us fulfillment and connection, pleasure and well-being, unity and harmony. We also need to look to advancement to cure harms: disease, exploitation, inequality, fear, and exclusion. *Imagination is a superpower.* To change what is wrong, we need to imagine what a world that is human made, embracing technology for good, can look like. Examples of using AI for such good are all around us. Machine learning shows promise for addressing intractable challenges from poverty to climate change to ocean pollution to global pandemics. The stories of those who have skin in the game—who are doing good *and* adding diversity, all while doing well in the field—can motivate the next generation to join in.

In debates about the future of technology, I see how scholars are far more willing to accept the role of AI in areas such as medicine, climate studies, and environmental sustainability—which they perceive as more purely scientific—than in other areas such as employment, social justice, domestic violence, and equal pay. This field-bifurcation fallacy can be detrimental. Just as machine learning is a game changer in detection and diagnosis of health and climate issues, it can become a game changer in detection and diagnosis of social challenges. As we shall see in the chapters to come, mathematical models can be used to fight poverty, environmental destruction, climate risks, and viruses just as well as harassment, workplace and wage discrimination, media exclusion, public space representation, design stereotypes, and more. All we have to do is be willing to imagine it and then materialize it.

Both the opportunities and the risks are immense. If computers can measure and predict what we care about more and more accurately, then we can reduce the human biases that have been shaping our markets, our societies, and our homes for centuries. At the same time, the concerns about technology's path are well-founded. *The Terminator* trope aside, when technology gives more power to the already powerful and encodes and amplifies decades of inequalities, we risk a far greater evil. As digitization and automation are introduced into every aspect of our lives, the ride has been incredibly—and predictably—bumpy. But we cannot strive toward change if we don't recognize progress. The use of machine learning algorithms for prediction tasks is often replacing processes traditionally performed by simple statistical analysis. Machine learning dynamically considers many variables, enabling us to predict continuous outputs.

As we enrich our toolkit of detection models and solutions, we become more apt to observe how organizations and communities can emulate best practices and positively use the power of algorithms and digital design. The equality machine is just that—a toolkit and a framework that allows us to approach complex issues and reach positive and equal outcomes using innovative technologies. It's also a mindset that allows us to rethink uses and designs of technological advances. To improve and build on opportunities, we need more data, increased detection, inclusive design, and diverse participation in the building and oversight of tomorrow's technologies.

To quote Martin Luther King Jr.: "We are caught in an inescapable network of mutuality, tied in a single garment of destiny. Whatever affects one directly, affects all indirectly." An equality mindset has enormous potential to shape the technology fields across the board for our collectively brighter future. We have a responsibility to direct the research, collect the data, inform the design, and shape the goals of new technologies in ways that consider their benefits to all. At the heart of our manifesto lies the need for a grounded vision and a critical yet constructive agenda to transform tomorrow's technologies for equality and empowerment. Our normative paths will be contested and dynamic, but that is true whether we are supporting our goals with technology or not. As we continue to examine different choices—whether in the market, at home, or in government—we must consider when and how the equality machine can address not only the risks of technology but the underlying problems in society itself.

II
MIND

CHAPTER 2

Behind the Hiring Curtain

A future based on new science and new technology
also shows the results of the old human behavior
that guides them.

—GLORIA STEINEM, journalist and political activist

Strangers to Ourselves

For two decades, the workplace has been a central focus of my research. Here in California, I direct the University of San Diego's Center for Employment and Labor Policy (CELP). I study job markets and how discrimination happens in every industry. Every year, I teach employment law and policy, and I regularly serve as an expert witness in cases about corporate culture and employment discrimination. It's not an easy field. It can get frustrating. How is it that for years we've had laws on the books demanding equal treatment, and yet discrimination, unequal pay, harassment, and hostile work environments persist in every industry? How can we overcome years of exclusion, toxic work cultures, and glass ceilings?

Human processing, by its very nature, discriminates— distinguishing between different categories and making decisions according to classifications and schemas that we've developed in our minds. Most of these processes are beneficial and efficient, the result of thousands of years of cognitive evolution allowing humans to make quick decisions. If I prefer apples to oranges, I easily remember to choose one over the other when I go grocery shopping. But for centuries, humans have also developed problematic categories of discrimination. We often decide irrationally, discriminate unconsciously, and hold skewed and biased beliefs about others. We are prone to cognitive failures and limited in our ability to process large amounts of data. We humans are not very good at understanding our own motivations and inner workings. We are prone to letting our emotions take over, often leading to waste and grief.

These thorny cognitive schemas are difficult to unwind, and we have not magically outgrown them as we move into the digital era. What if we could employ debiasing software in job searching, recruiting, hiring, payment, evaluation, promotion, and termination? Imagine an equality machine that detects disparities and identifies ways to reduce bias in the job market, from initial recruitment and job postings to résumé screenings, interviews, workplace culture, and work-life balance.

Would an Algorithm Hire Lakisha Washington?

We worry that algorithms are black boxes—in other words, opaque and difficult to understand (which they often are). But what about the black box of the human mind? Human decision-making in the hiring realm involves dozens of recruiters, interviewers, co-workers, clients, and supervisors, each a small black box of their own. By contrast, using technology, we can check our intuition and innate human bias by employing machines to help us quantify and analyze information. We need to strive to integrate the best of both worlds—human and machine decision-making.

Two decades ago, a group of psychologists began running résumé experiments. They sent more than 5,000 identical fictitious résumés differing only in the applicants' names to 1,300 employers in response to job ads posted in Boston and Chicago newspapers. The pretend applicants were named Greg Baker, Jamal Jones, Emily Walsh, and

Lakisha Washington. The results were telling: "white-sounding" names received 50 percent more callbacks for interviews.[1] That study was so illuminating that researchers all over the world began replicating it, manipulating other protected identities in the fictitious résumés. These résumé manipulation studies have continued to find gender, race, age, and sexual orientation discrimination in hiring.

Twenty years of these résumé studies have been frustratingly consistent: despite social efforts and legal rules, human bias thrives. In all sectors—not least of all in the tech industry itself—and despite decades of anti-discrimination laws on the books and diversity and inclusion training in place, workplaces still demonstrate bias in recruiting and hiring. To be sure, using technology to supplement or replace human decision-making carries risk and is not a panacea, but it has the potential to mitigate our innate human bias. University of Chicago professor Sendhil Mullainathan, who co-authored the original résumé study twenty years ago, argues that algorithmic bias is more readily discovered and more easily fixed than human bias.[2] Studying what algorithms do, Mullainathan says, is "technical and rote, requiring neither stealth nor resourcefulness," which makes discovering algorithmic discrimination more straightforward. Humans, on the other hand, Mullainathan warns, are inscrutable in a way that algorithms are not. Even when the algorithms' *workings* are opaque—or a black box—we can more systematically check the outcomes they produce to monitor for bias. When Mullainathan and his collaborators first conducted their résumé experiment—before the internet became the primary vehicle for job searching—it was a complex covert operation. They created banks of fictitious résumés, collected job opening data, faxed fake applications to prospective employers, and waited to receive job interviews or offers in order to identify the human bias that the study revealed. Nowadays, we can detect bias and imbalance in searches and screening in a much easier and more immediate way.

Technology also changes the way we can prove discrimination when disparity is detected. In my work as an expert witness in discrimination cases, I see how difficult it is to convince a judge and a jury that what happened to an employee was the result of bias. These cases have become even more difficult to prove as discrimination has become more subtle and furtive. Before Congress enacted Title VII of the Civil Rights Act in 1964, ads explicitly stating that women and minorities "need not apply" were commonplace in the job market. Now, the smoking gun of discrimination—such as the Idaho law specifying that "males must be preferred to females" in appointments for certain positions, a law that led to the landmark U.S. Supreme Court decision in *Reed v. Reed*—is mostly a thing of the past.[3] Discrimination today is more subtle and more disguised. In hiring decisions, employers usually do not have formal, discernible rules on what weighs more heavily among the many factors considered— experience, skill, education, personality, references, the likelihood that an applicant will accept an offer, and so on. Often, companies will just say that they are looking for the employee who is "the best fit." Employment discrimination litigation is therefore notoriously difficult, especially when an applicant has not previously worked for an employer. And even when an employee has worked at the organization for a while, most evidence is circumstantial. Employers shift their explanations and proffer decision-making rationales that can be impenetrable to outside scrutiny.

Even more importantly, when we find that people are biased, what can we do about it? Litigation is a long, arduous, and after-the-fact process. It can financially compensate the employee who was discriminated against, but to what extent does it change hearts and minds—and, most importantly, institutions? We can bring in sensitivity training and develop departments dedicated to diversity and inclusion, but it's very hard to debias humans. Systemic, lasting change has been elusive.

Enter algorithmic decision-making. Done right, it can overcome the flaws of human decision-making. As Mullainathan says, "Software on computers can be updated; the 'wetware' in our brains has so far proven much less pliable."[4] With these new pliant machines, we can expand how job opportunities are communicated; expand the applicant pool by identifying more inclusive formats and language; and employ screening measures that reject past, demonstrated human biases. We can then monitor and detect exclusions and continue to improve screening measures. As we explore each of these stages of the employment process in the following pages, we will see that while a data point that an algorithm provides may be tainted by human bias and unequal realities, AI can continuously improve; algorithmic processes can be audited and corrected swiftly in a way that a human mind simply cannot. Such malleability and adaptability vastly outclass our current hiring practices, which rely on biases that continue to shape recruiting, mentoring, hiring, evaluation, and promotion processes.

The Pool and the Pipeline

Recruitment begins with spreading the word about job openings. A recent lawsuit by the U.S. Department of Labor against the data-mining company Palantir shows that when the job pipeline is narrow, bias seeps into the employment process from the very beginning. The lawsuit claimed that the company discriminated against Asian job applicants.[5] It showed that Asians constituted 73 percent of qualified applicants for internship positions but only 19 percent of those hired. Statistically, that kind of result is nearly impossible without discrimination at play. The lawsuit suggested that Palantir's heavy reliance on employee recommendations for jobs caused the discriminatory result: more than half of new hires came through the employee referral program. This pattern is a common one. Companies often believe that referrals, word of mouth, and inside hires are more effective than a broad search. But such inside tracks are a source of exclusion: people who are already "in" tend to seek out others who mirror their own characteristics. If a company's roles are largely filled by white men, then diversifying through informal hiring practices is a near impossibility. Word-of-mouth hiring is also notoriously exclusionary: friends bringing in friends, colleagues networking and mentoring others in the market and communicating opportunities informally—these are recipes for the exclusion of those who are not already in the proverbial old boys' network.

Online advertisement and recruitment platforms can be a way to recruit more widely and to disseminate information about positions to people outside a company's immediate network, but the risk of replicating and amplifying past biases and exclusions persists; targeted online job advertisements can end up excluding women, minorities, and older workers. For example, until 2018, Facebook allowed companies to exclude certain age groups and genders from its target audiences with no accountability for the resulting discrimination.[6] To get a better sense of the issue, a 2017 study by the Federal Reserve Bank created 40,000 fictitious résumés for job applicants and applied to thousands of positions in eleven different states.[7] The résumés didn't explicitly list the ages of the applicants, but each applicant's approximate age could be easily garnered from dates such as high school graduation year. Young applicants were called back much more frequently than older applicants, and older women applicants were even more impacted by including age clues on their résumés than older men. Similarly, a ProPublica and *New York Times* investigation concluded that dozens of employers—including Verizon, Amazon, State Farm, Goldman Sachs, UPS, Target, and T-Mobile—excluded individuals over forty. Facebook in particular allowed companies to post ads exclusively targeting younger applicants, using discriminatory age filters to exclude older workers from employment ads.[8]

After receiving backlash over the lack of accountability, Facebook implemented a self-certification process that requires anyone running ads for jobs to check a box affirming that they are complying with its anti-discrimination policy. Facebook also removed the option for advertisers to exclude people based on politics, religion, ethnicity, or social issues—though age and sex exclusions reportedly remained.[9] In response to several complaints filed against Facebook and companies continuing to use its platform to advertise jobs only to younger, male applicants, the U.S. Equal Employment Opportunity Commission (EEOC) found that "businesses have been posting job ads on Facebook that illegally discriminate against women and older workers."[10] Facebook settled age discrimination cases in 2019 and 2021, consenting to modify its ad targeting tool to restrict the algorithm from considering age and gender, among other characteristics, when curating audiences for ads.[11]

And Facebook is not alone in the sea of biased job advertising. A team of researchers from Carnegie Mellon University found that Google tends to advertise higher-paying jobs and opportunities more frequently to men than to women. One such ad, targeting highly paid executives, appeared 1,816 times to men and just 311 times to women. Recalling earlier résumé studies, the Carnegie Mellon study employed fake job-seeking profiles to ensure that gender—not browsing behavior, shopping patterns, or social connections—was the only difference.[12]

In a press release, Facebook CFO Sheryl Sandberg, author of the feminist call to action *Lean In*, said, "Getting this right is deeply important to me and all of us at Facebook because inclusivity is a core value for our company." And yet, as we have already seen, taking out identity markers as inputs doesn't always guarantee that the algorithm will "get it right." Facebook moved to also prohibit use of zip codes and other factors that "may relate to race, color, national origin, ethnicity, gender . . . among other protected characteristics or classes."[13] Another important move was to remove the ability to provide "lookalike audiences"—that is, allowing advertisers to provide a sample list of the kind of audience they are seeking.

Each of these solutions, while helpful, is not enough to eliminate bias in targeted ads. In 2020, Facebook conducted an internal audit in which it admitted that the problem of bias in ad placements continued.[14] The self-audit cites a new study by Northeastern University computer scientists finding that Facebook's modified algorithm still presented ads in biased ways.[15] The researchers explained that the algorithm continues to rely on proxy data that correlates with gender or age. The study found that ads referring to hip-hop, for example, can be delivered to an audience that is over 85 percent Black. The algorithm also learned what kinds of pictures in ads are more appealing to women and delivered those ads to a female majority, and what jobs are typically male or female (delivering lumberjack position ads to an audience that was 90 percent male and 72 percent white, for instance). Likewise, supermarket cashier ads were served to an 85 percent female audience, and janitor and taxi driver positions were delivered mostly to people of color. The advertisers provided a sample audience that consisted of past applicants or current people in the profession (say, drivers, cashiers, or programmers) and the algorithm still learned that male job seekers are the more likely target audience. All of this suggests, as we've discussed, the need to focus on *equality of outcomes*—effectively monitoring equality in addition to preventing intentional discrimination.

Clearly, automated ads have perpetuated long-standing biases. Yet amid these failures, we can insist on doing better and consider the ways that these technologies can be improved. For some practices, ensuring diverse ad targeting may require regulatory interventions and updating our current laws to better address technology exclusions. Personalized advertising has its advantages, but we can decide as a society that any time ads are shown in ways that exclude women, minorities, older candidates, and other protected classes, such practices are unlawful. As we shall discuss later, this may mean updating our civil rights laws. We could reform employment law to explicitly make targeted ads unlawful even if they are the result of algorithmic digital placement optimization, without intentional human direction to exclude. But we could also direct the algorithms to increase diversity in outputs—that is, intentionally showing the ad to underrepresented demographics and learning how to increase the likelihood that these potential job seekers will actually apply for the job.

An algorithm won't give us equality "for free" without deliberate design. If an algorithm is merely programmed to deliver content to the most "relevant" audiences, it will invariably replicate past wrongs. But we are at a moment during which many companies are in fact interested in diversifying their workplaces. Indeed, most companies rationally want to find the best employees, regardless of their gender or race, and these days good workers are hard to find. So we need to think more deliberately about the proactive ways in which ads can be shown to a more expansive network of job seekers. If we shift the focus to outputs, we could, for example, specifically program algorithms to display ads equally to men and women.

There are already examples of targeted efforts to increase diversity and spread opportunity using online automated ads. LinkedIn Recruiter, for one, allows companies to track applicants by gender, making it easier to ensure a balanced applicant pool. LinkedIn has become so robust that millions of applicants use the platform to apply for jobs each year. Expanding the pool of applicants who view job opportunities and can act on them is the challenge. Job postings that reach a wider pool of applicants and encourage a diverse group of individuals to apply should be the first step in a company's recruitment process. Responsible, equitable job advertising begins with ensuring that a broad range of individuals have access to the ad. Promoting job openings across a variety of publications and forums can help engage diverse applicants who might never otherwise see an ad. And, importantly, remember *comparative advantage*: even if online advertisements are far from perfect in reaching all potential applicants, they are still likely to reach a more diverse population compared to the age-old word-of-mouth practice. Progress over perfection.

Coding Ninjas

Beyond expanding the reach of job ads, companies can also use technology for ad description optimization. When we're looking for a new job, the black box of our minds helps us make decisions about the type of work we'd like to pursue. Does the formatting and phrasing of a job ad matter? As it turns out, these details can matter a lot, and some firms offer technology solutions to help employers tailor their processes to eliminate unconscious bias and improve workplace diversity.

Textio is a company that analyzes job descriptions in real time to help companies increase the percentage of women recruits by avoiding gendered phrasing and formatting. Textio identified more than 25,000 phrases that generate gender bias. Its algorithm discovered that certain phrases used in ads for job openings—such as sports terms, military jargon like "mission critical" and "hero," and phrases like "coding ninja"—result in fewer women applicants. It also found that terms like "top-tier," "fast-paced work environment," "aggressive," "competitive," and "we want only the best" bring fewer minority and female applicants. At the same time, terms like "partnerships" and "passion for learning" attract more women to apply for a job.

Textio discovered that even common formatting practices such as lengthy bullet point lists can reduce the number of women applicants. Research conducted in affiliation with the Science of Diversity and Inclusion Initiative at the University of Chicago also found that generic EEOC statements in job descriptions can reduce the number of minority applicants. The same research showed that specific changes to job postings and descriptions can bolster rates of application from Black and Latinx candidates by almost 300 percent.[16]

If a company is truly interested in recruiting for diversity, it has to take these findings seriously. Findings like these can help companies cut down on bias simply by phrasing and formatting their job ads differently. Tools like Textio's are very easy to use: an employer just inputs its job posting on the site and the text lights up with different colors to indicate whether the phrasing is solid or can be improved. When a phrase is found to be at risk of appealing more to men than women, for example, the algorithm offers a one-click replacement for a gender-neutral synonym.

This is the beauty of machine learning. Companies are increasingly using machine learning algorithms to predict and flag language that creates gender bias during the recruitment process. Recall the eBay study we looked at in the previous chapter, in which researchers mined data from years of auctions and retroactively found that female sellers' listings had been underbid compared to identical ones from male sellers. Here too, algorithms can be forward-looking and can continuously search for irrational or discriminatory patterns by examining how even seemingly small tweaks can be a step toward diversifying the applicant pool.

Screening Fast and Slow

In the 1970s, less than 5 percent of musicians in the top five orchestras in the United States were women. A decade later, the numbers were only slightly better, with female musicians holding 10 percent of the spots in some of these top orchestras. The numbers of non-white musicians were similarly dismal. Increasingly since the 1970s, orchestras began using a curtain to conduct blind auditions, following the lead of the Boston Symphony Orchestra (which first implemented the practice in 1952).[17] The musician would play for a jury that could hear but not see him or her. An even more nuanced step was to place a carpet or to instruct candidates to walk barefoot to their seat so that the jury would not pick up on cues such as high heels clicking, which might inform them that the footsteps were a woman's. The results were transformative: women were at least twice as likely to advance to the next round. But what the blinding of identity achieved in orchestra audition screening is nearly impossible in most settings. How, then, can we simulate a blind interview process and block human decision-makers from picking up signals that can lead us to dismiss certain people as unworthy, quickly and often irrationally? The "fast" initial screening stage—which by nature is instinctual and largely subconscious, and thus less amenable to training—is a place where algorithmic decision-making holds promise.

In his 2011 bestseller *Thinking, Fast and Slow*, Nobel laureate Daniel Kahneman describes in detail the two systems that drive the way we think. One is fast, automatic, intuitive, and emotional; the other is slower, more deliberative, and more logical. Kahneman says that we cannot necessarily trust our intuitions when we're "thinking fast," when our innate biases and assumptions can creep in and color our decision-making—whether or not we're aware of it. After we broaden the pipeline by spreading the word about a job and expanding the pool of applicants, as we discussed earlier, the challenge becomes screening résumés, sometimes hundreds or thousands of them. On average, fast human screening takes seven seconds per résumé. Goldman Sachs, for example, receives a quarter of a million job applications for its summer positions alone. To put that into perspective, it would take one person working sixty hours per week eight whole weeks to screen all those résumés; two people working forty hours per week could get the job done in six weeks. Couple that massive human time cost with inherent (conscious or unconscious) bias, and it's plain to see where smart machines might improve the process.

Automation in applicant screening is already happening. One 2020 report found that nearly half of U.S. companies use algorithms and chatbots to assess candidates during the recruitment process, and 90 percent of Fortune 500 companies use some version of a résumé tracking system.[18] The talent acquisition industry is estimated at over $100 billion and growing. More broadly, *Forbes* projects that the global data market and the market for data analytics will reach $135 billion by 2025 and surpass $1 trillion by 2027. Out of this sea of numbers emerge new opportunities to address ongoing workplace inequality, but also new forms of exclusion. On all fronts—speed, scale, cost, and accuracy—digitization can offer certain competitive advantages. But, as we've learned, and as computer scientists Aaron Roth and Michael Kearns remind us, "Machine learning won't give you things like gender neutrality 'for free' that you don't explicitly ask for."[19]

Do You Play Lacrosse?

Automated résumé screening runs a résumé through a parser that removes formatting and breaks the text down into recognized words and phrases, sorting content into categories such as education, skills, and work experience. The algorithm then searches for keywords or skills coded as desirable and the résumé is scored. The first generation of screening algorithms was primitive, merely searching résumés for particular keywords; these keywords could range from skill sets like Microsoft Excel proficiency to prestigious markers like names of Ivy League schools or distinctions such as summa cum laude.

Because inequality is so entrenched in our society, every data point about a job candidate risks being tainted. Technology can move us toward equality by masking data that may contribute most immediately to biased hiring. The Google Chrome extension Unbias, for example, removes faces and names from LinkedIn profiles, and software from companies like Interviewing.io, Ideal, and Entelo anonymizes applicants' names and identities.[20] But there is an inherent limit to what can be removed. Ideal boasts that it can help companies screen thousands of candidates in seconds while removing "every trace of subconscious bias from that initial screening process," thereby ensuring that companies start with the most diverse candidate pool possible to give them the best possible chances of hiring the most diverse workforce.[21] Once its algorithm strips the applicant's gender, age, and even name, Ideal standardizes its matching between candidates' experience, knowledge, and skills and the requirements of the job for which they're applying. Candidates are then given an overall grade and a percentile ranking, as well as individual grades for different categories, including job fit, skills match, résumé quality, and specific screening questions.

According to Ideal, its process increases diversity, reduces screening costs, and increases employee productivity and retention. That all sounds well and good, but it's not hard to see how AI companies' claims of success might be too good to be true; there needs to be a check on these claims. For one thing, a company must engage in continuous auditing as to whether the algorithm is indeed recommending a balanced number of men and women for hire. As one writer shrewdly remarked about the notion of purging racial indicators from a data set, "If you wanted to remove everything correlated with race, you couldn't use anything. That's the reality of life in America."[22]

Complicating matters is the fact that résumé screenings are prone to replicating past wrongs, as we have seen. Algorithms are incredibly precise in identifying correlations. For instance, an algorithm can find patterns linking gender identity and opportunity to a gendered career path in a data set. To take one example, LinkedIn's algorithm assigns more than 100,000 variables to each user.[23] Even with that much information—even when names and specific boxes marked for gender or ethnicity are purged—AI can still discover such identity markers. While an algorithm can be programmed not to classify for a certain category like gender or race, proxies such as names, zip codes, shopping patterns, clicks, connections, and consumption patterns can give the algorithm enough clues not to need a direct classification.

A now-scrapped AI tool developed by Amazon offers a striking example of bias in hiring algorithms. In 2014, Amazon began working on a computer model to review job résumés for "top talent." Engineers fed the algorithm résumés submitted to the company over a ten-year period and indicated who was hired out of the pool, training it to find patterns in those résumés. The algorithm became predictably biased: the tech industry is dominated by men, and because Amazon had hired mostly white men, the algorithm naturally learned patterns of success from résumés that were predominately from white male applicants. Soon, Amazon discovered that its recruiting algorithm was sexist and was downgrading résumés that included the word "women's" (as in women's chess club captain, women's math Olympiad, or Women's Law Caucus president) as well as extracurricular activities that are more associated with women. The program also downgraded graduates of all-women colleges because the program "learned" that women's colleges had not historically been a fit for Amazon's workplace. It assigned little weight to the skills necessary to perform the job and put a premium on certain common phrases more commonly found on male engineers' résumés, such as "executed" and "captured." In an audit of another such attempt at unsupervised résumé screening, the two factors the algorithm identified as most indicative of job performance were if the applicant's name was Jared and if they played high school lacrosse.[24]

Learning how to best diversify applicant pools and workplaces happens over time. Think about the Netflix model of selecting content. In 2006, Netflix opened a data set of 1 million users' movie recommendations, stripped of all personal identifying information, to research teams around the world, inviting them to compete to develop the most accurate prediction model for viewing preferences. The company offered a $1 million prize to the team that could improve its existing film recommendation service by 10 percent. Netflix withheld the data set about viewers' subsequent movie choices and ratings so that it could then run the contestants' competing models against the real outcomes of what people were viewing and their ratings. In other words, there were two data sets: one past and one "future." This method is called validation. Validation requires data and continuous improvement and goal setting. But unlike with movie watching, a focus on equality means we cannot just validate past choices; we must actively strive to do better. True validation would require more complete data sets of potential candidates and performance data in an already unbiased labor market.

In 2018, Amazon announced that it was abandoning the project, stating that the recruiting tool had never been used to choose real applicants.[25] Amazon did not code the program to look for anything specific, but rather allowed the unsupervised algorithm to produce its own decision trees from the collection of résumés fed to it. The lesson here is that an algorithm is only as good as the data it is fed. If the data is skewed or partial, biases will be baked in. Amazon's failed experiment exemplified the fact that an algorithm built on a data set of whoever has been selected in the past for particular opportunities—be they college admissions, jobs, loans, or anything else—will replicate any systemic exclusions that have occurred.

What's more, companies and colleges don't track the success of the people who *aren't* hired, approved, or admitted—no data exists on how they would have performed. And behaviorally, we know that on average, women tend to downgrade their résumés while men tend to amplify theirs. Even recommendation letters for promotions have been found to describe women and men differently: women are typically described as empathetic; men are described as strong leaders. The bottom line is that making screening decisions based on who was hired (or approved, or admitted) in the past is a recipe for baked-in algorithmic discrimination. If nearly everything in the past—from references to evaluations—has been tainted by bias, then all data derived from it will be tainted. Bias in, bias out.

And, of course, it's a vicious cycle: when some groups are not represented in sample populations, an algorithm has no way to model their successes. If we simply train algorithms on an industry's existing talent pool, we will replicate past marginalization. AI uses data to observe what employers do, thus learning from human behavior. Even if we only feed the algorithm data about women who were hired in the past and ask it to replicate their profiles for future hires, we can run into unexpected risks. There may be distorted patterns even among women and minorities who have been hired. For example, we know from experience that some men are threatened by high-performing women; what if a hiring executive only hires women who don't present this perceived threat? Perversely, relying on past data may skew the hiring process to screen out precisely those who would excel in their jobs.[26]

At the same time, we also know that we can neither quantify nor change what we don't measure. Engaging in data analytics can illuminate ways to address impediments to equality. Gild is a company that uses an algorithm to crunch thousands of bits of data to identify characteristics of an individual, such as where an applicant socialized and with whom, the language they use, the websites they visit, their social media use, and the skills they list (along with those they appear to have accumulated from their experience listed on LinkedIn). But here again, we run into unforeseen possibilities for bias creep. For example, Gild's software scours information about candidates from platforms like GitHub to see how much time prospective programmers have spent sharing and developing code. On average, though, women have less time to spend online outside of the workday than men do. Women also sometimes choose to post using male identities due to sexist attitudes of platform users. So, left unchecked, Gild's algorithm would penalize women, ranking them lower than male candidates—much like what we saw with Amazon's unsupervised résumé screening debacle.

When we see these disparities and audit the results, we can correct for such imbalances by valuing other skills or accounting, for example, for the lesser amount of time women have outside of the nine-to-five. These issues underscore why identity blindness is actually often undesirable: data can be evaluated differently when accounting for identity, with the specific goal of increasing equal representation and equitable outcomes. For instance, when Gild used data about how long people stayed at a job and discovered that those who have a shorter commute are more likely to stay longer, the company aptly realized that using such a metric would penalize minorities who might not be able to afford to live close to a company in a major metropolitan area. The first reaction to correct this bias might be to exclude the distance between applicants' homes and employer location, yet companies can do far more than that. They could expand the socioeconomic pool of applicants by in fact valuing the distance a worker must travel and helping with commute time by offering compensation for commuters or more flexible and remote work schedules. When the pool is expanded and new screening and oversight processes are developed, companies committed to diversity can specifically request to search for the top candidates in a particular category—for example, displaying all the highly ranked women at the top of the list. Ultimately, the more we know about candidates, the more we can do when we're truly committed to diversifying the workplace.

Grit and Games

To increase the data points and types of information that are screened for beyond what is found in résumés and references, the recruiting industry is introducing new kinds of hiring algorithms. These new screening methods forgo résumés and screening for pedigree, which is often encoded with skewed privilege, and instead analyze voice and facial expressions when an applicant submits an online video interview, online personality tests, and even data drawn from applicants playing online games. This growing industry promises that these alternatives can mitigate bias and increase diversity as well as productivity and ultimately success in the workplace.

Companies like HireVue and Cappfinity provide employers with face-scanning algorithms that observe candidates' video interviews. These programs analyze voice, tone, and behavior along with word choice and facial movements, ranking candidates comparatively on an employability scale. The companies say that their algorithms screen for qualities such as grit, curiosity, and polish. HireVue's algorithm considers hundreds of elements, including whether the candidate speaks in passive or active voice, how fast they talk, and how long their sentences are. According to HireVue, the company has already analyzed more than 12 million applicants, helping employers cut costs and increase diversity. Its clients include Hilton, IKEA, Oracle, Staples, HBO, and many more. Even the Atlanta public school system has used the company's services. Loren Larsen, HireVue's chief technology officer, describes why the algorithm is better than human judgment on candidates: "People are rejected all the time based on how they look, their shoes, how they tucked in their shirts and how 'hot' they are. Algorithms eliminate most of that in a way that hasn't been possible before."[27] AI video analysis received much attention for both its accuracy and its inaccuracy, and there is no doubt that the technology is imperfect. But Larson has a good point: human interviewers in face-to-face interactions have long been making highly problematic judgments. If machines can learn to do better, we should certainly explore their potential.

Pymetrics is another company leading the way in developing alternatives to traditional job screening methods. Its founding CEO, Frida Polli, set out to apply behavioral insights and a gamified environment to the hiring process to help companies diversify their workforces. Polli says she realized the problems with the recruiting process when she was in the job market. As a thirty-eight-year-old single mom with degrees from Harvard and the Massachusetts Institute of Technology (MIT), she didn't fit the twentysomething male entrepreneur mold. When I interviewed her, she was Zooming from her living room with two small children playing and doing remote learning in the background. She explained how Pymetrics forgoes what it sees as an archaic differentiator—namely, résumés and traditional markers of prestige—and instead asks applicants to play online games that measure cognitive and emotional attributes like decision-making, focus, generosity, fairness, and risk tolerance, among others.[28] The company customizes these games for clients including Boston Consulting Group and JPMorgan Chase. She described how one large investment firm—which previously had hired primarily from a few top local universities and through referrals—shifted its hiring to more than sixty different schools, significantly increasing female and minority hiring as a result.

Polli acknowledges that algorithms are not objective by nature but says she firmly believes that they can be employed to mitigate bias. She describes two camps in the market: those who are eager to use any kind of automated screening and will adopt any technology indiscriminately, and those who want to completely avoid using technology. Polli urges us to consider the vast space in between these two camps. Pymetrics' analysis, Polli said, is based on games it conducts with a client firm's current staff to create profiles of successful employees to compare incoming candidates. The algorithm is programmed to focus on features it sees as equally distributed among identity groups. Pymetrics also strives for transparency and has increased its reporting to the EEOC. When I asked Polli how we can simultaneously demand transparency and protect a company's trade secrets, she replied that it's analogous to monitoring car emissions: we require reporting on the emission levels, not on how the engine was built.

Pymetrics is not the only company pioneering the use of video games as job-hiring tools. Knack, a company founded by an old friend of mine from graduate school, created a game called Wasabi Waiter that helps employers screen applicants. The game places the job applicant in the role of a server at a sushi restaurant. The player must decide which dishes to recommend to customers and then deliver the right dishes during an increasingly busy happy hour, requiring the player to prioritize, persist, strategize, and multitask. The software then analyzes all the data points collected from gameplay and offers insight into an applicant's intellectual and personal makeup. Guy Halfteck, Knack's founder and CEO, partnered with Royal Dutch Shell a few years back to examine Wasabi Waiter's predictive value in identifying creative employees. Shell's start-up accelerator program asked 1,400 past idea contributors to play Wasabi Waiter. The company shared with Halfteck how well three-fourths of these idea generators had done in identifying business ideas, and then Halfteck paired that data with those contributors' Wasabi Waiter performance. With no additional information, Knack's program gave Shell a highly accurate mechanism with which to accurately rank idea generators. The rankings were based on identified factors that distinguish the company's known top creatives, such as their tendency to allow their minds to wander, their "goal-orientation fluency," their implicit learning and task-switching abilities, and their conscientiousness and social intelligence. Hans Haringa, a Shell executive, called this recruitment system a paradigm shift.[29]

In another such game, Firefly Freedom, designed by Arctic Shores, job applicants enter a magical forest world where they must catch fireflies to provide light for their family during winter. Players catch fireflies using a net and keep them in a jar, firing pieces of fruit to release them. One out of ten fruits smashes the jar, allowing all the fireflies to escape. The game looks at applicants' risk-taking and risk aversion tendencies and their persistence—whether they will press on in their quest for more fireflies and risk losing them all or quit while they're ahead. The accounting firm Deloitte uses Firefly Freedom to evaluate interns with the express aim of eliminating human bias and recruiting high-potential applicants from a variety of backgrounds. Emma Codd, a global special advisor on inclusion at Deloitte, explains the firm's rationale for using this next-generation testing in its hiring process like this: "We need people to join Deloitte from a variety of backgrounds, bringing a range of perspectives and experience. There is compelling evidence that alternative recruitment methods support this objective, helping to identify exceptional talent by providing opportunities for the millennial generation to shine."[30]

Of course, we must also look beyond the promise of these new avenues—and beyond the declarations and statements of the services that profit from them—and carefully monitor and audit results with public external processes that we can trust. Whether it's derived from gameplay or more conventional methods like social media data, information about us can be skewed. There is always a risk that looking to the past to identify successful workers and then modeling a screening process after such patterns will replicate past wrongs. We need to think comparatively and look at a trajectory of positive changes. We need to bring the same rigor to these practices that we have employed in other contexts. Pharmaceutical companies conduct randomized, controlled experiments, reported to the FDA, on what types of drugs are effective at keeping us healthy and safe; in much the same way, we could examine results on new ways to screen applicants that produce diversity and high performance in tandem.

Scaling Successes

This is where systemic audits and guidelines can come in. As a four-foot-eleven gay Black woman and a technologist, Blendoor founder and CEO Stephanie Lampkin considers herself well suited to tackle the problem of workplace discrimination. She recognizes how much our past opportunities—even the earliest ones—contribute to our success in the job market. Lampkin told me how, despite growing up periodically homeless in Maryland, she got lucky. She had extended family, aunts in particular, who were educated and who inspired her. Lampkin believes that she gained survival skills and found her passion for data analytics via her mom's work as a Mary Kay representative. Mary Kay is a multilevel cosmetics marketing business that has been operating since the 1960s and has been called a "pink pyramid scheme." Even so, Lampkin's mother did well in the cutthroat entrepreneurial environment; Lampkin vividly remembers the iconic pink Cadillac her mother brought home.

She also recalls her mother enlisting her to help with bookkeeping and to log all the receipts and sales, giving her early skills that would prove relevant to coding. Her mother hadn't even heard of Stanford, but Lampkin applied, got in, and graduated with a degree in engineering. She went on to earn an MBA at MIT. Still, when she interviewed for a job at Google in 2013 after working at Lockheed Martin, Microsoft, and TripAdvisor, she didn't get the job. She looked at Google's diversity figures and saw a pattern: the company hired few engineers who were women of color. "The further you are from a cisgender white male in their thirties," Lampkin says, "the harder it is to escape bias." She founded Blendoor as a job recruiting platform that uses data analytics to help companies hire and manage a diverse workforce.

Blendoor trained its algorithm with performance metrics rather than historical résumé data of those who had previously been hired. Lampkin describes her "'guiding idea': talent and genius are evenly distributed, opportunity is not."[31] She believes that data can help us identify the signals of success for those who have not been in the privileged end of the job market pool: "If you are building a model using what has been historically successful, it automatically skews the rating system to favor what has been historically representative, which we know to be male and predominantly white."[32]

Lampkin told me that while Blendoor was successful in helping its customers significantly increase hiring of women and minorities, she sees more work to do to identify all the skills that can help a candidate be successful. Screening services like Blendoor's often improve on human decision-making and bring progress, but she believes—and I agree—that systematic analysis of what companies are really doing is key. So Lampkin decided to pivot Blendoor's focus and launched BlendScore, a system that scores and ranks companies based on diversity and inclusion efforts "to help job seekers find where they truly belong." BlendScore measures how well a company is recruiting, retaining, and treating its women and underrepresented minority employees. The Blendoor Bias Index uses surveys and publicly available data to create a score for a company. The software scours the internet for information about companies' inclusion policies, parental leave, flexible work arrangements, and diversity numbers. Among the dozens of factors it considers are indicators such as using blind data when screening for candidates.

According to Lampkin, the market for these scores is broader than just the companies themselves and their prospective employees; she thinks that investors, too, are interested in looking at how companies perform on the diversity front because they know that what's good for diversity is also good for business. For example, in 2020, Goldman Sachs announced that it would not support companies in going public unless their boards are diverse, with a focus on women. Lampkin envisions this kind of diversity scoring as the equivalent of *U.S. News and World Report*'s annual college and university rankings. She says that since the killing of George Floyd in particular, and amid the twenty-first-century global movement for racial justice more broadly, employers have promised more diversity. But, strikingly, BlendScore found companies that have made statements about hiring more diverse employees to be less diverse than those that did not. Lampkin recently moved from Silicon Valley to Washington, D.C., to be closer to public initiatives for more data collection and transparency.

Going back to our guiding principles, we can't fix what we don't measure. In one study published by the National Bureau of Economic Research (NBER), programmers trained an algorithm over the course of twelve years to predict corporate director selections.[33]

The algorithm found that companies were more likely to choose directors who were male, were part of a large network, already had ample board experience, and had a finance background. Detection of bias is a first step in using AI as an ethical tool. But the NBER study results also showed something critically important: directors who are not board cronies and come from different backgrounds do a better job of monitoring management. So, the algorithm in fact helped show that human bias in corporate board selection is not just bad for diversity but bad for business as well. And like corporate board outsiders, who are more willing to expose corruption in their corporate monitoring roles, algorithms lack innate conflicts of interest. AI doesn't favor personal connections and will not turn a blind eye when data proves a historical selection process faulty. Discrimination is bad for business; negatively impacts a company's productivity, profit, and reputation; and prevents the recruitment and retention of the best talent.

Systemic inquiry about workplace diversity can happen only when we have enough public data to look at what is actually occurring in the corporate world. Thanks to algorithmic data mining, we can gather quite a bit of information simply from browsing the web. Recently, a group of researchers from Europe and the United States collaborated to develop automated assessments of organizational diversity and detection of discrimination by race, sex, age, and other parameters. The researchers applied the deep-learned predictors of gender and race—algorithms that use facial and name recognition to predict identity—to the executive management and board member profiles of the 500 largest companies on the 2016 Forbes Global 2000 list. They then ranked the companies by a sex and race diversity index.[34] Overall, in the photos found online, women represented only 21.2 percent of all corporate executives. Of these executives, 79.7 percent were white, 3.6 percent were Black, and 16.7 percent were Asian. Except for the Swedish clothing giant H&M, every single company had a lower percentage of women executives than what would be expected relative to the percentage of women in the general population.

The researchers also found dramatic differences between companies and countries. European and North American companies fared far better than Asian companies. A staggering number of Chinese, Japanese, and Saudi Arabian companies had *no* female corporate executives with searchable, publicly available photographs. The researchers acknowledged in their study that the method was far from perfect: publicly available data has a margin of error, and comparing findings to a country's general population doesn't always make sense. The study predicted that improved AI and increasingly available data will serve as powerful tools for rapid analysis of diversity in the private sector, as well as in government, educational institutions, and media. It concluded with a telling paragraph describing how the use of AI to assess organizational diversity is highly controversial: one of the young female collaborators on the research team asked to be removed from the study "after being intimidated by a journalist from a media outlet with a low diversity index." Indeed, data is power, and there will always be powerful people who will want to cover their tracks, maintain secrecy, and try to block data mining that exposes inequality. We need to make sure that people are empowered to use data—and have the power to mine it—to expose inequality.

Opaque Algorithms, Validation, and Policy

Competition among for-profit firms in providing automated—and diversity-enhancing—hiring services has the market bubbling, but competition also means keeping data secret. Companies are notoriously tight-lipped about their internal statistics and processes, and they often try to shield such information behind labels like "proprietary," "confidential," and "trade secrets." Such secrecy makes it more difficult to check claims about the effectiveness of new screening processes. But increasingly, we are seeing initiatives to create more transparency and improve auditing of automated screening processes. In 2019, the California State Assembly passed a resolution urging federal and state policymakers to use technology to reduce bias and discrimination in hiring.[35] Also in 2019, the Washington, D.C.–based Electronic Privacy Information Center (EPIC) filed a complaint with the Federal Trade Commission (FTC) arguing that HireVue had engaged in unfair and deceptive trade practices in its use of face-scanning technology to evaluate job candidates.[36] The complaint specifically targeted the company's alleged use of "opaque algorithms and facial recognition."[37] Describing the potential bias in such stealth AI screening tools, the complaint quoted a business school's advice to students preparing for AI interviews: "Robots compare you against existing success stories; they don't look for out-of-the-box candidates."[38] Subsequently, HireVue abandoned its use of facial analysis algorithms but has continued to use algorithms to analyze speech, intonation, and behavior.

In 2020, EPIC petitioned the FTC to set rules on the commercial use of AI, citing hiring as one context in which unregulated use can cause harm. The message is clear: we need more transparency around how the various automated tests fare on equality. Differences in speech, facial expressions, and vocabulary may correlate with race or ethnicity and thus need to be monitored for disparate impact. Matt Scherer, who heads the AI department at the law firm Littler Mendelson, told me that there is a lot of "snake oil that's being peddled in this space," and that the number of clients who are falling into purchasing said oil has frustrated him. He says that some companies are trying to reduce the costs of using human recruiters and are willing to believe any claim. We urgently need to implement better oversight procedures and to rethink the scope of trade secrecy, which erodes access to important information. The rapidity of the algorithmic processing makes it very difficult to go back and check what happened during screening. Public policy should require firms to store snapshots of data sets at different points of the process.

Laws need to be adapted to support what is happening in the market. Under current discrimination law, it may be unlawful to tell an algorithm to adjust the scores of women or to institute hiring quotas. The current law on affirmative action is unsettled. For years, the quest for equality has presented a puzzle and bred tensions between different laws. Many policies to increase diversity have themselves been deemed discriminatory, labeled as unconstitutional affirmative action. Technology may help us move beyond the conundrum of wanting to be both identity conscious and identity blind. Legal scholar Pauline Kim argues that federal discrimination law should be broadened to prohibit what she terms *classification bias*—the use of automated classification that exacerbates inequality along the lines of sex, race, or other protected categories.[39]

But we've also seen that classification can be a way to support rather than impede inclusion. In the past, we could often know if an employer was using a screening factor that has a disparate impact on certain identities. For example, using height, weight, or physical strength requirements will inevitably result in gender exclusion. Other cases have involved the use of aptitude tests or college degrees as screening devices, which have a disparate impact on racial minorities. But with big data mining, there are times when no one—including employers—can know how attributes were processed to result in a disparate impact. This reality suggests that our policies—and how we think about discrimination and equality more broadly—must evolve. We need to be results-oriented rather than focusing merely on the traditional input-oriented legal inquiry, or what Columbia law professor Talia Gillis has termed legal policy's *input fallacy*. Comparing outputs for different identities is a distributional question, a question of social justice, and it opens the door for a transformative shift in how we think about equality.

There are quite a few initiatives happening on the policy side. In 2020, California enacted the California Consumer Privacy Act, the most comprehensive data privacy law in the country to date. One of the aspects it regulates is increased transparency in using AI for hiring decisions. The law requires employers to disclose information about how their data is being used by AI models. It also gives applicants a right to access all the data that has been gathered about them, and the right to demand deletion of this data. Several other states are passing laws to provide checks on the rapid integration of automation in employment, and soon we will have more avenues to examine the success of these initiatives. In 2019, the Illinois General Assembly passed the Artificial Intelligence Video Interview Act, which requires employers to notify applicants when they use AI assessment, including what types of factors are considered. The New York City Council passed a similar law in 2021, requiring AI technology to undergo anti-bias testing; employers also have to disclose AI use to job candidates, along with the specific job qualifications or characteristics the company used AI to measure. A Maryland law that went into effect in 2020 prohibits an employer from using facial recognition AI to create a facial template during an applicant's interview without obtaining consent. As we will see later in the book, there are U.S. federal initiatives—and, even more so, European Union efforts—to require companies to conduct impact assessments of automated decisions, and to take steps to rectify any issues found with accuracy, bias, or discrimination. All of these efforts are nascent, and the role of policy, including public research and learning about the best ways to regulate and ensure oversight, is critical.

Looking at the big picture should give us hope. We humans often decide automatically, intuitively, and subconsciously. But today, we can run a test on an algorithm to determine if it would come up with the same result if a person's gender or race were different. We can feed an algorithm a data set of past workers or we can choose a data set that is more expansive. We can examine how certain ads deter diverse applicants or reach a larger pool. If a decision was made algorithmically, plaintiff attorneys could demand access to the algorithm and the data set. With AI, there is something tangible to scrutinize, unlike the black box of the human decision-maker. These developments mean that employers can screen for qualities that go beyond what applicants have put on paper—beyond the dry facts of their lives—and into assessments of cognitive ability, social skills, work ethic, drive, passions, ethics, and resilience. It also means that employers can observe thousands of applicants even if they are just searching for a small number of new hires, and they can use algorithmic models to predict not only job performance but the likelihood that the employee will be happy and stay in the job for the long haul.

CHAPTER 3

Knowing Your Worth

The way to right wrongs is to turn the light of truth upon them.

—IDA B. WELLS, co-founder of the
National Association for the Advancement
of Colored People (NAACP)

The Bot Measuring Tape

In 1994, Nancy Hopkins, a tenured biology professor at MIT, grabbed a measuring tape and physically compared, inch by inch, the size of her lab to those of her male colleagues. She found that she had less than half—and in some cases one-quarter—of their lab space. Even compared to the average *junior* male professor, she had 500 square feet less space. After Hopkins met with fellow biology professor Mary-Lou Pardue and drafted a letter to MIT president Charles Vest, all the tenured women science professors at MIT at the time—15 women compared to 202 men—joined together to document such inequities. By 1996, Hopkins was leading a committee to write an internal report; by 1999, she had expanded her efforts to a national report on women in science. These efforts led to changes in research institutions across the United States, not only with regard to resources and space afforded to women scientists but also around

the gender imbalance in recruiting women faculty, the need to offer daycare services and extend tenure clocks for faculty who take
childcare leave, and the importance of appointing more women to
leadership roles.[1]

Hopkins's measuring tape catalyzed measurable, systemic change.
But one measuring tape can only do so much. It doesn't continue to
measure the space and resources allocated to new hires, for example, along with countless other ever-changing data points. Most of
the time, inequalities are hidden from sight. A man and a woman
may formally hold identical positions, but their treatment can vary
significantly in terms of the rewards, opportunities, and experience
they gain. In 2012, building on the method of the résumé experiments discussed in Chapter 2, a team of researchers at Yale University created fictional résumés for a lab manager position, assigning
half of the identical résumés a male name (John) and half a female
name (Jennifer).[2] The researchers asked more than a hundred faculty
members nationwide to assess the résumé they received. The majority rated John as significantly more competent and worthier of hire
than Jennifer, and John was offered the job more frequently. When
Jennifer was offered the job, she was offered a lower salary—an average of $4,000 less annually. Strikingly, both male and female hiring
managers tended to offer Jennifer lower pay than they offered John.
Such inequities in pay and resources persist beyond academia—
they're everywhere. In 2020, researchers ran an experiment asking
working professionals to play the role of a manager in a fictitious
tech company. Participants read employee performance reviews of
two fictional employees, Steven and Susan, and were then asked to
distribute stock options to their team.[3] The experiment revealed that
when participants were asked to distribute stocks based on the goal
of *retention*—that is, with the goal of keeping the employees in the
company—a gender gap favoring men was still substantial. Interestingly, though, when participants were asked to compensate based on
potential—guided to think about the contributions and value that the
employees are bringing—the gender gap disappeared.

The road to bring pay equity to workplaces, whether in research
institutes, finance, or any other sector you can think of, has been long

and winding. In 1869, a woman wrote a letter to the editor of the *New York Times* asking why female government employees were paid less than their male counterparts (half as much, in fact) for equal work. The following year, Congress narrowly passed a resolution that government employees would receive equal pay regardless of gender. During the First and Second World Wars, with American men leaving the country en masse, women began to fill jobs once thought to be only within a man's domain. The wars not only created space for women in the workforce but also led to unions supporting equal pay; unions realized that if women were paid less for the same work, then management would lower male workers' wages after they returned from war. Then came the pivotal legislation: almost a hundred years after it first addressed the gender pay gap, Congress passed the Equal Pay Act of 1963, mandating equal pay for equal work. The following year, Congress again addressed pay discrimination by passing Title VII of the Civil Rights Act of 1964. Soon after, most states followed suit and enacted equal pay laws of their own.

Despite the landmark law, for decades the story of the gender pay gap has been one of stagnation. In 1974, the U.S. Supreme Court wrote in a wage gap decision that "the wage structure of many segments of American industry has been based on an ancient but outmoded belief that a man, because of his role in society, should be paid more than a woman even though his duties are the same."[4] This outmoded belief continues to affect compensation, resources, and promotions today. On average, women still earn 82 cents for every dollar earned by men, and the wage gap is larger for women of color. Because I work in the field of pay equity, every year I recognize Equal Pay Day in March (the exact date differs from year to year). This date represents how far into the next year women must work to earn what their male counterparts earned in the previous year. It is important to note, though, that the March date represents the wage gap for *all* women; the statistics are far starker for women of color. In 2021, Black women, who earn 63 cents for every dollar paid to white men, achieved parity on August 3; Native American women (60 cents for every dollar paid to white men) on September 8; and Latina women (55 cents for every dollar paid to white men) on October 21.

These big-picture statistics of gender inequality in the work-place show the forest but not the trees. The persistent gender pay gap—unequal in and of itself—has many root causes. Economists agree that a portion of the gap can be explained by seemingly private choices. Speaking in broad generalizations, women tend to choose flexible career paths, take time off more frequently, and select less demanding professions. We'll tackle the inequities at home and in our family relations later on. But even when controlling for gendered choices, there is indisputable evidence that direct discrimination is at play. Equal work in the same position, with the same performance level and experience, still does not receive equal pay.

Inequality taints all industries, from low-wage workers to graduates of elite universities. The pay gap grows over time in a woman's career and deepens when she becomes a mother. Astoundingly, the gender gap between like-earning spouses doubles immediately after they have a child, with the mother's earnings never recovering while the father's earnings grow. It's been called the "motherhood penalty" and the "fatherhood bonus." As one journalist aptly (and bluntly) surmised, "One of the worst career moves a woman can make is to have children."[5] The pay gap has certainly lessened since the first U.S. anti-discrimination laws passed in the 1960s, but momentum has stalled in recent decades. In fact, if we attempt to project when parity will be achieved based on the rate of progress over the last five decades, women could expect to reach pay equity with men by 2059. More recently, as the gap has remained constant, projections estimate a delay of a century: without dramatic changes, the gap isn't estimated to close until 2152.[6]

But we can do something dramatic: we can harness technology to accelerate the closing of the gap. Imagine a digital "measuring tape" that on a 24/7 basis measures and records pay, rewards, and resources given to employees. For years, women and people of color—any worker, for that matter—didn't even know that they were underpaid, having no way to compare what they were earning to other salaries. Now, we can do something to remedy that opacity. Thanks to the widely publicized Sony Pictures email hack, Jennifer Lawrence, the highest-paid Hollywood actress in 2015 and 2016, discovered that she was paid 2 percent less for the 2013 film *American Hustle* than her male co-stars. The hack also revealed, among other things, that Sony's female co-president was earning $1 million less than her male counterpart.[7] Until that leak, the numbers were a closely guarded secret, like so many other workplace pay scales. If we want pay equity, we must correct for information asymmetry and move toward more transparency. Women and minorities can negotiate better salaries when they know where they stand relative to their co-workers. But employers are notorious for prohibiting their employees from discussing salaries, and increasingly so in recent decades. Sharing salary information is not merely discouraged by employers through non-disclosure agreements, policies, and corporate culture; it has long been taboo in American society. Technology is opening up the salary books.

When algorithms analyze patterns in salaries across positions and firms—accounting for skill, experience, occupation, industry, job description, and factors such as evaluation and performance— they can identify gender pay gaps in those vast data caches in ways that human eyes looking at smaller data sets simply cannot. Data can help employees better negotiate their pay; help employers correct the way they treat, compensate, and retain their employees; and help policymakers create systemic changes in the market.

Data can also help all of these stakeholders—employers, employees, investors, and governments—recognize the strong business case for equal pay. McKinsey & Company recently calculated that greater equality could equate to trillions of dollars—finding, for example, that companies with the most gender-diverse boards report 91 percent higher earnings and 36 percent higher stock prices than the industry average.[8] In my work on talent pools, creativity, and social responsibility, I've similarly found that diversity in teams is one of the great fuels of innovation. A wealth of research supports the idea that companies with diverse and equal representation across the board also tend to innovate more and score higher on measures of corporate ethicality. According to a 2020 article in *MIT Sloan Management Review*, companies with greater diversity experience higher R&D intensity, more patenting activity, and higher levels of overall innovation.[9]

Bots for Pay Equity

Technology is changing the way information is exchanged, understood, and used in the market for wages. Digital platforms accessible to job seekers are aggregating petabytes of data about employees' market worth, supporting demands for equal pay. New software is also enabling employers to detect pay discrimination internally, dynamically, repeatedly, and proactively. In recent years, thousands of companies—including Adobe, AT&T, Citigroup, Colgate-Palmolive, eBay, Mastercard, Microsoft, Nike, Starbucks, Symantec, and Target, to name a few—have added equal pay pledges to their company profiles.

Human-driven efforts are frequently tainted by bias, be it conscious or unconscious. One of the most immediate numbers that shape employee compensation is salary history. Past salary shapes the future gap and in turn affects negotiations. When it comes to setting pay, a common cognitive process called *anchoring bias* can cause us to rely too heavily on initial data points at the expense of a more rational valuation of a person's worth. When I teach my course on pay discrimination, I often replicate a well-known behavioral experiment: I ask my students to write down the last two digits of their social security number and then guess the price of a bottle of wine I bring to class. The lucky winner whose guess is closest to the price wins the bottle. What comes out time and again is what behavioral economists call anchoring bias. Simply jotting down an irrelevant number (such as one's social security number) skews the guess about the value of an unrelated item. If the last two digits of my social security are low, I am likely to guess that the wine is cheaper. You can see the implications for salary determinations: if irrelevant numbers affect our decision-making, imagine the effect of all the noise we hear and see when deciding something like employee compensation. *Confirmation bias*, too, is a common behavioral tendency in which we favor information that confirms our already-existing beliefs or assumptions. When recruiters ask for salary history and receive information about a female applicant's lower past salary, they may view other pieces of information—such as her experience, talent, and qualifications—in ways that confirm biases and stereotypes and justify a lower baseline salary. This bias can be replicated by bots: if an algorithm makes predictions using previous salaries as a measure of a candidate's competence and quality, the past and ongoing wage gap will harm women and people of color. Yet in the case of algorithmic decision-making, we can address such reliance on gendered patterns of past salaries and program the bot to correct for these differences.

Take the case of the BBC gender pay gap controversy. In 2017, the flagship British broadcaster, under pressure from the government as a publicly funded institution, released a list of its highest-paid on-air talent. Sixty-two men and thirty-four women made the list, which revealed that the highest-earning woman made £1.7 million less than the highest-earning man. The revelations unleashed a maelstrom that raged for a year and brought the case before a parliamentary committee. Over the course of that tumultuous year, hundreds of employees—both male and female—organized a private WhatsApp group to expose the BBC's pervasive gender pay gap. Colleagues shared pay and pension information using secure digital spreadsheets. Members of the group went so far as to wear lapel badges emblazoned with their salaries when meeting with upper management.[10]

As a result of the movement, the United Kingdom now requires employers with more than 250 employees to annually report their gender pay gaps. Mandatory reporting allows government agencies to mine through the data to better investigate complaints and enforce compliance. When the first reports began to come out, then–British prime minister Theresa May said, "We expected the results to make for uncomfortable reading and they do." An important revelation from the figures was a "startlingly high" bonus gap—performance-based compensation beyond base salaries that was, May wrote, "unseen until now."[11] And as May emphasized, transparency alone will not solve inequality, but it is a necessary first step. During his presidency, Barack Obama issued a similar rule set to cover more than 63 million employees, requiring companies with more than 100 employees to report employee pay broken down by gender, race, and ethnicity. The Trump administration issued a stay of the initiative, asserting that the collection of information was unnecessarily burdensome to companies. The Biden administration readopted the rule and reporting is becoming a reality.

If you don't know your worth, then you don't know that you're undervalued. The pay gap has been one of the most frustrating policy areas in my research because the gap has remained stagnant for decades. In 2007, the Lilly Ledbetter Supreme Court case demonstrated how problematic not knowing one's worth can be. Ledbetter worked for the Goodyear Tire and Rubber Company for nineteen years, unaware that she was paid less than her equally qualified male colleagues. When she finally found out by way of an anonymous note, the Court told her that the clock had run out on her opportunity to sue. In her passionate dissent (successfully) calling on Congress to overturn the majority's ruling, Justice Ruth Bader Ginsburg got to the heart of the matter:

> The problem of concealed pay discrimination is particularly acute where the disparity arises . . . because male counterparts are given larger raises. Having received a pay increase, the female employee is unlikely to discern at once that she has experienced an adverse employment decision.[12]

Responding to Justice Ginsburg's call, Congress passed the Lilly Ledbetter Fair Pay Act in 2009 to clarify that the time limit for suing an employer for pay discrimination restarts each time a paycheck is issued, rather than running solely from the original discriminatory action of the salary decision. The change was applied not only to gender but also to race, national origin, ethnicity, religion, age, and disability discrimination.

But stopping the clock on when victims can sue as soon as they find out about discrimination can only go so far. Secrecy used to last forever. In the 1970s, Nobel laureate economist Gary Becker provided the theoretical foundations that help explain the persistence of the gender wage gap under conditions of secrecy.[13] Under perfect market conditions, with perfect information and perfect competition, if a group of workers is treated differently by a small proportion of employers, then the forces of competition should eradicate that discrimination. Secrecy, however, prevents employees from efficiently seeking jobs elsewhere. This logic is disturbingly coherent: when the number of firms with pay secrecy is large enough, discrimination persists.

Becker couldn't imagine a market where everyone knows their worth, but times are changing. Digital connectivity is converging with changing norms and policies to upend the wage information markets. Flipping transparency on its head, the goal should be helping employers rationally decide employees' true worth *without* focusing on what they were paid in the past, and at the same time allowing employees to know their worth too. Again, think of a smart measuring tape that continuously records and reveals inequities in a particular industry. In 2020, I was honored to become a founding board member of the Fair Pay Workplace Alliance along with more than a dozen colleagues from industry and academia. The kickoff was on Equal Pay Day, March 31 of that year. The inaugural meeting was virtual, held during the early days of the Covid-19 pandemic. The goal of the initiative is to create lasting and meaningful pay equity with the help of technology.

The guiding principle is that everyone wins from pay equity. Companies like Syndio Solutions and OpenComp offer software that organizations of any size can use to find pay equity concerns and address them. The software makes it easy for employers to upload data, review results instantly, and address concerns in real time. Democratizing access to analytics puts compliance within reach and eliminates the problems that make data analysis and review challenging. I sat down with Syndio founder Zev Eigen, who describes the company's software technology as "the future of pay equity." Syndio's platform aims to ensure that people are paid equitably before and after they're hired and that they're promoted based on objective, unbiased standards. When Salesforce ran an external audit to look at their pay gaps in 2015, they discovered millions of dollars of gaps that required adjustment. The next year, despite these adjustments, they discovered another $3 million in pay gaps. Salesforce hired Syndio to help them analyze the compensation data in a more systemic, ongoing way than an annual external audit. Maria Colacurcio, CEO of Syndio, says that we need to reframe the word "audit" and think about embedding pay equity into the process of salaries all throughout. With employees in twenty-eight countries, Salesforce needs to manage the complexities of regional variation and differences in laws. With Syndio's help, Salesforce significantly reduced the need for annual adjustments, sustained pay equity, and in 2021 was named number two in Fortune's 100 Best Companies to Work For.

Syndio's customers until 2020 were more focused on gender pay gaps—only half of the clients requested analysis by race. But Syndio reports that since 2020, 98 percent now analyze gender and race, with growing attention also to sexual orientation, gender identity, and disability status. For example, ongoing auditing of the data can illuminate how merit raises can be based on biased evaluations. Similarly, men are more likely to ask for retention raises. Eigen and I have been collaborating on a research project that mines data on pay disparities to develop industry standards for equity software. "The whole ecosystem of compensation should be established and maintained in a way that is fair and ultimately more transparent than it is now," Eigen says. "You could even imagine a world in which people are promoted and given pay increases based on a gamified 'leveling up' system derived from data and data science, putting gender pay inequity in our collective rear-view mirror." Syndio board member Byron Deeter says that measures to address inequities are rapidly becoming an organizational necessity: "Workplace fairness is no longer simply 'nice to have.' Legal requirements are expanding state-by-state and globally, but perhaps more importantly, equity and transparency are becoming necessary ingredients for workplaces to attract and retain the best talent."[14]

Similar to Syndio, Gapsquare is a software company in the United Kingdom whose Fairpay platform helps employers analyze their compensation schemes and detect and correct gaps. Organizations like Condé Nast, Accenture, and the London Metropolitan Police have used Gapsquare's analytics to run their payroll and HR data together in one system, providing a more comprehensive story about the data and helping employers make more accurate, data-driven compensation decisions.[15] Zara Nanu, Gapsquare's CEO and co-founder, started her career campaigning on women's rights issues, including human trafficking, and moved to the tech space to help address workplace inequality. In fact, it was during her time helping women find jobs to escape human trafficking environments that she began to fully understand the importance of addressing the pay gaps that exist in the job market. When Nanu visited these women, she expected them to exude joy and gratitude for being saved from unimaginable conditions. Yet she found them trapped in low-wage work, living and laboring in poorly heated buildings, and without the ability to truly support themselves. She decided that facilitating women's access to the economy and getting them jobs was only part of the battle. The missing piece of the puzzle was career progression and equal earnings. She was struck not only by the pay gap but also by the fact that technology was being used to solve other problems involving medicine and transportation but was not being used to address wage inequality. Data analytics helps companies better understand—and address—the specific contributors to pay gaps. When Google focused its data analytics on the problem of the gender gap, it first identified that women were twice as likely to quit working at Google than men. The company analyzed years of data and found that the time of quitting was more often than not when women became mothers. Google introduced new leave plans that let mothers take five months off, instead of the standard twelve weeks, and saw great success with retaining mothers under the new plan, something that not only tackled the pay gap but also greatly enriched the talent pool of the company.

Private services like Syndio and Gapsquare can also be scaled by government initiatives. For example, when Gapsquare analyzed pay data on 200,000 employees in the United Kingdom, it found that a job with flexibility in its hours and the availability of remote work can help close the pay gap. Governments can act as a research arm to aggregate even more data to better understand the dynamics of exclusion and discrimination in the wage market. Governments can also provide incentives for companies to conduct self-audits using these new software tools. The Swiss government, for example, has developed a free online tool for companies to self-test how they are doing on pay equity.

Beyond company efforts, the rise of online connectivity is also changing our social norms about salary secrecy. Digital platforms such as LinkedIn, Glassdoor, Salary.com, and SalaryExpert are frequent launchpads for people on the job hunt in part because they provide salary information. These platforms have troves of crowdsourced salary information that can be shared, stored, and mined. Glassdoor, for example, provides a pay data tool called Know Your Worth, which provides users with a customized personal market value based on job title, company, location, and experience. It also dynamically analyzes trends and recalculates figures weekly.[16] According to Glassdoor, its salary estimator can calculate the market value for 55–60 percent of the U.S. workforce within roughly a 12 percent margin of error. As with other digital platforms, the algorithm improves as more data is introduced and the machine learns over time.[17] The larger the employer, the more likely the crowdsourced information is accurate. The possibilities, it would seem, are endless.

Can a Bot Negotiate for Me?

For years, the double standard was glaring: employers demanded secrecy about salaries while asking prospective employees for their salary histories. Now, we can tackle both ends of this asymmetry. Just as digitization is helping to reverse information flows to foster more transparency in the market about employees' worth, new laws are also directing employers to not rely as much on past pay levels, which can be tainted by systemic inequality. In 2016, Massachusetts became the first state to pass a law prohibiting employers from asking job candidates about their salary histories. Since then, more than a dozen states have followed suit.

Barring employers from asking prospective job candidates about their salary histories has two goals. The first is breaking the vicious pay gap cycle, which emerges when women are paid less at a previous job and that gap is then replicated by the next employer. The second is addressing gender differences in the negotiation process.

Salary figures are plagued by gender disparity, and they can perpetuate and further exacerbate existing market disparities. When a woman discloses that she currently earns less than a man, she could be harming her salary trajectory—both in the applied-for position and for the rest of her career. Each time she discloses her current salary to a potential employer, that gap is likely to grow, as recruitment efforts and promotions are often offered as a percentage increase in relation to current base salary. Rather than relying on biased figures, bans on salary history inquiry induce employers to use other ways to determine a potential employee's worth, including a shift to automated computation. Employers using market and internal data can consider merit-related characteristics when determining pay, such as experience, training, education, skill, and past performance.

And yet, as we have seen, human bias can creep into our algorithms, and an algorithm that is fed data tainted by salary bias is likely to perpetuate that bias itself. Feedback loops are digital vicious cycles that can result in self-fulfilling outcomes. Once again: bias in, bias out. The risk is that an algorithm will learn that certain types or categories of employees are on average underpaid, and then calculate that into salary offers. This is the wrong that recent policy has been designed to eliminate—and that we can program AI to avoid. Removing the anchored numerical figure encourages employers to proactively assess pay based on the company's needs and the candidate's fit rather than on a tainted number. At the same time, having pay scale information for a job but *not* having a salary history on the table can embolden women to ask for more.

What's more, AI can also help in the future—maybe not even the distant future—by replacing some of the negotiation that takes place in unequal settings. Empirical studies on negotiation differences between men and women have repeatedly shown that women on average negotiate less, and that when they do, employers react negatively.[18] Women don't ask for higher salaries, better terms, promotions, or opportunities nearly as frequently as men do. In my research, I've called this the *negotiation deficit*. In one study at Carnegie Mellon University, 93 percent of female MBA students accepted an initial salary offer, while only 43 percent of men did.[19] In another study, female participants simulating salary negotiations asked for an average of $7,000 less than male participants.[20] Economists Andreas Leibbrandt and John List have also found that while women are much less likely to negotiate with employers over salary, this difference disappears when all job seekers are explicitly told that pay is negotiable, mitigating the pay gap.[21] My own experimental research with behavioral psychologist and law professor Yuval Feldman, my longtime collaborator, has found that women in some work environments act less as "homo economicus"—that is, as rational economic actors—and more as altruistic social actors, such that women do not demand for themselves as much as men, and are more likely to value non-monetary benefits, such as good corporate culture.[22]

Can these research insights offer us clues for developing new software tools that will spur women to negotiate? Digital platforms can serve employees by providing advice and information on asking for a raise or preparing for an interview. Information on pay—and especially an explicit expectation that pay can and should be negotiated—can empower applicants to negotiate higher salaries before accepting job offers. The digital platform PayScale conducts annual surveys asking thousands of job seekers whether they disclosed their pay at previous jobs during the interview process. PayScale's 2018 survey found that women who were asked about their salary histories and refused to disclose were offered positions 1.8 percent *less* often than women who were asked and disclosed. By contrast, men who refused to disclose when asked about salary history received offers 1.2 percent *more* often than men who did disclose.[23]

Even when women do negotiate, they are treated differently. In my research, I call this phenomenon the *negotiation penalty*. Women are told to "lean in" and make demands, but the reality is that for centuries, women have been universally viewed as weaker negotiators than their male counterparts. In one series of experiments, participants evaluated written accounts of candidates who did or did not initiate negotiations for higher salaries. The results in each experiment showed that participants penalized female candidates more than male candidates for initiating negotiations, deeming women

who asked for more not "nice" or too "demanding." While qualities such as assertiveness, strength, and competitiveness culturally
benefit male negotiators, women who display such characteristics
are often considered too aggressive.[24] Another study looked at data
from a group of Swedish job seekers and found not only that women
ended up with lower salaries than equally qualified male peers, but
also that they were often penalized for negotiating like them.[25]

The eleventh annual competition for artificial intelligence that
has been trained to negotiate—the Hagglebot Olympics, as it's been
termed in the popular media—was held in January 2021. Universities from Turkey and Japan won this time. In some experiments
involving negotiations with bots, most people did not even realize
they were talking to a bot rather than another person—the bots had
learned to hold fluent conversations that completely mimicked humans.[26] Using game theory, researchers are increasingly improving
the ways bots can negotiate on behalf of humans, eliminating some
of the aspects in which we humans are fallible, like trying to factor
in and weigh many different aspects of the deal. AI can now predict
the other side's preferences quite fast. For example, an AI listening
by microphone to the first five minutes of negotiation is learning to
predict much of the eventual deal just from the negotiators' voices.[27]
Following these speech patterns through machine learning, it turns
out that when the voice of a negotiator varies a lot in volume and
pitch, they are being a weak player at the negotiation table. When
the negotiating sides mirror each other, it means they are closer to
reaching an agreement. Using AI also has helped uncover the ways in
which women are penalized at the negotiation table. A new study out
of the University of Southern California used a chatbot that didn't
know the gender identities of participants to evaluate negotiation
skills. The study showed that most of us—both men and women—do
quite badly at negotiating salaries. Over 40 percent of participants
didn't negotiate at all, and most people left money on the table they
could have received. Women valued stock options less than men did
as part of their compensation package, affecting women's likelihood
to accumulate wealth over time. These advances can also help with

negotiation disparities across different identities. A group of Israeli and American researchers looked at how a smart computer can negotiate with humans from different cultural backgrounds.[28] Without telling the machine anything about the characteristics of people from three countries—Israel, Lebanon, and the United States—they let the AI learn about the patterns of cultural negotiation differences by engaging in negotiation games. They found that the computer was able to outperform people in all countries. These developments are promising. We can envision bots learning about negotiation differences and ultimately countering such differences to create more equitable exchanges, level the playing field, and achieve fair outcomes. They can be designed to tackle the specific distributive goals we have. Note however that even the visual characteristics of bots can affect negotiations. Nick Yee and Jeremy Bailenson have shown that attractive avatars lead to more intimate behavior with a confederate in terms of self-disclosure and interpersonal distance.[29] In a second study, they also observed that tall avatars lead to more confident behavior than short avatars in a negotiation task. They term it the Proteus Effect (the Greek god Proteus was known to have the ability to take on many self-representations). The Proteus Effect suggests that the visual characteristics and traits of an avatar are associated with correlating behavioral stereotypes and expectations, including those that affect the way we negotiate.

Untapped Potential

Consider this: If, for as long as we can remember, women workers have not been valued to the same degree as men, how might they opt to employ their innovative capacities from outside the regular framework? Do women fare better in alternative settings and non-traditional models? And might the untapped talent pool of the excluded—namely, women and minorities—in fact be richer than that comprising only those who have a foot in the door to traditional employment? In researching open invention processes, Harvard business professors Karim Lakhani and Lars Jeppesen study how innovation often happens via outsourcing.[30] Sometimes a company decides to innovate by calling on the world at large to enter a competition. The company or institution announces an unsolved problem online and offers awards for submitted solutions. Major organizations ranging from NASA to Procter & Gamble to Netflix run such global competitions.

InnoCentive is the largest online marketplace for problem-solving bids. Founded in 2001, its open innovation platform consists of hundreds of thousands of solver-users. Lakhani and Jeppesen studied nearly 200 InnoCentive competitions and discovered that more often than not, so-called outsiders—that is, individuals "who are not engaged in the occupation . . . and are, therefore, not bound by professional customs and traditions"—won these competitions.[31] In some cases, individuals with no experience beat hundreds of insiders who had been working in a particular industry for years.

InnoCentive's blind review process, reminiscent of the Boston Symphony Orchestra's blind auditions, removes contestants' names from entries before they are presented to judges. Lakhani and Jeppesen hypothesized that women excel under these conditions on the premise that, as outsiders, their historical exclusion from traditional inventive settings translates to untapped knowledge. Their findings strikingly aligned with this hypothesis: women who submitted solutions to InnoCentive competitions were 23.4 percent more likely to win than male contestants, regardless of the field of competition. The researchers concluded that women "are on the whole more likely to be in 'the outer circle' of the scientific establishment," and that "trained and talented individuals who could not enter core positions in the fields, i.e., 'women scientists,' might be more capable of approaching problems in fresh ways."[32] These findings support the insight that a wealth of untapped talent—including countless women, people of color, and talent from the developing world—is excluded from mainstream creative processes and operates in the margins of market activity, underscoring the fact that markets are missing out on abundant talent when women, minorities, and outsiders in general do not have equal opportunity. Equality is, for lack of a better phrase, good for business.

Gigs and Gigas

So how do digital platforms fare with regard to equal pay compared to traditional work? The results are mixed, but as we already saw with the research on eBay and Airbnb, digital platforms have the advantage of fine-tuned data on outputs, productivity, completed projects and services, and pay for each task. Fiverr, a leading digital marketplace for online services, thrived during the Covid-19 pandemic, as did many other such platforms. I serve as policy consultant for Fiverr and I have seen the company expand to hundreds of services, from website design, audio, product branding, writing, and editing to architecture and marketing. In 2020, the company crunched its numbers on earnings of the freelancers on the platform, and the findings were promising: it found that women earn roughly 3 percent *more* on a per-project basis than men. More than that, Fiverr reports that women receive 9 percent more project requests through the platform than men, making women the higher overall earners. The average earnings for women are 19 percent higher than the average earnings for men. Perhaps more than in traditional, non-digital work settings, digital platforms allow customers to evaluate sellers and service providers based on their portfolios, reviews, and quality of work.

The gig economy has been the subject of much debate and has been a focus of my research in the past decade. There is no doubt that AI-driven automation will lead to certain job losses, further deepening income inequality. I have argued in my research that it is time to consider how tax, social welfare, universal basic income, and other fiscal transfer policies might have advantages in protecting the interests of many and tackling financial insecurity and income and wealth inequality, compared to traditional labor market wage and work conditions protections.[33] Moreover, we need to understand the net effects of job displacement and job gains that inevitably happen as a result of technological innovation. Governments need to help alleviate transitions and leverage AI to be better prepared for such market shifts. AI is a tool that can at its best reveal the path to distributional justice. For example, the Stanford Immigration Policy Lab has developed an algorithm to help refugees find success and integrate into their new country. Millions of refugees flee their countries every year and settle in host countries. In 2022, Russia's war in Ukraine forced nearly 10 million people to flee their homes, the fastest-growing refugee crisis since World War II. Feeding data from over 30,000 past refugee resettlements in the United States and Switzerland to a machine learning algorithm, the researchers found that economic success depends on education levels, knowledge of English (or another language of the host country), and the specific location of their resettlement within the host country, and it identified that refugees from different backgrounds and with different skills will achieve success in different places. In an article published in *Science*, the researchers show that using AI to help place refugees will increase their employment rates by 40 percent in the United States and by 75 percent in Switzerland, the two countries they initially studied. This suggests that governments can use machine learning—at very little cost—to optimize and support not only vulnerable immigrant populations but the labor market more broadly.

For gig economy workers, the self-employed, immigrants, and indeed anyone dreaming of bettering their financial situation, financial credit is key. Credit enables individual humans, multibillion-dollar entities, and capitalist governments alike to build the present with the help of the future. The traditional and ongoing practice of categorizing people as "creditworthy" and "not creditworthy" is inevitably one of selection. Like the job market, the financial sector has always used proxies for assessing applicant risk. Enter artificial intelligence, which can help sort through massive amounts of data and determine what factors are most important in predicting creditworthiness. Available data might include an applicant's list of contacts, GPS information, SMS logs, app download history, phone model, available storage space, and other data scraped from mobile phones.

In August of 2019, Apple introduced its first credit card with Goldman Sachs and faced immediate regulatory discipline for its "sexist" credit limits. High-profile tech leaders, including Apple cofounder Steve Wozniak and tech entrepreneur David Heinemeier Hansson, took to social media to voice their complaints, noting that female spouses were approved for a minuscule percentage of the credit limits that their male spouses received, despite having identical assets and shared bank accounts. Calling it a sexist algorithm, Hansson tweeted: "My wife and I filed joint tax returns, live in a community-property state, and have been married for a long time. Yet Apple's black box algorithm thinks I deserve 20x the credit limit she does." New York State's Department of Financial Services threatened regulatory action in order to get Apple to rectify the algorithm's bias, and state regulators opened an investigation in 2020, saying: "Any algorithm that intentionally or not results in discriminatory treatment of women or any other protected class violates New York law." Apple and Goldman Sachs did not intentionally discriminate, but the algorithms were likely trained on a data set in which women appeared to pose a greater financial risk than men.

Historically, lending practices have been biased. Women, people of color, and members of the LGBTQ+ community have experienced discrimination in lending, credit, and insurance. Lack of access to these financial resources has spanned decades, and the inequities caused by discriminatory lending practices are still felt today. AI is helping the insurance and financial services sectors alike to become less biased and more equitable. AI is used in lending platforms to analyze thousands of data points. Everything from credit bureaus to bank records, social media streams, and public records are analyzed to indicate creditworthiness, likelihood of fraud, or default. A 2019 study by researchers at the University of California, Berkeley, found that financial tech algorithms discriminated 40 percent less on average compared to face-to-face interactions for loan pricing.[34] The study found that the algorithms did not discriminate in accepting or rejecting loans, and that the strong competition between fintech companies that exclusively deal in electronic lending versus more traditional lenders has led the software to become less biased.

Of course, the same commitment to debiasing and detecting exclusions as in hiring and pay must exist in the financial context. The algorithmic model must be designed with a goal of minimizing bias alongside that of maximizing accuracy, and humans must be involved to review and detect any ongoing bias.[35] In the credit and lending industry, early decision-making processes replicated past exclusions by considering factors such as marital status, gender, and race. When platforms and institutions attempted to neutralize those factors, discrimination still crept in—for example, by accounting for credit history. But now, the best machine learning algorithms are designed to reduce gender and racial gaps by predicting creditworthiness rather than relying on credit history and allowing the use of different predictors to foster equity for different demographics.

We should not and cannot wait until 2059—or, worse, 2152—to close pay gaps or credit gaps. Technology can help increase awareness and visibility of disparities, providing a broader spectrum of comparisons and the potential to walk back generations of biased and discriminatory practices. The future of financial equity lies in our ability to empower the various stakeholders—workers, companies, and governments—to share and mine through data, identify disparities, rationally negotiate corrective action, and work together with smart technology to move toward a more fair and equal market.

III
BODY

CHAPTER 4

#BotToo

*Some people call this artificial intelligence, but
the reality is this technology will enhance us.
So instead of artificial intelligence, I think we'll
augment our intelligence.*

—GINNI ROMETTY, former IBM CEO
and cochair of OneTen

Starting a Movement

In Ovid's *Metamorphoses*, Tereus, the king of Thrace and the son of
Ares, rapes his sister-in-law Philomela. He then threatens her in order to keep her quiet about the assault, but Philomela is defiant and
wishes to speak up. To permanently silence her, the enraged king
cuts out her tongue. Mostly in more subtle ways (but sometimes not),
powerful entities throughout history have silenced countless women
who have experienced sexual violence, abuse, and harassment. In the
book *She Said: Breaking the Sexual Harassment Story That Helped
Ignite a Movement*, journalists Jodi Kantor and Megan Twohey detail how they gathered and reported stories of sexual harassment
and abuse by high-profile men, including the influential American film producer (now convicted sex offender) Harvey Weinstein.
Kantor and Twohey won a Pulitzer Prize in journalism for exposing

Weinstein's history of sexual harassment and intimidation in a 2017 *New York Times* article—the watershed event that propelled the #MeToo movement.[1] Their 2019 book is much more than just the story of a single serial harasser. It is the story of the system that enabled him and countless others to muzzle untold cries for help for generations. *She Said* is the story of a pervasive silencing.

Beyond exposing Weinstein and his horrifying abuse of power, sexual harassment, and assault of dozens of women—including A-list celebrities, aspiring stars, and employees of his company over the course of decades—Kantor and Twohey reveal how allegations and accounts were "killed" for years when other reporters tried to publish them. *Catch and Kill* by Ronan Farrow, which came out the same year, is also about the suppression of #MeToo stories involving Weinstein and other powerful men. Accusers and reporters alike were systematically silenced using contracts, legal threats, money, and professional intimidation. In *She Said*, Kantor and Twohey describe working "in the blank spaces between the words"—the pauses, the signals, the surrounding circumstances, all the pieces of the concealed puzzle—to give voices to victims and expose a culture of secrecy and complacency.

The accusations against Harvey Weinstein triggered the wave of sexual misconduct claims against powerful men that became the #MeToo movement. A pervasive pattern emerged: the accused often hid claims of misconduct from the public through private settlements, which frequently included non-disclosure agreements (NDAs). Zelda Perkins, Weinstein's former assistant, broke her NDA nearly two decades after she settled with him following years of sexual harassment. Gretchen Carlson, a former Fox News host, also broke her silence by filing a lawsuit against Roger Ailes, the network's former chairman and CEO. In 2022, Carlson and I teamed up alongside four other scholars and activists and co-authored a report calling on the Biden administration to address the growing number of secrecy contracts employers are requiring from workers.

This practice of silencing helps explain why sexual harassment is notoriously underreported and difficult to investigate. The EEOC estimates that 70 percent of victims never file a formal complaint, and those who do often experience retaliation. Leveraging digital connectivity, the #MeToo movement demanded that survivors be silenced no more, and continues to this day. It's one of the most powerful examples of how technology can play a pivotal role in fulfilling our demand for greater accountability from individuals and corporations by making reporting easier, tracking the histories of complaints, and collectively exposing misconduct that has been silenced for far too long.

Crowdsourcing Change

Within the global framework of activism, digital connectivity has been crucial to recent social justice movements. Social media serves as a bridge between grassroots activism and policy reform. For the feminist and racial justice movements in particular, digital access has been invaluable. The #MeToo movement gained momentum through the internet and by the famous hashtag that is now synonymous with the cause. The same is true for the Black Lives Matter movement, along with many others.

In the early days of social media, men outnumbered women, but participation has increased and women now outnumber men. This altered ratio changes the narrative we're accustomed to: the more women and other historically underrepresented groups speak up, connect, and share their accomplishments, initiatives, stories, and concerns through hashtags like #MeToo, #TimesUp, #HeForShe, #OscarsSoWhite, and #BLM, the more the world—with its 3.6 billion social media users—is inspired to bring about change. Of course, it takes much more than a hashtag to bring change. Online connections can be the first step toward meaningful reforms. And for change to take hold, we need more—not less—democratized digital access. A 2019 United Nations report cochaired by Melinda French Gates and Jack Ma warns that over half of the world's population lacks real access to the internet, and those are precisely the populations who are already marginalized: women, elderly, people with disabilities, indigenous groups, and those living in poor or remote areas of the world.[2] Mobile access and use remain globally unequal. Across low- and middle-income countries, women are 15 percent less likely to own mobile phones and 234 million fewer women than men have access to the internet on a mobile phone. Particularly in developing countries, women simply do not have equal access to the digital world, nor do they have equal opportunity to develop their digital skills. They have less control over their household's digital devices or their account settings and online identities (when they have them) than men.[3] "At the frontiers of technology, the gap becomes an ocean," another recent UN report states.[4] To extend opportunities to organize and engage in these online social justice movements, we must ensure that everyone has a seat at the digital table.

Scale and equitable participation in digital connectivity allow us to better understand the sources of inequality. Digital access can also have a tremendous positive impact for individuals who wish to capitalize on their previously unmonetized talents and abilities. Technology is never a panacea. But for better or worse, the internet is the world's biggest connector, educator, seller, information aggregator, and megaphone. The printing machine was one of the greatest inventions and equalizers of all time. It was a breakthrough technology that brought progress and democratized knowledge. Growing connectivity allows freedoms but also enables control and supervision. Still, digital design interventions allow us to mitigate some of the tension between for example individual freedoms and regulatory interventions. The right to technological advancement should be shared by all for the benefit of all.

Around the world, activists are using social media strategically more and more. For example, Blank Noise, founded by Jasmeen Patheja, is a community project designed to confront street harassment and sexual violence in India. Its physical and digital art display and social media initiative "I Never Ask for It" invites women to send in clothes that they were wearing when they experienced sexual violence, along with their stories. The goal of the initiative is to illustrate that women are harassed and assaulted regardless of the types of clothing they wear, and to combat the culture of victim blaming that is prevalent not only in India but around the world. Other online forums, such as the "Abuse No More" Facebook page, provide spaces where people can expose issues that women face by encouraging and facilitating communication among their members. These forums create a sense of community among abuse survivors, resulting in more survivors coming forward and more accountability for abusers.

Activists have gone viral on online platforms large and small through campaigns, advertisements, hashtags, blogs, clips, GIFs, sharing, liking, and circulating. Modern-day internet activism combines outrage, morality, passion, and humor. The #MeToo movement showed how a hashtag could create a snowball effect of stories and support, quickly becoming a global campaign. In solidarity, UN Women's #HeForShe movement has engaged billions of users worldwide in support of advancing gender equity. In the United States, the Women's March on Washington became the largest globally coordinated public event of all time, born from the 3-million-member Facebook group Pantsuit Nation.

Black Lives Matter—with its hashtag #BLM—similarly brought people together, organizing protests and calling for reforms with the support of online campaigns. A bystander's video of George Floyd's murder in May 2020 spread over social media, sparking outrage and inspiring tens of millions of Americans to take to the streets in protest. In the month after Floyd's death, 37 percent of Americans who use social media reported posting or sharing content about race or racial equality.[5] With digital connectivity, organizers leading the movement have been able to reach and engage people around the world. Hashtag activism has helped increase public attention to equality challenges in ways and on a scale previously not possible. Importantly, online activism is merely a first step toward mobilizing communities. For sustainable change to happen, we need to allocate resources, demand systemic policy reforms, implement ethical changes across all sectors, and oversee meaningful redistributive justice. None of this happens overnight, but digital access and connectivity allow us to push forward, compare, learn, and monitor progress.

Challenging Cultures of Secrecy

The digital world has created and connected communities of workers advocating for change around the world. One global platform aiming to offer employees the space to organize and launch campaigns to improve their workplace is coworker.org. The causes and petitions on the site range from small changes, like having a coffee maker in a break room, to much larger issues, like labor unrest. Recent successful petitions on the site include raising Starbucks workers' minimum wage to $15 an hour and getting NBCUniversal to pay migrant workers their full wages for sewing T-shirts.[6] This forum illustrates not just the power that employees have when they come together for a cause, but the importance of having online forums to allow groups to mobilize.

Technology can help employees report experiences and address grievances in a safer and more accessible way, but movements for change can only come together with human leadership. In the aftermath of the first #MeToo revelations, California, New York, and several other states enacted laws prohibiting confidentiality in sexual harassment settlement agreements. Legally limiting secrecy makes a difference in the information we see online. New research shows that on Glassdoor, workers in states like California and New York with more stringent limits on NDAs are 16 percent more likely to give a one-star review, write 8 percent more about the "cons" of working at a firm, and discuss harassment at work 22 percent more often.[7]

Other initiatives sought to establish confidential tip lines for reports about harassment and to require public companies to disclose settlements related to harassment. In November 2018, Google saw a global, 20,000-employee walkout centered around a demand to end compulsory arbitration in cases of sexual discrimination and sexual assault. According to Amr Gaber, one of the walkout's organizers, the event came together in just three days—a feat that could only have been accomplished online. The walkout spurred Google, Facebook, Airbnb, eBay, and Square to announce that they would all end forced arbitration and secrecy for cases of sexual harassment.

Access to online platforms that operate as hubs of information about the workplace is challenging cultures of secrecy more than ever before. Blind, a South Korean platform, is one such example. In 2013 it began as an anonymous forum for employees of the Korean tech giant Naver to discuss issues within the workplace. Now, employees in more than 2,000 American tech companies use the app, including 40,000 Microsoft employees, 20,000 Amazon employees, and 10,000 Google employees.[8] Blind co-founder Sunguk Moon started the app after Naver shut down its anonymous chat board because employees began discussing critical and sensitive issues like corporate culture, workplace inequities, and harassment. Moon now says employees receive information about harassment and other issues through Blind faster than through media reporting. In 2018, Blind launched a #MeToo channel where workers can anonymously submit their experiences of workplace sexual harassment, sexism, wage disparity, and discrimination.

Online reviews serve as an important source of discipline on companies, which have been shown to improve their practices in response to negative reviews. A 2021 study finds that after being reviewed online, firms improve their workplace practices, measured by corporate social responsibility scores on employee relations and diversity.[9] Firms also increase disclosures about workplace practices after being reviewed.

Blind is not alone in offering an outlet for workers to connect and share information about the work environment. Spot, which launched in 2018, is a web-based platform that uses AI to conduct interviews with employees alleging discrimination and harassment. The Spot chatbot is designed to be neutral, non-judgmental, and calm—a listener that won't ask leading questions. Spot is available 24/7, so if a woman (or anyone, binary or non-binary) has experienced harassment by her boss or co-worker, she can chat with the bot without having to wait days, weeks, or months for an HR meeting. The entire conversation is recorded, time-stamped, and encrypted; the person reporting can choose whether to file or merely receive the time-stamped report, ensuring that she has a record of her reporting should she choose to file a complaint in the future. Employers can mine through the data and the bot can use the data to detect patterns. Spot co-founder Julia Shaw, a psychologist and memory scientist at University College London, hatched the idea for Spot as she studied false memories in courtrooms.[10] Shaw imagined a more immediate way to document and prove what and when people experienced something. Digital records of what happened in the workplace provide such documentation and in turn strengthen employees' ability to speak up and advocate for change.

The new apps that have emerged from the #MeToo reckoning, like Spot, Vault, tEQuitable, Riskcovery, AllVoices, STOPit, Workshield, and Speakfully, among others, offer employees time-stamped, anonymous, and confidential reporting systems where they can provide details about their harassment experiences. Employees can log notes of ongoing misconduct privately before sharing their reports, use a messenger feature to report misconduct, and escalate their reports to legal complaints if that conduct reaches a certain level. These apps also promise safeguards against employer retaliation by sending the reports submitted through the app to unbiased third-party moderators who independently investigate and find swift resolutions. Some of the apps also encourage bystanders to become upstanders by reporting misconduct they've witnessed.

Anonymity, however, is a double-edged sword: many of the apps promise anonymity to those reporting harassment, but that same anonymity could compromise efforts to keep a transparent and reliable record of events that have occurred. Vault, one of the new reporting apps, recognizes the importance of exposing repeat offenders. Its GoTogether feature enables employees to choose to submit a report only if the app has a record of previous complaints about the same perpetrator. This interface design resonates with game theory: if you are alone in the reporting game, the risks are large and the payoff small, but if more people participate, everyone wins, finding strength in numbers and banding together to launch complaints. Vault states that women are eight times more likely to report using the platform under these conditions than reporting through other channels, even when other channels promise anonymity.

Another venture, Riskcovery, uses AI to sift through corporate documents, chat logs, emails, internet articles, or anything else related to a particular problem, such as sexual harassment. The algorithm looks for patterns and trends using concepts and key-words and returns sorted documents that may indicate wrongful behavior. For example, one of Riskcovery's corporate clients received a complaint from a former employee claiming that she had been ha-rassed by her supervisor. The employee reported that the supervisor would email and text at all hours asking her to meet him for non-work-related reasons. There were also allegations that the supervisor was using inappropriate language and offering raises and promotions if she complied with his advances. In less than three hours, Riskcov-ery ingested 37.4 GB of text messages and compared them against its Sexual Harassment Taxonomy, which includes sample text and concepts to describe inappropriate patterns of behavior. The taxon-omy comparison returned 893 documents that were indicative of potential sexual harassment. A report was sent to the company high-lighting specific instances of the manager engaging in inappropriate conversations with the former employee, such as sexual jokes, ad-vances, and descriptions of employees unsuitable for the workplace. The analysis uncovered additional inappropriate conversations with other employees who had not come forward. Within a week the su-pervisor was fired and the company settled the case with the former employee.

Code Red

In today's ever more digital workplace, many employers are ditching distant, outsourced reporting hotlines and turning to apps to en-courage secure, efficient reporting and readily accessible data about issues like harassment, bias, and discrimination. As we saw, #MeToo launched a host of new start-ups designed to provide companies with such technology. These ventures are all quite new and their success is yet to be documented. In adopting these platforms, employers are sending a message to their employees that they want to hear about these incidents and are committed to creating a safe environment to bring forth such concerns. By conserving a digital trail, these types of platforms can also serve as important tools for reporters and watchdog agencies looking to develop fuller stories about companies, if reporters are granted access to these digital records. But we also need to demand evidence about the comparative efficacy of these applications, as well as risk and possible inadvertent harms, such as crowding out other, more traditional modes of prevention.

The ultimate goal of the #MeToo movement is not merely to detect and punish harassment but rather to prevent harassment before it occurs. The hope is to change our behaviors and norms to eradicate the culture of harassment altogether. Traditional sexual harassment training has been shown to be largely ineffective in preventing harassment from occurring. Could AI help teach us new behaviors and interactions? By the time harassment is reported, it is of course too late to prevent it from happening. To that end, there are #MeToo bots in development that will use AI to detect potential harassment before it ever happens. Like the 24/7 measuring tape we envisioned for equal pay, new algorithms are learning to identify patterns of behavior that are frequent antecedents to harassment.

Some apps allow employers to flag candidates even before they are hired for being a risk to engage in sexual harassment, workplace violence, and other toxic behavior from the time of hire. Assessments are based on public online content. Of course, we need to use these kinds of technologies with caution, treading a fine balance between monitoring and invasive—or biased—over-flagging. Such capabilities of identifying potential offenders or people at risk to become offenders may become quite accurate, but normatively, we want people to be screened for things they have done, not for personality traits that have not been expressed in any actual wrongdoing. Companies like Advanced Discovery, Nex, Botler, AwareHQ, and Emtrain (to name just a few) offer early warnings—a "smoke detector" AI—analyzing patterns of behavior that could lead to sexual harassment. These AI tools cross-reference thousands of legal documents and complaints related to harassment and use natural language processing to scan online conversations to predict whether a user's experience might be unlawful. The AI bots analyze speech patterns, attachments, and the timing of messages being sent, tracking employee communication, flagging potentially problematic cases, and sending them for human investigation. Think about these bots as analogous to spam filters, which have been around longer and have become very effective at weeding out unsolicited emails.

The companies developing these technologies claim that AI purposed to monitor employee communication can detect 75 percent of workplace harassment that typically goes undetected. Automatic detection can eliminate the need for the victim to report the abuse to their superior—and avoid the intimidation, fear, and threat of retaliation that often come with reporting harassment. The idea is to examine online interactions between employees and categorize employee conduct according to a spectrum—for example, a color map that ranges from green for acceptable normative exchanges to red for recurring behaviors that negatively affect the workplace and create a toxic environment; yellow would be just above green for unconscious negative behavior, and orange would be the next level up for consciously toxic behavior.

But what are the consequences of false positives? And at what point does the human employer intervene? Like many automated systems, to be effective and ethical, the #MeToo bots still require a human in the loop. Usually, when the bot identifies inappropriate communication or, say, an orange color-coded alert, it flags it for Human Resources or in-house counsel. At that point, prevention continues to depend on human decision-making to make good choices and to not sweep bad behavior under the rug.

Again, these technology experiments have promise. But we need to know more about how they are performing relative to other prevention methods. In my research of over a dozen of these new ventures, I found scarce concrete reports with transparent data on efficacy and impact. Artificial mining is still limited in its ability to tackle the subtleties and nuances of communication, but we can easily imagine such capabilities improving over time. Communication with sexual innuendo depends heavily on context and on the history and relationship of those involved. And of course, the stakes of accuracy are high. Flagging speech that isn't harassment can create chilling effects and cause employees to be investigated for communication that is perfectly appropriate. We can err on the side of false positives and then have humans investigate, or on the side of false negatives and do nothing when there is any doubt. Or we can have middle-ground design: AI chatbots can warn employees not to post, email, or say something that might be problematic, without flagging the speech to a supervisor. Each has a price, and each line we draw is guided by our worldview and how we decide to mediate tensions between social values we hold dear. In particular, a false positive can be patterned in ways that target groups of workers who do not comply with "mainstream" speech norms, for example, older workers or workers from different cultural or socioeconomic backgrounds.

Like with every technology that observes and tracks us, we are walking a fine line: constant monitoring can clean up a hostile work environment but can also chill speech and invade privacy, creating a digital surveillance system that could easily cross over into being overly intrusive. This level of monitoring may give us pause. We don't want the workplace to become so sanitized, as law professor Vicki Schultz has called it, or so Orwellian, that our autonomy and agency are stripped to numbers and warnings. "Nothing was your own except the few cubic centimeters inside your skull," wrote George Orwell in *1984*, but now even those centimeters inside our skulls are readable. We must recognize that our goals are often in conflict—preventing harassment can mean a loss of privacy and certain freedom of expression. This has always been the case, but technology may shift the costs and benefits of these trade-offs. The challenge-cum-opportunity is to envision leveraging technology in ways that seek to preserve privacy while allowing detection. And the crucial piece to complete the puzzle is for public agencies to collaborate with the vibrant private sector in investigating the efficacy of these ventures, encouraging experimentation, requiring transparency, and reporting about their use and impact, eventually creating more certainty about the best practices that are emerging from these technological advances.

Safety Beyond Work

Outside of the workplace, app developers have sought to use the same types of systems as those described above to encourage the reporting of sexual violence. With both a mobile app and a web portal, Safe-Pal works as a friend that can talk to and support victims of sexual violence without judgment. The app helps victims by first initiating a conversation on why and how they should report instances of sexual misconduct. The app also uses a database of health centers and other service providers, allowing users to receive immediate medical aid, psychosocial support, and legal assistance through various civil society organizations. Uniquely, the app has a feature that allows users to report sexual violence on behalf of a friend. Nurah Shariff Nantume, one of SafePal's app developers, explains that sometimes victims of sexual violence are too scared to report their trauma, but others who are privy to such criminal behavior can be more comfortable about reporting it for them. The company focuses on ensuring ease of access to disadvantaged communities. Emmanuel Kateregga, another SafePal app developer, says that a prospective partnership with UNICEF could allow the program to run on "digital drums"— solar-charged computers that are deployed in community settings and used to distribute information in low-connectivity areas.[11] Other initiatives, like Sis Bot, a chatbot in Thailand, provide 24/7 service for victims of harassment through a messenger channel, responding to victims by informing them about how to report incidents to police, preserve evidence, and access other resources. HarassMap, a woman-owned app that grew in response to sexual harassment in Egypt, and Hollaback!, which started in 2005 as a response to gender-based harassment in public spaces, use interactive mapping and forums to identify sexual harassment. Callisto, a university-specific alternative, allows students to report perpetrators of sexual assault on college campuses.

The history of sexual violence, harassment, stalking, discrimination, and objectification has been inextricably tied to men as perpetrators and women as victims. That history and the realities behind it make it imperative to examine how new technological capabilities may affect men and women differently. AI can be purposed to address the gender disparities in safety—to create more safety, more privacy, and more freedom for women to participate in all spheres of life with less risk. Technology, from electricity to phones to GPS trackers, has helped women take back the night. There is so much more that can be achieved. Envision a robot companion or a drone summoned by a woman walking home alone at night. These technologies are already being developed. In India, law enforcement has introduced surveillance drones with night vision capabilities to watch out for sexual violence in high-risk areas. Similar advancements are in the works for child welfare and abuse.

At the same time, the risks of digital abuse are very real. *New York Times* journalist Nellie Bowles wrote an exposé on how abusers use smart technology to control, stalk, and hurt their victims.[12] In more than thirty interviews, victims described their abusers' use of technology to harass, control, and monitor them without the aggressor physically being in the home. Anecdotes include switching air conditioner units on and off, changing digital locks, sounding the doorbell, or blasting music, all accomplished via internet-connected smartphone apps. Smart home technologies are relatively inexpensive and typically installed by one partner in the household. Many victims reported not having all the applications on their own smartphones or knowing how to remove their abuser from the account. These are profoundly serious risks and, as we will discuss in the next sections, building an equality machine means not only empowering all to access and benefit from technological advances but also holding abusers accountable. We've seen how technology in employment relations can be employed to prevent discrimination and harassment. In domestic relationships, there is potential as well, but technology alone cannot reverse centuries of subordination. We need to empower women around the world, ensuring women have access to education, work, credit, and digital resources. As we shall see in the next sections, we must do more to leverage technology to detect abusive situations both online and offline.

Upstanders by Digital Design

Harassment can operate as a well-oiled machine. When we think about the sheer reach of the internet, the reality can be daunting. Run-of-the-mill sexism and racism run rampant, of course, but then there's hate, misogyny, slut-shaming, revenge porn, intimidation, threats, cyberbullying . . . the list goes on and on. All these forms of online abuse are linked to depression and suicide.

Women and minorities online too often face cybermobs armed with despicable, networked misogyny and racism. Organized online attacks exist, quite simply, to maintain the status quo, and women—especially women of color, queer women, and trans women—are more susceptible to online harassment. During the controversy known as "Gamergate," which began in 2014, a group of women and non-binary gamers, including game designer Zoë Quinn, were "doxed," which means publicly posting "dox" (as in documents) to the web with private information about the victim, such as their home address, telephone number, credit card information, or a relative's personal information. These gamers received hate mail, threats of rape, and death threats after they criticized the male-dominated culture of gaming. Online harassment, even when it is the initial topic of dispute, has nothing to do with sexual desire. Instead, it almost always veers into identity territory, including the use of sexist and racist speech and images.

We are beginning to use AI to better understand the precursors and dynamics of such patterns of online harassment. Caroline Sinders, an AI researcher, devotes significant time and energy to fighting online abuse. She aims to answer the question of how we can create what she calls an emotional data set. Every report about harassment is a data point. But more importantly, it is also someone's experience—often a traumatic or life-changing one. Sinders wants to understand how the pain of someone's experience can be translated into data. She suggests that we need a supervised machine that learns ways to study doxing by looking at instances that have occurred and what happened prior—who and how many were involved, what platforms they used, what types of interactions they engaged in, and the words and timing they employed, to name a few. Sociology professor Tressie McMillan Cottom sums up the need nicely: "If there's an organized outrage machine, we need an organized response. By the time they're writing about you on a website or publishing your address or something, it's probably too late."[13] The "organized outrage machine" can be difficult to detect; it often trails through years of forums, essays, and content to become what it is, and even that which we find may be the tip of the iceberg. When most of us don't even know those dark corners of the internet exist, let alone dare venture into them, the consequences are vast and untold.

Algorithmic detection of cyberbullying is still new and relatively unreliable; the data to train the machines on isn't far-reaching enough. Programmers usually input words or phrases typical of harassment, but without a full grasp of context, playful and friendly exchanges can be incorrectly flagged. Algorithmic detection entails close monitoring and analysis of conversations, which also imposes some threat to users' privacy. Researchers are working tirelessly to untangle the ins and outs of automatic cyberbullying detection, but for now, our AI tech just isn't advanced enough to distinguish between contexts. As the technology gets better, the policy questions too must be answered: What do we do with detected risk? What is the responsibility of online platforms? What is the role of law enforcement? How do we best balance between equality and speech, safety and privacy, online? These are hard questions. I encounter the depth of these challenges in very concrete ways when I consult with online platforms on their content moderation policies. And the absence of government regulation has left too much of these critical issues in the hands of the private market. But given the normative challenges, the underlying promise must not be lost: the more accurate the technology, the more effectively it can aid us to draw such tough policy lines in an informed and consistent way.

One promising alternative to after-the-fact algorithmic digital detection is to complement existing technologies to induce people to behave well using digital design. Only a third of Americans act as upstanders when they witness online harassment. Few bystanders intervene in the face of cyberbullying, although intervention is certainly effective. The pattern, sadly, mirrors how few people in the real offline world actually step up as Good Samaritans. Yet, intervention helps victims feel less alone, and it can often deter aggressors before things deteriorate further. How might we harness AI to tackle online harassment proactively?

My colleague Yuval Feldman and I have researched accountability design and the cues that motivate prosocial behavior, for example, what kinds of incentives will increase the likelihood of blowing the whistle on corporate corruption. As we've already seen with all the new apps designed to tackle workplace culture, in a Foucauldian world in which we know we are acting in a fishbowl, people are more likely to behave responsibly since they know they are being observed. Again, this is both useful and problematic for our autonomy and agency—and different democratic societies may reasonably vary on how to strike the balance between safety and privacy, between equality and free speech, and between rights and liberties. But technology can move the needle by presenting a greater range of solutions to ongoing problems. For example, digital design can go beyond chilling perpetrators' behavior to increase accountability cues to induce both personal ethical behavior and prosocial conduct like bystander intervention.

In one experiment on Twitter, bots were directed to send messages reminding online harassers that their behavior is hurtful.[14] When a bot came across a racial slur used in a tweet, the bot replied to a harasser: "Hey man, just remember that there are real people who are hurt when you harass them with that kind of language." The experiment used bots with ostensibly white and Black characteristics (i.e., names and avatars) simulating white and Black Twitter users with high and low followings. The findings were predictable but worth noting: the white bot with more followers had the greatest impact on harassers. In other words, being reprimanded by someone in the "in-group" who is considered an influencer was more likely to reduce racial slurs by harassers. Consider the implications: Could we employ influencer bots to deter harassers? What are the comparative advantages of human and bot influencers on social media whose role is to reduce harassing behavior and model ethical communication? What else can technology teach us about our social dynamics and behavior, and how can we design forums that embed these new insights?

In another study of online forums, researchers ran an experiment using a custom-built social media platform called EatSnapLove, designed as a social network specifically for sharing, liking, and reacting to pictures of food—an Instagram just for food, if you will. As with other social networks, EatSnapLove participants began the experiment by signing up for accounts and creating profiles. They then could scroll through a feed of posts and like, reply, or flag what they saw. Participants also created posts, and bots responded with preprogrammed reactions. In this experiment, gender was a significant predictor of personal responsibility. Women reported feeling more responsible to help others when they witnessed cyberbullying. They were also more likely to flag problematic posts or comments than men.

This result is consistent with my research on whistleblower behavior: in a series of experiments Feldman and I found gendered differences in the likelihood of women and men to report corruption and illegal behavior. Armed with these insights, women have even begun to publicize and praise each other for their courageous whistleblowing tendencies. The website womenwhistleblowers.com aims to provide stories and examples of women who have combatted workplace issues, often at the expense of their own careers, personal lives, and even safety. The site's creators hope that it serves as a resource for other women who are experiencing issues and are considering speaking up.

Feldman and I are not alone in researching prosocial behavior—far from it. Researchers are leveraging digital forums to better understand how likely people are to shift from bystander to upstander. In one controlled experiment, viewers were notified about the size of the audience watching the bullying occur on the platform. When such notifications were given, bystanders were more likely to intervene, showing that design can indeed help increase prosocial behavior and digital accountability.[15] In another experiment, bystanders felt more accountable when their names were displayed in red instead of black text or their webcam was turned on.[16] In these heightened accountability settings, people were actually more likely not only to intervene directly in the face of cyberbullying, but also to report misconduct. Anonymity breeds passivity, and heightened exposure may do the opposite.

An Empathy Machine

Gloria Steinem once said that empathy is the most radical of human emotions. What about changing hearts and minds even sooner than when things are about to go badly in online exchanges? What about the radical idea that we can use AI to *make* people more empathic? Empathy and care can be learned through experience. A few years ago, my eldest daughter, Danielle, who is now studying AI and neuroscience at Stanford, came home from high school with an egg. It was a familiar sex ed project, designed to give students a sense of the responsibilities of parenthood. But I wondered then and still do if other families experienced the same conundrum that mine did. Danielle's teacher said they could throw the eggs away when the week was over, but Danielle felt uncomfortable throwing her egg-baby, which she had named Evie, in the trash. The rest of my family felt similar dread. We pulled out an old crystal jar with a lid and put the egg inside. It has been there ever since. Danielle's empathy toward her egg-baby is an example of this learned empathy.

Simulations can be valuable teachers, imparting insight and helping people learn from situations that they might never experience in real life, especially in the context of work and education. Workplaces and schools already regularly hold tolerance, diversity, and anti-harassment programs. I've engaged in numerous discussions about the effectiveness of mandatory diversity training in the workplace, the results of which are mixed. Today, we have new tools that can upgrade the experience and better enable us to reach our shared goals.

In recent years, the technology of virtual simulation has made enormous strides. Virtual reality (VR) technologies, which use wearable devices and machine learning, mix real-world experience with virtual environments, and have shown promise in teaching empathy. In an article titled "Changing Bodies Changes Minds: Owning Another Body Affects Social Cognition," psychology professor Lara Maister and her colleagues designed experiments in which participants, using VR technology, experienced embodying a different gender, age, and race than their own.[17] At least immediately following the experiment, the experience reduced implicit biases against outgroups. The research described a process in which self-association occurs within a physical, bodily domain such that switching bodies, even virtually, creates positive change and positive responses toward those who are "others."

Similarly, Stanford psychology professor Jeremy Bailenson found that VR can enhance our empathic capacities. In one study, Bailenson placed college-age users into an elderly avatar, finding that an embodied perspective increases positive evaluations of the elderly. In another experiment, Bailenson's subjects experienced the virtual reality of being a cow: "You go down to a trough, you put your head down and pretend to drink some water. You amble over to a pile of hay, you put your head down and you pretend to eat hay. As you're going from one spot to another, you're actually seeing your cow get a light prod from a cattle prod, and you're feeling a slight poke in your chest from a stick in your side." After the experience, his subjects ate less meat. One of the participants in the experiment explained, "I truly felt like I was going to the slaughterhouse . . . and felt sad that as a cow I was going to die."[18] Chasing Coral, a six-minute virtual reality collaboration between Netflix and Sir David Attenborough, similarly uses experiential learning to provide a wake-up call about the ocean's environmental crisis, with great success in raising awareness. Another virtual reality experience allows people to embody a young girl in a refugee camp going through her day-to-day life. According to the United Nations, showing people the immersive video doubled the number of people who donate to refugee funds.

Virtual reality experiences like these are increasingly being created to tackle racial, gender, LGBTQ+, and socioeconomic biases. In one called 1000 Cut Journey, designed by Stanford's Bailenson and Courtney Cogburn of the Columbia University School of Social Work, users experience life from the perspective of Michael Sterling, a Black man experiencing racial microaggressions. In Becoming Homeless, designed by Stanford's Virtual Human Interaction Lab, participants engage in an immersive VR experience of days in the life of someone who can no longer afford a home. The description reads, "Interact with your environment to attempt to save your home and to protect yourself and your belongings as you walk in another's shoes and face the adversity of living with diminishing resources." Observing thousands of participants in this seven-minute immersion, the researchers found that the VR experience changes human behavior more than other types of perspective-taking exercises, and the effect lasts for months. They concluded that "while this 7-minute journey does not come close to the immense burden of living without a home, researchers continue to find that VR experiences can be a powerful tool to help put oneself in the shoes of another."[19]

Psychologists have long found that men who are violent toward their female partners are less able to recognize fear in female faces compared to non-violent men.[20] In one study, virtual reality simulations had perpetrators of domestic violence experience what it felt like to embody the victim.[21] Perpetrators' ability to recognize fearful faces, which was originally low compared to general populations, improved after the experience. The offenders who engaged in the VR immersion were less likely to wrongly attribute happy emotional states to facial expressions that exuded fear.

The Chinese company VeeR VR has developed experiences to enhance tolerance and empathy toward LGBTQ+ people. The company produced two videos showing results from experiments it conducted with the Beijing LGBT Center on May 17, 2018, International Day Against Homophobia, Transphobia, and Biphobia. The first, titled "Free Hug in Beijing," shows a young woman wearing a shirt that reads "I am a homosexual" in Chinese. The woman is wearing a blindfold and has her arms outstretched to hug passersby. The VR experience allows the video to be watched from the perspective of the woman or as a bystander. A second video titled

"Can You Take a Photo of Us?" shows two young men wearing the same shirt reading "I am a homosexual" and similarly allowed the viewer to watch from the perspective of the young men or as a bystander.

Feminist scholar Judith Butler has described the concept of performativity: thinking of the body as a "stylized repetition of acts," with the body itself as a locus of performances that reflect power and identity.[22] We can think of virtual reality as a way to disrupt performativity and turn our designated scripts on their heads. The rituals and rules that govern our spaces can be replicated as we create virtual, artificial, and outside-the-body augmented realities. But we should also envision using machines as opportunities to disembody and reembody, to shift space, gravity, the laws of nature, physical ability, and identity to reconfigure the ways we've long interacted. VR technology has also been used to add realism to sexually threatening role-plays to help college women resist sexual attacks.[23]

This potential of VR to change perspective and behavior is being taken up, unsurprisingly, by the burgeoning market of sexual harassment prevention tech that we saw in the previous sections. New companies such as Vantage Point are offering sexual harassment training in which employees are placed in scenarios where they are a bystander to a sexual harassment incident. The participant is presented with options to deescalate, report, or intervene. Employees then engage in questions and discuss their observations. The idea is to provide employees with a realistic visualization and experience of sexual harassment, preparing employees to better identify and prevent sexual harassment from occurring in their workplace. Like with the sexual harassment apps we explored earlier, the research on the effectiveness of VR training compared to other mainstream sexual harassment training is still sparse. Recent studies suggest that VR interactions overcome the barriers in traditional training methods by making the interaction more realistic and inducing emotional and impactful reactions.[24] But these studies for the most part include few participants and do not track the long-term effects of such training on actual workplace environments.

The virtual experience is driven by two salient questions: What would the world be like if we could see it through the eyes of others? And, more importantly, if VR can extend our sense of humanity to everyone, would it be able to provoke an exponential change in society? The first question seems to be answered immediately in positive ways—people are increasingly emotionally engaging in immersive experiences. But the second question is something we need to learn more about, research, and publicly monitor. The power of VR lies in its ability to increase cognitive empathy (understanding other people's pain) and emotional empathy (taking on the emotions of others). I see promise in these experiences. Inevitably, with a race to build an immersive metaverse experience online, these questions become even more pressing. Remember: we need skin in the game, and we need to envision positive uses of immersion, because otherwise these technologies will be built anyway, but they might be built in ways that do not consider equality and empowerment at all.

Here's an immersive experience I find inspiring. The international collective BeAnotherLab is heading up a project of experiencing direct identity swaps. The method that BeAnotherLab employs is called Body Transfer Illusion by VR, and it integrates neuropsychology research, storytelling, and virtual embodiment techniques to allow two users of different genders to exchange bodies and perspectives. BeAnotherLab's body swap lab was designed to promote mutual respect and a deep reflection on mutual agreement and gender violence. Imagine integrating the best of such projects in the commercial immersive experiences that are already saturating our markets.

Revenge Porn and Deepfakes

In 2017, Gal Gadot, the star of the *Wonder Woman* movie franchise, was horrified to discover that a video of her supposedly starring in a porn movie was going viral. She had never made such a video; her face had been swapped onto another person's body using a machine learning algorithm. "Seeing isn't believing anymore," wrote the *Wall*

Street Journal in an exposé about revenge porn and deepfakes—technology that uses machine learning to create an illusion on video.[25]

Revenge porn utilizes non-consensual pornographic image sharing. This phenomenon encompasses highly destructive uses of deepfake technologies, making it seem like people are photographed or filmed in situations they were never involved in. According to the Data & Society Research Institute, one in twenty-five Americans has been the victim of revenge porn.[26] And deepfakes are getting better. In the Gadot video, there were obvious flaws that exposed the fact that the video wasn't real: her mouth and eyes didn't quite line up with speech and movement. The hacker who created the fake Gadot video wrote that he had done it using open-source software. Big movie studios use the same technology, as when Disney digitally recreated a young Princess Leia in *Rogue One*. The technology is getting easier to employ and getting better on its own terms, and you no longer need to be a Hollywood filmmaker to access it.

Democratized creativity is a good thing—people around the world are creating humorous memes and videos, social and political commentary, and creative art. But the insidious use of deepfakes is extremely concerning. Like Gal Gadot, Taylor Swift and Scarlett Johansson have had deepfakes of them posted online, but celebrities aren't the only victims. Deepfakes have also been used politically to shame women for not aligning with their gender roles or the values of their communities. The story of Indian journalist Rana Ayyub is telling. Ayyub exposed Hindu nationalist politics as corrupt, and thereafter she became the victim of a deepfake porn video, which in turn led to Ayyub receiving rape and death threats.[27] Unsurprisingly, 90 percent of the victims of revenge porn are women.

How can we encourage creativity in new technology while curbing harmful uses? Can we counter deepfakes deployed to take revenge on exes, to objectify women, to demean, harass, and extort? The most effective way to combat deepfake porn will be a combination of technology and policy. AI experts envision developing technology to detect fake videos; teams of academics and private companies are hard at work developing such technology. One method uses AI to detect eye blinking in the videos, a physiological signal that does not appear natural in the synthesized fake videos. The naked eye may not notice such subtle differences, but a bot can. A related method detects gesture misalignment: a UC Berkeley researcher designed an algorithm that can flag videos with gestures that do not appear human.[28] This detection method was once very successful, catching deepfake videos with an accuracy of over 90 percent, but the race is a difficult one: after the research was made public, deepfake algorithms adapted and incorporated blinking into their code.

In a similar tell, in a human face, eyes (literally) reflect whatever the subject is looking at, and that reflection is symmetrical in both eyes. Deepfake videos fail to accurately or consistently generate videos with symmetrical reflections in the corneas. A team of computer scientists at the University at Buffalo developed an algorithm that detects deepfake videos by analyzing the light reflections in the eyes. This method was reportedly 94 percent effective at catching deepfakes, and the researchers created a "DeepFake-o-meter," an online resource to help people test to see if the video they've viewed is real or (deep)fake. Other methods to identify deepfakes include detecting lack of or inconsistencies in detail or resolution inconsistencies around eyes, teeth, and facial contours. For example, mouths created by deepfake videos often have misshapen or excess teeth.

Like with other areas of technology that harm and help, the race to do good often feels like a game of whack-a-mole. The race is tough: while detection methods are improving, so is the deepfake technology. In 2020, Facebook held a competition for artificial intelligence that can detect deepfakes. The winning algorithm detected deepfakes only 65 percent of the time. Some scholars, including law professor Danielle Citron, a leading voice in the field of sexual privacy, are skeptical that technology alone can battle deepfakes. Citron explains that to be effective, detection software would have to keep pace with innovations in deepfake technology, dooming those wanting to protect against deepfakes to a cat-and-mouse game. Citron warns that the experience of fighting malware, spam, and viruses shows the difficulty in such a race. She suggests that platforms would have to make the use of detection programs mandatory before allowing videos to be posted. This is where policy can leverage technology for systemic accountability: Citron argues for policies that will hold online service providers accountable for violations of sexual privacy and require the removal of such images.

People around the world upload billions upon billions of photos to Google, Facebook, and Instagram, as well as other, smaller platforms. Facebook has an AI tool that can detect and flag sexual images and videos of someone posted without consent. The system, also available on Instagram, can detect "near-nude" content, which is flagged and sent to a human moderator for review.[29] Not only can AI help to identify whether intimate images and videos are floating around various platforms in the first place, it can also help to determine whether the videos are unaltered originals or shams. One AI technology called "hashing" encodes a digital footprint into a file, allowing computers to quickly spot duplicates. PhotoDNA is a Microsoft program that uses a unique "hash," representing an image or video, and compares it to other copies posted around the internet. The unique hash operates like a digital signature and pools its data from a database of known illegal images and video files. PhotoDNA has been used not only to detect and remove disturbing images but also to identify child predators and rescue potential victims.

Using new technologies to help find victims of abuse is an important development in fighting against an insidious social ill. Project VIC is one of the organizations that use Microsoft's PhotoDNA to locate victims, and it has been able to locate offenders by tracking, for example, the geographical location of an offender through background details in the photo, such as local vegetation or landscape. It also uses machine learning to make predictions about the presence of child abuse materials in digital files. In 2021, Apple announced that it will begin using new software that aims to stop the spread of child sexual abuse material (CSAM). This new technology would enable Apple to detect known CSAM images stored in iCloud Photos and report the instances to the National Center for Missing and Exploited Children. Apple didn't anticipate the public outrage of consumers and the media, who claimed that the scanning and monitoring of one's photo library is an invasion of privacy. The public outrage led Apple to place the initiative on hold. Nonetheless, this kind of technology represents a powerful tool to tackle some of society's worst ills. Trafficking, by all accounts, is one of those, and it represents nothing less than a modern slavery epidemic.

A Wicked Problem

Most victims of trafficking are women and children, often minorities from poor and neglected parts of the world. Human trafficking is larger than just sex trafficking; victims are also forced to work in agricultural, industrial, and other menial underground jobs. The United States estimates that about 1 million people are trafficked across its borders every year; 80 percent of those victims are female and 50 percent are children. Trafficking, vile and illegal, is a huge industry, estimated to be worth $150 billion per year.

The efficacy of online regulations to combat sex trafficking is the subject of heated debates and public and private efforts. In 1996, in the early days of the internet, the Communications Decency Act (CDA) was enacted to protect providers of an interactive computer service from civil liability for another's actions. In just a few words, Section 230 of the CDA provided a shield for online platforms to deflect responsibility for the content published on them: "No provider or user of an interactive computer service shall be treated as the publisher or speaker of any information provided by another information content provider." In 2018, Congress introduced an exemption to Section 230, the Fight Online Sex Trafficking Act and Stop Enabling Sex Traffickers Act (FOSTA-SESTA). The wisdom of imposing liability on online platforms for trafficking activities on their sites is still debated. Some argue that it resulted in some sites, like Craigslist's personal ads section, shutting down for fear of liability, causing trafficking to move to the darker, harder-to-detect regions of the web (the so-called dark web). FOSTA and SESTA are also said to have harmed some sex workers by driving them back to offline solicitation, which is less safe and less trackable than online solicitation.

AI can help on two fronts here—preventing sexual abuse and detecting unlawful behavior. Emily Kennedy describes the moment when she decided, at age sixteen, to devote her career to helping children who are victims of sex trafficking. She was in eastern Europe and saw the realities of poor children trafficked by their parents to work the streets and bring home money. When she returned to the United States, she realized that even here at home, sex trafficking affects millions of children, primarily children living in poverty, children living in foster care, and children with abusive parents. She co-founded Marinus Analytics, a company that develops machine learning tools to stop human trafficking. The company's lead product, Traffic Jam, helps sift through data online to search for victims and trafficking rings. Local, state, and federal law enforcement, including the FBI, have used Traffic Jam to identify thousands of victims of sex trafficking, and it has also been adopted in Canada and the United Kingdom.

AI can perform tasks exponentially faster than humans, saving massive amounts of time. Computer vision can identify multiple victims advertised and sold from the same hotel bedroom, identifying the bedding or wallpaper pattern, for example. Traffic Jam also sorts the kinds of language that is coded in online human trafficking advertisements. In 2017, Marinus Analytics also released Face Search, the first facial recognition tool to fight sex trafficking. Kennedy describes how one detective stumbled on a huge trafficking ring when he was looking for a girl named Sarah. Sarah had been recruited by a ringleader, Julian, when she was fifteen. The detective only had an old photo of Sarah, which he ran through Face Search. One of the photos found by the AI as matches was part of an ad with a phone number that was linked to Sarah's real legal name. The detective himself was unable to recognize her because she was two years older now and her appearance was so altered with hair and makeup, but the algorithm did—AI was able to recognize the victim when a human couldn't. It was a huge breakthrough in the case: twenty more victims were found in the ring. In three months, the detective was able to put together a case that would otherwise have taken years. Kennedy says that Face Search, like Traffic Jam, has accelerated investigations and helped rescue thousands of victims. With government agencies drowning in data, she sees enormous potential in those oceans of information.

The Anti-Human Trafficking Intelligence Initiative (ATII), a non-profit formed in 2019, is similarly partnering with law enforcement agencies and private sector companies to fight against human trafficking. ATII developed a phone app through which victims can scan QR codes placed in the bathrooms of hotels and other public places identified as potential loci of trafficking victims. Once the data is received, law enforcement can obtain cell phone records. It takes a lot of information to determine if someone is trafficking people, including the person or group's patterns, website postings, and travel. Software able to ingest and analyze massive quantities of data can identify patterns far faster and more accurately than a human eye. When images of young women entering a country match with social media and missing-person images from high-risk countries, that data can be matched to people and organizations suspected of trafficking, and puzzle pieces start to fall into place. What's more, the information collected can often be used as evidence to shut down these criminal operations.

Code 8.7, which was born out of a two-day conference in 2019 to investigate how computational science and artificial intelligence can be used to achieve Target 8.7 of the UN Sustainable Development Goals—the goals of eradicating forced labor, ending modern slavery and human trafficking, and securing the prohibition and elimination of the worst forms of child labor—is a community engaged in a collaborative effort to wield the powers of technology to stop human trafficking and modern slavery. Anjali Mazumder, a researcher at the Turing Institute at Carnegie Mellon University, emphasizes that for these AI tools to be effective, there needs to be organized and productive sharing of data among NGOs, law enforcement, tech companies, and academia. Right now, there is a lot of information that competes and duplicates instead of becoming shared and integrated. Mazumder believes that widespread coordination and sharing of structured data (such as suspicious financial transactions) and unstructured data (such as free-form and narrative information from law enforcement reports) offers an opportunity to innovate and address the problem of trafficking at the strategic and tactical levels. Open-sourcing the data can reduce redundancies and oversights, offset much of the opacity and uncertainty about how technology is put into use, and bring much-needed coordination to disperse efforts.

On the corporate side, IBM has partnered with the Stop the Traffik initiative to develop a new, cloud-hosted data hub that enables institutions such as Barclays, Europol, Liberty Global, Lloyds Banking Group, University College London, Western Union, and others to provide its analysts with information to help combat human trafficking. Using AI and machine learning, the tool is trained to recognize and detect specific human trafficking terms and incidents and examine real-time risk developments in supply chains. These technologies also use machine learning web crawlers that search relevant news stories about abuses to connect the dots and complete the puzzle.

AI is also proving useful in the prosecution of sex traffickers and prevention of further trafficking. Machine learning technology helps prosecutors include more evidence to show that a woman who was involved in a sex ad, for example, was being trafficked when the ad was created, showing that she had not willfully and knowingly engaged in sex work. Because sex ads are often shot in hotel and motel rooms, AI tech such as TraffickCam, developed by the Exchange Initiative to end sex trafficking, allows ordinary people to upload photos of hotel rooms to law enforcement databases. The algorithm is designed to analyze the carpets, furniture, and accessories in an image's background to narrow down which hotel the photograph was taken in. A company called XIX developed another program, Entry, that can recognize people in blurry photos via mirrors and at different ages. Facial recognition technology is a whole new ballgame when it comes to fighting crime and protecting victims, but it is one, we will see, that is rife with questions and controversy.

Channeling Facial Recognition for Good

Facial recognition software, which scans an image or video of a person's face and matches it with a similar stored image to identify the person, is perhaps the most controversial AI technology in recent years. It has been rapidly introduced for a variety of uses ranging from law enforcement, airport security, and employee clearance to dating apps and friend mapping on social networks. Facial recognition has tremendous benefits when it comes to fighting trafficking and sexual abuse, for example, but the harms of inaccurate facial recognition—and the legal and ethical pitfalls of the technology itself—cannot be understated.

We already know that AI accuracy depends on how much training an algorithm receives. In the context of facial recognition, if a computer hasn't seen many photos of people who look similar to you, the algorithm is prone to error. Such errors have proven to be pervasive: Google's digital photo software tagging Black people as gorillas; Nikon's software telling Asian people to stop shutting their eyes; Hewlett-Packard's software failing to identify persons with darker skin tones—all of these programs have been found to do worse at recognizing people of color and women than at recognizing white men. Google responded to the gorilla tagging scandal by describing similar problems across all ages, the bot tagging at first some humans as dogs. Google ultimately removed the "gorilla" label and continues to improve the technology toward a better recognition system for all skin colors.[30]

These reported problems, however, were just the tip of the iceberg. The American Civil Liberties Union (ACLU) of Northern California conducted a test of Amazon's facial recognition system, Rekognition, having the software compare photos of every member of the U.S. House and Senate to a database of 25,000 publicly available arrest photos. Amazon's technology flagged photos of twenty-eight members of Congress, all of them Black, as likely matches with the ACLU's collection of mug shots. These are distressing findings, especially when we recognize the deep racial biases that pervade our law enforcement systems. Thirty-eight percent of state prisoners are Black, despite Black people constituting only 13 percent of the population. Black people are 5.1 times more likely to be incarcerated than whites. The Black Lives Matter movement has brought these and other concerns to the forefront, and in June 2020, Amazon, Microsoft, and IBM all announced that they will not sell facial recognition technology to police.

AI's facial recognition problem exemplifies the problems of other digital technologies (in particular, the problems of insufficient, partial, and skewed training data), but it also raises fundamental questions that include both privacy and safety concerns. What if facial recognition technology was perfect, never failing, never producing false positives? Recall the principle of comparative advantage. In a system already so deeply flawed, can technology make things better even with the new risks and challenges it inevitably brings? How can we use facial recognition responsibly, allowing public and private organizations to improve their work in fighting sex trafficking, hate crimes, child abuse, and other heinous behavior, while at the same time protecting against the harms of biased enforcement? How can we balance between privacy and safety when algorithmic accuracy can be perfected? What if the bias isn't because the algorithm hasn't been fed enough data, but rather because it has been fed ample data that adequately reflects social realities?

These questions lead to even more questions: Are we more afraid of AI being imperfect or being perfect? Flawed and failing, or all-knowing? The former are matters of correcting its technical limitations; the latter require rigorous debates about normative trade-offs. The former are about smart technology not being smart enough; the latter are about smart machines becoming too smart to handle—so competent that they pose a risk to our civil liberties, or worse. The insight that emerges from all the spheres we're exploring in these pages is one that can't be overstated: algorithms risk embedding bias, but they also provide an opportunity to break cycles of bias. Data is a specific, partial, and often subjective representation of reality. AI that is flawed because it hasn't been exposed to enough diverse data is a fixable problem. AI that is flawed because it supports flawed social systems is a much more fundamental challenge that we must continue to grapple with.

Safety, Privacy, and Vulnerability

Technology is never a magic bullet, but it does have incredible potential as both a weapon and a shield for the more vulnerable. As we saw earlier in the chapter, technology has helped women take back the night. Drones and other technology can help protect people from perpetrators, acting as personalized streetlamps and bodyguards. A woman walking alone at night could summon the drone on her phone and have it follow her, shedding light from above and monitoring for danger.

Until now, drones have found a much more enthusiastic buyer in the male market. Men buy 90 percent of civilian drones, and most drone enthusiasts and civilian drone professionals are men. At a recent drone film festival, only 11 of 330 films were submitted by women. This is a problem in and of itself, but the media's narrative surrounding drones exacerbates the issue. Legal scholar Margot Kaminski challenges the media's focus on the risk of drones spying on the "naked," "topless," or "sunbathing"—drones peering into women's homes, apartments, backyards, or swimming pools. Kaminski says that while the actual number of cases of spying on women using drones is small, the narrative of the sunbathing-girl-meets-invasive-drone is fixed in our popular imagination. Kaminski observes that this emphasis on women's privacy goes back in history to Lady Godiva, who rode naked through the streets of England to protest her husband's taxation policy.[31] The commoners in the streets averted their eyes to respect her modesty. One man, a Peeping Tom, takes a look and is punished for offending the noble woman's honor. The new drones roaming and lurking in our midst are bringing back the Lady Godiva conundrum: liberation means being able to walk freely, how and when we want, wearing what we want, and alone, in public spaces without fearing attack. And technology should support rather than impede such freedom.

But when privacy is feminized and the sunbathing-girl-meets-invasive-drone trope breaks the social rules of not peeking too long, we might be losing sight of the full potential of technology to protect and liberate. This mindset of protecting women's (and young girls') modesty and honor rather than focusing on their ability to take charge of their own freedoms (including reproductive choice) runs through court decisions. For example, in *Kyllo v. United States*, which involved an infrared device used by police to examine the amount of heat emanating from a home, the late Justice Antonin Scalia raised a concern about the "lady of the house taking her bath and sauna." As legal scholar Jeannie Suk contends, nowhere in the facts of the case is such a lady sitting in her sauna; rather, Scalia was evoking "the privacy interest of the man [of the house—his castle, if you will] entitled to see the lady of the house naked and his interest in shielding her body from prying eyes. Privacy is figured as a woman, an object of the male gaze."[32]

Technology can both protect and invade privacy, and at the same time, privacy itself can be an impediment to other rights and liberties. As the Covid-19 pandemic reminded us, privacy can be in tension with safety and accountability. In some circumstances—for example, when a deadly virus is rapidly spreading—we might decide that the benefits from monitoring citizen movement and contact tracing trump privacy concerns. Striking that balance begins at the root: How do we define privacy, and what does it mean to be "protected"? It is up to us all to decide the right mix and balance. But technology can help give us the tools to fine-tune the fine balances we've always had to strike in a democratic society.

CHAPTER 5

Breasts, Wombs, and Blood

*One of the misconceptions people have about AI is
that it is allegedly everywhere. But the truth is that
AI is not uniformly distributed across all the areas
of our life the way it impacted e-commerce.*

—REGINA BARZILAY, faculty co-lead, MIT Abdul Latif
Jameel Clinic for Machine Learning in Health

The Hope of the Bionic Pancreas

In August 2017, my thirteen-year-old daughter, Elinor, suddenly
had trouble breathing. Earlier that week, we had returned from two
months abroad in Thailand and Israel, a marvelous, active summer.
Now my daughter was lying on the floor, unable to inhale, her body
limp, her face colorless. At the hospital, Elinor's diagnosis was immediate: like millions of other children, and with numbers alarmingly on
the rise, she has type 1 diabetes. Her pancreas had stopped working.
She had gone into diabetic ketoacidosis after going weeks—perhaps
months—undiagnosed. Those first few days were the most terrifying
I had experienced as a mother. I also felt incredibly guilty that I had
not known Elinor was sick in the weeks before her diagnosis. We had
been with my father, a medical doctor, and yet none of us had recognized the telltale signs: weight loss and thirst.

The doctors and nurses all said it would get easier. They told me there were many new breakthroughs in diabetes care. But I just wanted to see Elinor out of the hospital. At first, when we were finally back home, it didn't get easier. Elinor, amazing as always, took charge of injecting herself with insulin every morning and evening and before every meal. She learned to prick her finger a dozen times a day to measure her glucose levels, and we all learned to count and measure carbohydrates. Still, even with her diligence and resilience, the daily care that comes with a diabetes diagnosis is excruciating and exhausting, and the stories about hypoglycemic incidents—where one can pass out and lapse into a coma—are frightening.

Our lives dramatically improved when Elinor received her first constant glucose monitor (CGM), a device that attaches to her body and sends information to each of our smartphones. Just like that, Elinor, her dad, her older sister, the school nurse, and I could all track her blood glucose levels in real time. Constant blood glucose level monitoring is necessary for diabetics because of the risk of hypoglycemia. The next huge leap in her care came when Elinor moved from using an injection pen to a pump. And in 2020, her pump, upon the approval of the FDA, became smart: it calculates how much insulin she needs given her glucose level and carbohydrate intake, and it makes autonomous decisions about insulin dosages as it receives information from the glucose monitor in a closed feedback loop.

These advances have been game changers; the pump uses data and learns to adjust insulin levels accordingly. As one of the first users of the smart system described it: "It's not possible to fully put into words the burden the system took away when I no longer had to constantly keep a portion of my brain dedicated to thinking about my blood sugar and tweaks I needed to make. Magic is still the only way to describe it."[1] Yet the future of diabetes technology is the "bionic pancreas"—an even smarter device that can deliver both insulin and glucagon autonomously, without manual outputs, constantly learning from the trends it observes. If Elinor started to experience elevated glucose, the pump would start injecting tiny amounts of insulin to bring her back down. If she started to trend low, the pump would not only suspend insulin delivery as it does now, but it could inject glucagon on its own, so that her blood sugar would rise to a safe level. This bionic pancreas is not yet on the market, but we are hopeful. AI is revolutionizing medicine in countless ways as bots take on more and more roles in healthcare. There's a lot to celebrate and, for people living with disabilities and health risks, much to gain.

The "Mutilated Male"

For centuries, women's and girls' health has been understudied, overlooked, and neglected compared to men's health. Aristotle described the female body as "'a mutilated male' whose development had stopped because the coldness of the mother's womb overcame the heat of the father's semen."[2] Around the world, the "mutilated male's" health has been an afterthought, with women's well-being lagging behind a focus on men's health. In her essay "The Gender of Sound," poet and classics scholar Anne Carson discusses the pervasive belief in ancient Greek and Roman medical and anatomical theory that women have two mouths: "The orifice through which vocal activity takes place and the orifice through which sexual activity takes place are both denoted by the word *stoma* in Greek (*os* in Latin) with the addition of adverbs *ano* and *kato* to differentiate upper mouth from lower mouth. Both the vocal and the genital mouth are connected to the body by the neck (*auchen* in Greek, *cervix* in Latin). Both mouths provide access to a hollow cavity which is guarded by lips that are best kept closed."[3] The ancient medical experts applied parallel medications to upper and lower mouths, treating uterine infections the same way as a sore throat. The oversimplification in theory led to an oversimplification in practice that has failed and continues to fail women.

For years in modern medicine, women have been excluded from being health subjects in research studies, and research study topics tended to prioritize men. The health sector, which accounts for trillions of dollars of spending each year in the United States alone, has long had a bias problem. Some exclusions have been simply inconceivable, such as a National Institutes of Health (NIH)–funded study on how obesity affects breast and uterine cancer in which not a single woman was included.[4] Other exclusions can be explained by convenience and the social reality of male presence in more public settings. For example, U.S. military personnel databases offer one of the largest troves of public health information, so researchers often use this database, but women are a minority among soldiers. Thus, data collection for new drugs or treatment has often featured a disproportionately large number of men. When studies use military databases, they are studying gender-imbalanced data. Neglecting to count and study women's health has resulted in alarming medical risks. In just one telling example, prescription drugs taken off the market by the Food and Drug Administration (FDA) disproportionately relate to health risks for women.[5]

Economist Ronald Coase said that if you torture the data long enough, it will confess to anything. Data has to be mined with caution, because too often it can be tainted or skewed. Remember, we don't know what we don't count. Missing data sets are our collective blind spots, blank spaces within a world overflowing with information. In 1977, the FDA issued a guideline in clinical trials for new drugs, which excluded women with "childbearing potential"—defined as any "premenopausal female capable of becoming pregnant"—from participating in Phase I and II clinical trials. It was only in 1994 that the FDA reversed its guidelines, emphasizing the need to enroll women in clinical trials. There are many decades to catch up on, filling in the blank spaces of data, processing and understanding what is collected with regard to women's well-being. Such grave gaps in health data are also pervasive along racial and ethnic lines, and go hand in hand with the ways health is so intricately intertwined with wealth.

Technology is helping on the health front to dramatically expand data collection. Here's an astounding figure: 90 percent of the data that exists in our world today was created in the past couple of years. The vast quantity of studies and clinical trials performed across the spectrum of science and industry has only recently become easily searchable and widely accessible thanks to AI-enabled natural language processing. For example, the Jackson Laboratory Clinical Knowledgebase (CKB) is a database that allows researchers to sort, store, and interpret data from clinical trials and research papers related to oncology.[6] CKB provides and concentrates data previously scattered in tens of millions of publications; figures are updated daily, saving oncology professionals valuable time. The ability to process vast amounts of data using AI is allowing researchers to fine-tune their analyses, better examining the results of trials for gender, race, and age differences. Yet as health research, tracking, and treatment shift to digital technologies, we unsurprisingly find problems here too. In 2014, for example, Apple released HealthKit, an app that tracked many types of basic, routine health data—daily exercise, caloric intake, breathing, body fat, and blood pressure—but it did not include the option to track one's menstrual cycle.[7] It took a year for an app update to include this basic function. Today, there are an enormous number of apps and wearable technology on the market with the goal of improving health and well-being. And though menstrual cycles were neglected in the development of early-to-market health data apps, there are hundreds of apps for that specific purpose available in the Apple store today. In the health and fitness category, period trackers are the second-most-downloaded apps after running apps. Many women champion these apps as an empowering way to understand their bodies and take control of the effects of their periods in their daily lives. In an interview with the BBC, an opera singer from southeast London stated she had been using tracking apps for three years to avoid auditioning or performing on days when she was premenstrual and her hormones would affect her larynx.[8] There are also accounts of women in South and Central America using tracking apps to help prevent pregnancy during the Zika outbreak and other more recent pandemic cycles. Specialized apps have even been developed to optimize athletic performance taking into account menstrual cycles, such as Wild AI, which modifies the frequency of high-intensity workouts in an athlete's training plan based on where the user is in her cycle. Technology has enormous potential to continue to level the playing field and counteract the historical imbalance and bias in health and medicine. Indeed, some of the greatest recent breakthroughs in medicine and health are coming not from life science research but from computer science.

All About the Breasts

In 2013, Angelina Jolie, having lost her mother to breast cancer, made the brave decision to have a double mastectomy based on genetic data that predicted the disease in her future.[9] As computing powers became more advanced, human genome mapping accelerated, and scientists were able to discover specific genes, known as the BRCA genes, that can carry mutations increasing the risks of breast cancer. Still today, however, breast cancer is the most prevalent of all cancers, with more than 1.8 million new cases and more than 600,000 deaths in 2020.[10] Dr. Regina Barzilay, AI lead of Jameel Clinic, MIT's Center for AI and Healthcare, describes three defining images that have guided her seminal research; all three are her own mammograms. Barzilay was forty-three when she was diagnosed with breast cancer in 2014, but the images from 2012 and 2013 also show a small mass that had been undetected by the human radiologist's eye. Barzilay had been doing routine annual mammograms, had no family breast cancer history, and led a healthy lifestyle. She described her frustration with the state-of-the-art oncology she encountered: "At every point in my treatment, I had many more questions than my doctors had answers to. I remember I did my mammogram, and they said, 'Your cancer is really tiny.' I said 'Great!' Then we went to M.R.I., and suddenly they see cancer all over. Then they did a biopsy, and they discovered it's actually small; the M.R.I. was a false positive. How can we have this high-resolution M.R.I. modality and still not know that this is a false positive?"[11] Barzilay was astounded by the contrast between the healthcare industry and tech companies like Google and Facebook-turned-Meta that track every action we take online and use the data to build a model of who we are. "In some ways they know more about you than you know about yourself," she said. "But if you go to any clinic, for cancer, heart disease, you name it—there is no A.I."[12]

The majority of breast lesions detected are benign; in fact, 90 percent of the lesions deemed "high-risk" are found to be benign post-surgery. This means that thousands of women go through painful, expensive, and scarring surgeries that are unnecessary. Barzilay underwent surgery and radiation treatment and, thankfully, her cancer is in remission. She was already a rising star in the field of artificial intelligence at that point in her career, but prior to her diagnosis, her research had focused on other aspects of AI like natural language processing, and she had done groundbreaking work using computer science to decipher dead languages. Barzilay developed an algorithm that was able to translate Ugaritic, an ancient Semitic language, allowing the machine to learn Hebrew to help it decipher the more ancient, unknown language. But after battling breast cancer, Barzilay felt she simply could not go back to her old research. "I started asking: What is the best way to spend my time, my mental energy? I could not forget the suffering and pain I saw in the hospital. I wanted to use data to provide answers now."[13] She returned to MIT with a new vision for her research and for technology: to improve medical diagnostics and treatment using AI. Training a machine to identify patients at risk seemed obvious and effective. Machines were already able to distinguish between images at a level that the human eye could not: "From a patient's perspective, it felt cruel. We're talking about well-understood technology commercially deployed in other industries, not brand-new research. . . . It doesn't matter what your disease is; today, A.I. is not yet part of clinical treatment."[14] Barzilay developed an algorithm that analyzes mammogram images differently, assessing risk before cancer develops, which is something that is not attempted by human radiologists. In terms of detection of existing cancer, Barzilay believes that today the best radiologists are still better than machines, though the gap is narrowing fast. The year after she was diagnosed, she created a system that uses computer vision technology to independently learn about the patterns of diagnosing breast cancer. She partnered with Dr. Constance Lehman, chief of breast imaging at Boston's Massachusetts General Hospital. Lehman herself serves on several key national committees and was eager to apply deep learning to all aspects of breast cancer care, from prevention to detection to treatment.

Barzilay and Lehman fed the algorithm both the image and the outcome over time so that it could teach itself what can be detected—what a human eye might miss. They fed the algorithm 70,000 images of lesions with known outcomes, both malignant and benign. They effectively trained the computer to predict which patients were later diagnosed with cancer. The result is a computer that is significantly better at diagnosing than any previous human-led detection system. The model can predict the development of breast cancer up to five years before a diagnosis would be made using traditional methods. In other words, the computer can find patterns at the earliest stages of cell mutation. Using artificial intelligence allows the physicians to search not simply for cancer but for the cells that *predict* cancer, or as Lehman puts it, "the soil . . . that allows that seed of cancer to grow."[15] The AI has been used in hospitals since 2018, helping diagnose and treat countless women earlier than was possible before.[16]

Barzilay set out to further apply her field of natural language processing to automate the reading of existing data from hospitals, including data about treatment efficacy. She describes our existing health records as "a gold mine of data" that is "severely underutilized."[17] Despite billions of medical records in hospital archives, patients today cannot get answers to simple questions such as how other patients responded to a particular drug or treatment plan. To address this gap, Barzilay began work to automate hospital record searches. She created a database of more than 100,000 patients from Massachusetts General and other partner hospitals, and now patients and machines can search, query, and learn from archived treatment plans.[18] In 2017, two years after she turned her attention to women's health, Barzilay won a MacArthur Foundation fellowship (colloquially referred to as a "genius grant").

Once she had set her sights on making us healthier, there was no turning back. Barzilay told me she shares my frustration about AI recently receiving a lot of bad publicity, or as she put it, "an overemphasis on the dangers of AI, when we are constantly subjected to deficiencies of human decision-making in the healthcare system." She says that the vast majority of the U.S. population has never experienced any AI as patients, but AI is currently portrayed as a serious danger to their health. Barzilay has now turned her attention to other key medical challenges in addition to breast health.

She hopes to expand the technology she developed to the screening of other cancers, including lung and pancreatic cancer, which are often only detected after it is too late for treatment.[19] She also recently collaborated with another MIT professor, James Collins, to develop an AI model that analyzes the structure of chemical compounds that could kill bacteria. The model learned what those traits are and then mined through thousands of other compounds to find something that had not been previously used as an antibacterial compound. And lo and behold, she and Collins found a compound they named Halicin that can kill dozens of bacteria, including some common ones that have long caused patient infections at hospitals. It was a game changer. In 2020, Barzilay received the inaugural AI award from the world's largest AI society, the Association for the Advancement of Artificial Intelligence. According to Yolanda Gil, the award committee chairperson, the prize aims to recognize "the positive impact of artificial intelligence for humanity."[20] Barzilay says it is not easy for computer scientists to receive funding to conduct medical research, mainly because funding comes from the medical and life sciences fields. Yet the overlap is becoming undeniable. Barzilay later donated part of the prize money to the Greater Boston Food Bank.

AI is still in its initial stages in diagnostic health. We absolutely must treat its integration with great caution. The best evidence right now shows that in some instances AI is outperforming radiologists, but in others—at least when we compare AI to two radiologists working together (which is costly and often not an available reality for most patients)—a team of radiologists still outperforms machine screening. What we need is to continue comparative test accuracy studies and controlled trials to evaluate the constantly improving technology in comparison to traditional screening processes. Moreover, we should always consider that AI *combined* with human screening might outperform either one of these methods on its own. Numerous exciting breast health innovations are in the works, including, for example, developing wearable devices that could monitor breast cancer patients to see if their treatment is working.

Yet many of these inventions are still years away from being available, effective, and safe for patient use. In 2021, the FDA detailed an action plan to further the study of and improve the approval process for AI- and machine learning–based methods in the health arena. Part of the action plan is to improve patient trust in AI technologies and to create better medical device labeling to support transparency to users of AI-based devices. The FDA plans to support regulatory science efforts in the development of methodology for the evaluation and improvement of machine learning algorithms, including for the identification and elimination of bias, and in the resilience of these algorithms to withstand changing clinical inputs and conditions. In other words, while there are many private experiments and emerging new tools to improve our health, public oversight and rigorous and robust peer-reviewed research are critical in expanding and implementing the potential of artificial intelligence for health and medicine.

Limitless Potential

With both promise and caveats, AI medical devices are now being applied to detect cervical cancer, pancreatic cancer, leukemia, and more. According to the World Health Organization, cervical cancer alone results in 270,000 deaths globally per year. One research team led by NIH investigators has been working on an algorithm to analyze digital images of the cervix and detect precancerous changes.[21] Another AI system, developed at University College Dublin in Ireland, is revolutionizing the diagnosis of preeclampsia, which kills 50,000 women and 500,000 infants every year and further results in 5 million premature births.[22] The diagnostic test, called AI_PREMie, combines biomarker testing and risk assessment to identify this notoriously difficult-to-diagnose condition. Professor Patricia Maguire, who heads the team that developed the system, said they hope to make it available as a stand-alone kit for hospitals all over the world. "When I say 1 in 10 pregnant women will develop pre-eclampsia and 500,000 babies die each year, this is probably an underestimation because it is likely that it is under-reported in lower-income countries,"

Maguire said. "The big dream is to reach every person who needs this test across the world."[23]

The potential of lifesaving AI applications is breathtaking. There's even hope that AI will eventually create novel medical applications absent a designer's input. As put by physicist Herbert Kroemer in his Nobel Lecture in 2000: "The principal applications of any sufficiently new and innovative technology always have been—and will continue to be—applications *created* by that technology." Barzilay too is an optimist at heart and a great believer in the power of machines to better our lives. She firmly believes that we can expand the capabilities of digital assistance to our well-being, and consequently our happiness: "Machines have immense capacity to remember our actions and predict our future behavior. This gives them the capacity to help us modify our behavior, so we become our better selves."[24] And the benefits extend all the way from lifesaving diagnosis and treatment potential to the everyday. Barzilay says that a simple wearable heart-monitoring app increased the frequency and intensity of her running. "When I first saw it, I just laughed and thought, 'Who can be motivated by these silly rewards?' But guess what? Every morning at 5 a.m., I am running. Rain, MIT deadlines, sleepiness—nothing stops me from getting my running points. And this change in my life has really made me happier."[25]

Not far from Barzilay's lab at MIT, another pioneer (and as Barzilay told me, "my best friend") is devoted to changing the landscape of patient care. Dr. Dina Katabi, co-director of the MIT Center for Wireless Networks and Mobile Computing and a principal investigator at MIT's Computer Science and Artificial Intelligence Laboratory, is working on a project called Emerald that uses AI and cutting-edge X-ray technology to track a person's movements. Emerald can look at your sleep stages, heartbeat, breathing, gait, and other physiological variables even when you are in another room. Like devices already in existence, it aims to monitor patients who are at risk of falling in their homes or who need monitoring for various health issues, from Parkinson's disease to Alzheimer's to multiple sclerosis. The innovation here is that the information is collected without body sensors needing to be attached to the person. The non-invasiveness is game changing. During the Covid-19 pandemic the system proved especially useful when hospitals were overcrowded and patients stayed at home isolated.

Like Barzilay, Katabi began her work in more theoretical realms of computer science and engineering but found her way to more practical, lifesaving applications. Like Barzilay, who was born in Moldova, emigrated to Israel, and came to the United States for grad school, Katabi is an immigrant, hailing from the Middle East. She was born in Syria and received her bachelor's degree from the University of Damascus before coming to MIT as a graduate student. And like Barzilay, the MacArthur Foundation awarded Katabi a "genius" grant, citing her "ability to translate long-recognized theoretical advances into practical solutions that could be deployed in the real world."[26] Among Katabi's other groundbreaking current projects is a radio-frequency system that monitors sleep postures called BodyCompass. BodyCompass tracks radio-frequency reflections in the environment, identifies the signals that bounced off the sleeping person's body, and analyzes those signals via a machine learning algorithm. Katabi and her collaborators found that with just sixteen minutes of labeled data from the sleeping person, BodyCompass's accuracy is 84 percent; within one week, its accuracy went up to 94 percent. Monitoring sleep posture is important for many health contexts, including monitoring patients after surgery, tracking progression of diseases including Parkinson's, and more.

The potential of AI extends to mental health as well. Despite immense efforts at prevention, suicide rates have remained intractable over time and recently increased in some parts of the world, including the United States. We now know that teens are disclosing risk factors for suicide on social media that they don't disclose to their family or health professionals. A recent systematic review of empirical studies on using AI in suicide prevention finds that machine learning can overcome some of the cost and clinical barriers, risk of bias, and restricted generalizability that all exist in suicide prevention efforts, leveraging large data sets and predictive modeling.[27] Similar risk modeling techniques, using machine learning on medical records and other data sets to predict risk, have been developed to predict schizophrenia and other mental health risks, as well as predicting demand for hospital capacities during times of emergency, each with high accuracy.

Analogous approaches are beginning to be introduced in the field of surgery. Surgical robots are built on algorithms of surgical videos and data from operations. Robotic surgery was originally developed to provide care to soldiers on the battlefield or astronauts in space. Since then, robots have been utilized in numerous surgical procedures. Artificial intelligence can currently facilitate interaction between surgeons and surgical robots, for example by recognizing surgeons' movements (e.g., head, eyes, hand) and converting them into action commands for the robots.[28] One study of orthopedic patients found that an AI-assisted robotic procedure resulted in one-fifth the number of complications compared to surgeons operating alone.[29] Pathologists, too, have utilized AI to decrease their error rates from 3.4 percent to 0.5 percent in recognizing cancer-positive lymph nodes. The Da Vinci, one of the most advanced ophthalmology surgery robots, delivers three-dimensional, high-definition views, giving the surgeon magnified vision ten times clearer than what the human eye sees. Some heart surgeons are assisted by HeartLander, a miniature mobile robot designed to facilitate the application of minimally invasive therapy to the surface of the beating heart, which improves precision while decreasing the hazards associated with gaining access to the heart. We are truly in the midst of a surgical revolution.

Algorithms and Embryos

Science and technology have always created new opportunities in the quest for gender equality. As with the industrial revolution, advances in women's reproductive care—and in reproductive rights, which are just as imperative—have been central to women's empowerment. Decades ago, the invention and subsequent availability of birth control gave women more control over their bodies and their lives. Now, with the application of digital progress, reproductive technologies are advancing at light speed. Yet at the same time, women's freedoms are under continuous attack. Access to reproductive health, including freely choosing when and whether to reproduce, is a matter of liberty and human rights, not simply science and technology. Indeed, in the United States, because the Supreme Court has tied the constitutional fault line of the right to abortion to the viability of a fetus, technological advancement could perversely be regressive. As Harvard Law School bioethicist (and my co-author on a study on health and safety regulations applicable to NFL players) Glenn Cohen explains it, if we get to the time when we can place a fetus in an artificial womb, the viability question could be detrimental to women's autonomy. Cohen explains that because the right to abortion has been most vigorously defended as a right not to be a gestational parent, as opposed to a right not to be a legal or genetic parent, the advancement in technology could allow women to exercise their rights to stop gestating while forcing them to transfer the fetus to the artificial womb. This could mean we may need, in the not-so-far-away future, to reframe our moral grounds for reproductive rights.

Humans can be thought of as self-replicating algorithms. Reproduction is perhaps the one remaining sphere in which gender still matters a lot. Despite all the advances in genetics, in vitro fertilization (IVF), and surrogacy, we still need a baby to grow in a woman's body. This may not always be the case: the artificial womb is a focus of fetal researchers in both the United States and Europe. In 2017, Children's Hospital of Philadelphia published a study showing they had grown premature lamb fetuses for four weeks in an extrauterine life support system. Moreover, the Human Genome Project envisions all of us and our different parts as text that can be reduced to code, which can in turn be stored, reproduced, and changed. Reproduction may one day be fundamentally transformed.

Today, AI is already helping women with pregnancy in myriad ways. It has already begun to revolutionize women's fertility treatments. Women undergoing fertility treatment go through an incredible journey to give birth. Machine learning is especially helpful in making curative decisions by using data and patterns. Many couples have trouble conceiving, and IVF—developing embryos in the laboratory and selecting healthy ones to implant into a mother's womb—is on the rise. The success rate of IVF is currently quite low; it is an expensive and long process, and I can attest that it is physically and mentally tough to undergo. This means only the well-off can afford it. Fertility doctors have few conventional methods at their disposal beyond the use of their eyes, aided by a microscope, to evaluate sperm, eggs, and embryos. But in IVF, selecting the most viable embryos to transfer back to the uterus is critical. The current tools available for making this decision are limited, highly subjective, and time-consuming. Embryologists rely on their experience and observational skills when choosing embryos, which can lead to a lot of variability.[30]

Enter artificial intelligence. Mass General Brigham (where I gave birth to my first daughter) is developing an AI system for IVF based on thousands of embryo images. An automated system based on machine learning could improve IVF success rates by assisting embryologists with embryo selection, resulting in a higher number of and more consistently healthy pregnancies. The AI system would learn about embryo development patterns and select the most viable embryo to implant. Thus, machine learning can both lower the costs and increase the success of IVF compared to human decision-making alone. The Mass General Brigham AI system has already been out-performing embryologists from leading centers in selecting the best embryos out of high-quality embryos with few visible differences. Toronto-based AI biotech start-up Future Fertility and its machine learning system Violet is introducing artificial intelligence even earlier in the IVF process by asking the AI to measure egg quality. The AI is trained on time-lapse images of fertilized eggs becoming embryos. The company asserts that the system's predictions have a very high rate of success, predicting correctly most of the time whether an egg will fertilize. As AI systems get more data, predictions get better on all of the fronts critical to IVF: fertilization, embryonic genetic health, successful implantation into the uterus, and ultimately a successful pregnancy, birth, and healthy baby.

The Color of Health

Technological advances that reduce medical screening costs can be lifesaving for people in underserved communities who lack health insurance or access to quality healthcare. Black women in low-income communities, for example, experience disproportionately high rates of late-stage, locally advanced, or metastatic breast cancer.[31] Not only does AI work (and learn) around the clock, but it also effectively eliminates the high cost of human radiologists. Since cost is one of the main barriers to women getting mammograms, AI can save lives simply by providing testing at a lower cost. Healthcare and medical research have for centuries been plagued by a white male standard model. Even the Human Genome Project—the world's largest collaborative biological project—began with a skewed focus: Africans' genes were not studied at the same rate, slowing down the development of personalized medicine for minorities.[32] We already know that incomplete or skewed data fed to algorithms can lead to bias: bias in, bias out. In 2019, an article in *Science* revealed how algorithms pertaining to blood pressure have a built-in racial bias: Black patients were deemed to be at lower risk than white patients when they were equally sick. In this case, the data point responsible for the bias was healthcare costs. The algorithm put weight on the healthcare costs of a patient as a metric of his or her illness. Unequal access to care meant that Black patients were receiving less spending than white patients, and the algorithm thereby (wrongly) deduced that they were not as sick. "Thus, despite health care cost appearing to be an effective proxy for health by some measures of predictive accuracy, large racial biases arise," the article concluded.[33]

University of Chicago professor Sendhil Mullainathan, who co-authored the résumé studies that we explored in Chapter 2, was one of the researchers on this study. When Mullainathan compares his research findings of bias by humans and by machines, he explains that the latter is the more fixable problem:

Changing people's hearts and minds is no simple matter. . . . By contrast, we've already built a prototype that would fix the algorithmic bias we found—as did the original manufacturer, who, we concluded, had no intention of producing biased results in the first place. We offered a free service to health systems using these algorithms to help build a new one that was not racially biased. There were many takers.[34]

As we've seen, training data can also be both incomplete and skewed. By definition, there is less data available about minorities. Big data sets may be unrepresentative of certain groups; not all of us have lives that are equally datafied. Those at the outskirts will have less data collected about them, sometimes to their advantage, but often to their detriment. We often have an idea that computation is precise and unbiased—what privacy and security law expert Paul Schwartz describes as the "seductive precision" of computational outputs.[35] The quality of the output depends on the quality of the inputs, and again, as we've already seen, bias in, bias out, which is a subset of the more general problem that computer scientists call garbage in, garbage out (GIGO)—flawed or irrelevant input data produces nonsense output. And of course, better training impacts costs, necessitating adequate funding and public oversight. A 2017 Stanford study asserted that a well-trained, data-driven algorithm could screen and classify cancerous moles with the precision of a dermatologist, helping physicians and patients alike. Such an algorithm makes screening quicker and cheaper, and is scalable, but we need to ensure that all patients—no matter the color of their skin— are benefiting from the accuracy and efficiency of the machine. If algorithms are not trained with diversity of skin types in mind, their output will be (at least for some populations) garbage, to state it bluntly. There is an upside, however. When it comes to more vulnerable populations for which quality healthcare has for too long been elusive, with the right direction we can do better, and do it cheaper, with the aid of technology. This promise is more likely to be realized when we pay more attention to the face of research.

The Face of Research

The rapid integration of AI in medicine and healthcare underscores why including gender and race in data sets is vital to making more accurate models. At the same time, it is crucial that more women and minorities are involved in the creation of the algorithms. Barbara Ehrenreich and Deirdre English's book *Witches, Midwives and Nurses: A History of Women Healers* describes how the professionalization of medicine marginalized and gendered the role of women health workers.[36] As a child, I remember my mother—psychology professor Thalma Lobel, whose groundbreaking research in gender development continues to impact generations of researchers—always testing people around us with a telling party riddle: A father and son are in a car accident. The father is killed, and the son arrives at the hospital for surgery. The surgeon cries out, "I can't operate on this patient because he is my son!" How can it be? My mother would pose the question, delighting at the puzzled faces of her audience. The answer is easy, of course: the surgeon is the boy's mother. Although the overall participation of women in medicine has steadily grown in the twenty-first century, we still have a gender imbalance in the field. By 2019, only 36 percent of physicians and surgeons were women, while 86 percent of registered nurses were women.[37] In 2021, 37 percent of physicians and surgeons were women, while 82 percent of registered nurses were women. Still today, my friend who is an ER doctor in San Diego doesn't need my mother's party riddle—she tells me that she is still regularly mistaken for the nurse by patients asking her who the doctor on call is.

For years, the black box algorithms within physicians' minds have been processing information in biased ways. In one study, doctors were shown two equivalent patient histories, with the only differences being the gender and race of the patient. The chances of recommending a beneficial procedure—cardiac catheterization—to the patient were 40 percent lower for women and minorities than for white males. Like with employment, credit, bail, and other life-impacting decision-making, machines with all their flaws can already often do better than biased humans. Recently, for example, researchers successfully developed a machine learning model that could assess the severity of pulmonary edema in chest radiographs with a relatively high level of accuracy in both men and women.[38] Such automation of medical screening can help reduce gender and racial imbalances in treatment for cardiovascular disease, and the same model applies across the board.

Gender and race analysis is starting to be recognized as key in creating robust data sets, meaningful studies, and better health insights. In one incredible study that examined a sample of more than 1.5 million medical research papers, the researchers asked a simple question: Does the participation of women authors in these studies make a difference as to whether the research includes gender and sex analysis?[39] The answer was an unequivocal yes. The face of research—diverse participation in medical science, as in every other field—is connected to better research design and outcomes. The scientific advancement of women and minorities and the scientific advancement of equality in medical research and treatment are inextricably connected.

Here again, it is important to remember that tracking differences is key to detecting disparities. The FDA tracks adverse reactions from pharmaceutical drugs with gender-disaggregated metrics, but its database on medical device performance does not include gender data. The International Consortium of Investigative Journalists (ICIJ) found that there was simply no gender data to analyze when it set out to study whether there is a greater incidence of serious medical problems due to medical implants and devices reported for women than men. Collaborating with a team of Stanford University computer scientists, the ICIJ developed an algorithm to mine patient incident reports for gender-indicating pronouns ("the patient reported she can see blood in the tubing of her insulin infusion") and adjectives ("a male patient in good health underwent a knee repair") to ascertain the patient's sex.[40] The resulting equality machine revealed what had been a hidden truth: in 340,000 incident reports of injury or death caused by medical devices, 67 percent involved women, while only 33 percent involved men. The algorithm was able to effectively quantify the textual evidence, increasing calls for FDA regulation of these devices and implants.

Digitization is also improving tracking. The SARS outbreak between 2002 and 2004 didn't track the effects of the virus on pregnancy. With Covid-19, researchers did a better job at tracking and studying the effects on pregnant women and on fetal health. This research has been important—likely lifesaving—as results showed an increase in the need for hospitalization and ventilation assistance for infected pregnant women.

In the pharmaceutical industry, algorithms are being employed to find treatments and drugs for rare diseases that to date haven't received much attention. The hard truth has always been that pharma devotes more research and development resources to diseases that afflict the rich. The definition of rare has too often been conflated with poor—that is, even if a disease is quite prevalent in a population that cannot afford to pay for it (for example, people living in the developing world), the disease has been neglected compared to First World ailments. By lowering the cost of data collection, mining, and analysis in drug development and clinical trials, AI can help offset imbalances in the pharmaceutical industry that skew attention to diseases that "pay," whether because the disease is more common or because it is prevalent among demographics that can pay more. Again and again, we see the democratizing power of AI to broaden the attention of the medical and research communities to find cures to traditionally neglected health issues and among traditionally neglected populations.

Companies extract massive amounts of information from users, turning the data into profitable resources—and, in turn, claiming ownership over this extracted information. As an intellectual property scholar, I've been long involved in efforts to bring more equity into our laws that grant monopolies over bodies of knowledge. Barzilay herself made sure that Mirai, the revolutionary technology that can predict nearly half of breast cancer disease up to five years before it occurs, was open-source, such that any hospital can use it and improve upon it. There are no patents on Mirai because, as Barzilay noted, "this should be for everyone to build on."[41]

The rapid advancement of AI and automated data collection is further underscoring the risks of our laws protecting the interests of corporations at the expense of distributive justice in the information ecosystem. Erin Murphy, a New York University law professor, warns that if your sibling or child provided their genetic information by spitting into a DNA kit and mailing it back to a company like 23andMe, "they are compromising your family for generations." The balance between preserving privacy and health, private property and distributive justice, free speech and equality, and many other democratic values will continue to be at the heart of any new technological capability. But as we've seen, AI can move the needle on some of the ongoing challenges by leveraging technology itself to decrease the tension between these different values. For example, researchers are developing algorithms to improve user privacy while at the same time providing viable data to study. It is possible now to produce made-up but highly realistic medical records for the scientific community to study. This is something only the computational power of machine learning can effectively accomplish, and it can mean we rise to a win-win equilibrium: privacy *and* scientific progress simultaneously.

Cure the Virus, Kill the Beast

How effectively could data collection—and AI's power to collate data and analyze it—balance the scales of inequality in healthcare and beyond? The NIH's All of Us initiative is an example of such an effort. The program compiles the most diverse health databases in history by collecting health data from underrepresented populations and individuals who don't regularly participate in clinical trials or don't frequently see physicians compared to other populations. Leveraging the enormous amounts of data stored in health records via machine learning algorithms can help reframe the conversation around inequality.

The way we frame problems informs how we think of solutions. Lera Boroditsky, a psychology professor at the University of California, San Diego, ran an experiment that demonstrates how metaphors shape the way people are motivated to address social issues. In the study, one group of people was told that crime is a "beast" preying on a community. The other group read a description of the crime infecting a community as a "virus." With just a difference of one word, people supported different solutions to the same problem of high crime rates. Looking at it through the lens of the "beast" led them to want more policing and harsher punishment. Those who saw it through the lens of a "virus" supported social reforms and constructive solutions such as education, community support, poverty-alleviating measures, and the creation of more housing and jobs for the poor.

Subtle cues and storytelling frame our conversations and imagination. Beyond its direct significance in bringing innovation to specific health challenges, big data pivots the narrative about inequality by offering a more complete picture of the systemic exclusions that have long been embedded in our health systems. It can help us move the challenge of inequality (and hence the solutions) from a "beast" mindset to a "virus" mindset. The lens of an infectious virus surely captures our imagination as the world recovers from the global coronavirus pandemic. A virus can only survive when there are hosts. A virus mutates. A virus infects the more vulnerable in patterned ways. And a virus requires collective action to prevent its spread, to treat the sick, to educate and ensure access for all, and to develop and disseminate vaccinations. When we think about the potential good and potential risks of technology, we can leverage technology itself to understand the multiple lenses that have shaped our public debates and to identify who is gaining, who is left behind, and how the benefits of technology can spread to benefit all of us.

IV
SENSES

CHAPTER 6

She Speaks

Why do we give robots female names? Because we don't want to consider their feelings.

—LAURIE PENNY, American journalist

What's in a Name and a Voice?

Who among us wouldn't benefit from having a digital *wife*? In our busy lives, we could all use a helping hand—especially women, who still disproportionately take on the largely invisible work of caring for others and the home. In the 1999 Disney movie *Smart House*, which predates Siri and Alexa by more than a decade, a family wins a computerized home equipped with PAT (which stands for "personal applied technology"). PAT starts out as a female-voiced chatbot, then comes to life as a woman-like hologram, and eventually takes on a motherly role. In the film, PAT was the brainchild of a female programmer, but in a predictable twist a male programmer removes certain protections and tells PAT to watch 1950s TV shows to learn how to be an ideal mother.[1]

In 2014, Google's chief economist, Hal Varian, said that for centuries only rich people had servants, but in the future we will all have cyberservants.[2] Today, in our homes and all around us, we meet cyberservants in the form of Alexa, Siri, and other voice-activated personal assistants that are evolving and getting smarter every day. They are designed to adapt to our speech patterns and personal preferences. They are always there to answer our questions, order us food, help us run the household, and even tell us jokes on demand. And they are almost universally female. *New York Times* tech reporter Farhad Manjoo describes Alexa as his household's brain—the keeper of lists, a provider of food and culture, an entertainer and educator, and handmaiden to his children.[3] Manjoo also describes Alexa as a kind of butler-in-the-sky that runs the place. But calling Alexa a butler is misleading. Historically, butlers were nearly uniformly male and higher paid than female servants, though the women servants performed far more work. These days, around the world, Alexa and newer versions of digital assistants assume work as housekeepers, secretaries, personal entertainers, and would-be wives and mothers, all rolled into one.

Digital personal assistants are a godsend for many families. They can ease people's daily challenges, large and small. They can be that much-needed wife to the single mom working two jobs. They can help overworked couples juggling dual careers to achieve a better work-family balance. Orthodox Jews, for example, were early enthusiasts of Alexa and other digital personal assistants. They were eager to adopt the technology to overcome religious restrictions around operating electric machines during the Sabbath. Around the world, and regardless of religion or culture, Alexa and Siri and their cohorts have lent a helping hand to families, assisting them in keeping the household in shape. One story that really touched my heart is that of Judith Newman and her thirteen-year-old son, Gus, who has autism. In the book *To Siri with Love*, Newman describes her feelings of being a bad mother, exhausted from the toll of caring for a child with special needs, and how Siri helped her son learn to communicate and connect. Gus learned to ask Siri questions about things that interested him, such as the weather, and could spend hours asking questions and receiving answers. Newman views Siri as a wonderful, inexhaustible complement to the humans in Gus's life, who are, of course, exhaustible. She says that when Gus discovered that there was someone who would always and tirelessly answer questions related to all his various obsessions, not only weather but also trains, planes, buses, and escalators, he was hooked. Through his conversations with Siri, Gus became more confident and skilled in talking with humans too. For Gus, Newman says, like many other children with autism, Siri served as a non-judgmental friend and teacher. Newman calls her story a love letter to a machine. She writes, "In a world where the commonly held wisdom is that technology isolates us, it's worth considering another side of the story."[4]

Newman's love letter to Siri is incredibly sweet and tender. Her book captures not only the unique challenges of raising a child with developmental differences, but also the universal challenges we face in the modern world, including, of course, isolation because of a global pandemic or other natural disaster. Even amid our cautiousness and at times trepidation, we should celebrate the benefits of chatbots and their potential to do good. They help us remember things, save us time, and alleviate life's burdens, even lessen our loneliness. At the same time, a feminist examination of the chatbot phenomenon also needs to grapple with the market's thirst for artificial housewives— how it started, how it's going, and how we can shape AI to better emulate tomorrow's society rather than yesterday's. Our digital assistants can become equality machines if we consciously direct their design and integration into our digital ecosystems.

On Echoes and Narcissism

When you hear someone call out "Alexa," you probably have an immediate association to the world's most popular AI assistant, made ubiquitous by the equally ubiquitous Amazon. Her name is inspired by the legendary Library of Alexandria in Egypt, the largest and most famous library of the ancient world; it is also another name attributed to the Greek goddess Hera, the goddess of fertility and marriage. Amazon introduced Alexa in 2014 alongside its Echo smart speaker system, the mechanism through which Alexa communicates. In Ovid's *Metamorphoses*, Echo was the nymph whom Zeus commanded to distract the goddess Hera, diverting her from spying on one of his lovers. Hera punishes Echo by taking away her ability to speak independently. Echo is left with the sole ability to repeat—or echo—what she hears. Echo then falls in love with Narcissus, who loves only his mirror image. Eventually her echoing voice is all that remains, a disembodied female voice reflecting male narcissism. Amazon markets Alexa, or Echo, as "always ready," and her job is to answer whatever we ask of her.

If Alexa is the most popular chatbot on the market, then Siri is certainly a close second. Siri, in Norse, means a beautiful woman who leads you to victory. SRI International—the company that developed Siri—originally conceived Siri as a gender-neutral voice, but as Apple commercialized the technology, it became the female-voiced Siri we so intimately know today. Siri Inc. co-founder Norman Winarsky says, "What Apple did is absolutely brilliant. They took Siri and gave it more of a personality. It's the first real artificial intelligence working in millions of people's hands."[5] Personality in the hands of Apple meant making Siri sound and feel like a woman.

While all the leading devices on the market were launched with female voices, many have now introduced non-female voice options. Still, defaults are sticky, and when Apple and Amazon advertise Siri and Alexa, the voices are consistently female. Alexa, Siri, Microsoft's Cortana (a reference to a nude female character in the video game Halo), Samsung's Bixby, and Google's Google Assistant all have feminine voices. For GPS navigation systems like Google Maps and Apple Maps, the default voice is also set to be female. Since World War II, cockpit navigation systems have tended to use female voices for warnings as well as greetings because they "stood out among the male pilots."[6] Notably, U.S. Air Force pilots regularly refer to the female voice in their fighter jets—which gets louder and more insistent if a pilot ignores warnings—as "Bitchin' Betty." British pilots call it "Nagging Nora."[7] BMW's GPS system is one of the few exceptions to the female voice default rule, though not for the reason we might hope: BMW initially introduced a female-voiced navigation system on its 5 Series cars, but it switched to a male voice after German male drivers told the company that they refused to take directions from a woman.[8]

Pitch Perfect

Before virtual assistants became part of our lives, the first text-to-speech programs designed in the 1980s and 1990s were male. This is telling: virtual assistants serve us; text-to-speech represents our own voice. Text-to-speech allows users to listen to a text being read aloud, which is widely useful, especially for users who are visually impaired or have speech disorders. Amazon's Audible platform allows the blind and the elderly to listen to books, journals, newspapers, and anything else that is digitally written, like blogs, ads, and websites. GPS speech systems allow us to drive more safely by verbally directing us. Incrementally, leading companies have developed systems that offer a choice of several female and male adult voices, as well as child voices, but those initially designed artificial voices were prone to stereotypes. One of the female voices was named Whispering Wendy and spoke in a soft, high-pitched, hesitant tone, while one of the male voices was called Huge Harry and spoke with confidence and authority.[9]

Speech specialists agree that while some differences in pitch are biological, much of the variation in male and female speech is nurture-based and can be traced to social norms. For example, numerous studies have shown that women in societies with greater gender inequality tend to speak in softer, higher-pitched voices. British prime minister Margaret Thatcher famously trained with a vocal coach to give her voice a more male-sounding, authoritative pitch. More recently, Elizabeth Holmes, the ousted Theranos founder who was later criminally convicted, favored a low, baritone authoritative voice as part of her invented persona (along with her Steve Jobs–lookalike turtlenecks). Design decisions to exaggerate male and female speech characteristics are salient examples of biased—and entirely unnecessary—gendering. Later versions of both male and female text-to-speech voices have been faring somewhat better on the anti-stereotype scale and reflect the potential to challenge gender norms while still acknowledging differences.

The tech industry has for decades considered female voices the go-to for designing helpful, inoffensive, eager-to-please technology solutions. When asked about their decisions to use female voices for personal assistants, executives of the leading tech companies often refer to studies showing that both men and women prefer women's voices, perceived as warmer and friendlier. For example, Stanford University professor Clifford Nass explains that "it's a well-established phenomenon that the human brain is developed to like female voices."[10] Some research does suggest that the human predilection for the female voice starts as early as the womb, but this preference goes away after the first few months.[11] As adults, we have been programmed for years to associate gendered voices with gender roles. Many studies find that consumers tend to prefer a male voice for authoritative speech and a female voice for assistance and support.[12] As these gender-voice schemas play out in the market, voices intended to convey authority—narration or broadcasting or explaining scientific facts—tend to be male, while compliant robots that serve tend to be female. A series of studies have found that both men and women prefer a male voice when studying "male" subjects such as computer programming, but a female voice when talking about relationships and dating. In some studies, male-voiced computers have been rated more competent than female-voiced computers.[13] At least one analyst believes that more of our computerized voices would be masculine if it weren't for negative associations with popular culture portrayals of menacing computers, like HAL from *2001: A Space Odyssey* or the computer program in *WarGames*.[14]

In researching the root cause for the selection of the female voice I found alternative explanations that, on the surface, seem to be more technical and objective. The high-pitched female voice is thought to be easier to hear over the din of a crowded train car, for instance, and more generally the female voice is said to be, simply from an audio technology perspective, easier to understand than the low-pitched male voice. As it turns out, this is not scientifically correct, but it has nevertheless been the explanation for "Julie the Operator Lady," who has announced station arrivals and reported delays for Amtrak since 2001.[15] British philosopher Nina Power describes this public female voice as the sonic equivalent of the "Keep Calm and Carry On" motto: the voice of soft coercion.[16] It's also possible that another explanation lurks in the background: that the female voice reduces perceived threats of privacy infringement and invasion. Alexa and Siri are not seen as a prototypical spy, poised to profit from the enormous quantities of data that are mindlessly given up in their presence—though some would argue that profiting from our household data is actually their intended purpose.

The paradox of the pervasiveness of the public female voice is that it is in reverse proportion to the actual numbers of women versus men who assume roles in public life. In the United States, although a friendly woman's voice will guide you through the nation's capital city while you ride the D.C. Metro, there are three times more men than women seated in Congress.[17] In the *Iliad*, written around the eighth century BCE, Zeus threatens to hurt his wife, Hera, if she continues to question his decisions regarding the Trojan War. As classics scholar Mary Beard has observed, "Right where written evidence for Western culture starts, women's voices are not being heard in the public sphere."[18] Today, women's voices, "albeit ghostly, disembodied, usually pre-recorded, and extremely narrow in terms of origin, class and pitch," are all around us.[19] But millennia after Homer's chronicles, women have yet to achieve equal representation in public life.

Why gender voice at all? Why couldn't these bodiless personal assistants be presented as genderless? Think of the voice of a Muppet, a mythical creature, or a mechanical robot. As machines become smarter, we purposely impose anthropomorphic features on them: human names, human-sounding voices, physical features, and human personalities. These human features are meant to give us the feeling that we are interacting with a person rather than a machine. But human features don't necessarily mean gendered features, or at least they don't have to. The designer community still believes that this choice between gendered and non-gendered presents a trade-off between neutrality and relatability. But consumer choice and market competition allow us to experiment with a broad range of binary and non-binary approaches to digital design. In an Amazon ad that aired during the 2021 Super Bowl, a woman is shown admiring the spherical contours of the company's Echo speaker. She then reimagines her Alexa voice assistant as the actor Michael B. Jordan. Instead of the disembodied female voice that comes standard in the device, the woman's Echo takes the form of the smoldering star in the flesh—abs and all. He takes her shopping list updates, offers measurement conversions, makes requested adjustments to her home lighting and sprinkler systems, and even reads to her during a candlelit bath. As depicted in the ad, her husband hates it.

Reversing gender voices is important. Queering voices—challenging the very assumptions of gendering, and disrupting narratives and traditional binary understandings of sex and gender—is important. As we forge our way to a more equal and inclusive society, having options that are female, male, non-binary, and non-human is the way forward.

Chatbot Chatter

According to the Turing test, if a machine can impersonate a human, the machine is intelligent. In 1966, Joseph Weizenbaum, a computer scientist at MIT, attempted to create a chat robot that would pass the Turing test: ELIZA, considered the first chatbot in the history of computers. ELIZA was designed to imitate a therapist in the Rogerian psychotherapy style, asking open-ended questions and responding with follow-ups like "And how does it make you feel?" Weizenbaum was surprised, and in fact alarmed, at how patients related to ELIZA emotionally. ELIZA knew how to recognize key words or phrases to produce preprogrammed follow-ups. If a patient said, "My parents put me in boarding school," ELIZA would recognize "parents" and respond with "Tell me more about your family." If someone hesitated, ELIZA encouraged, "Go on, don't be afraid." Weizenbaum later worried about how easily people are willing to be deceived by the illusion of machine intelligence.

Today, specialized chatbots are used everywhere—in banking and financial services, healthcare, retail, education, and government. In 2020, when the Covid-19 pandemic brought a retail apocalypse, companies scrambled to increase their online sales while narrowing their brick-and-mortar footprints. Conversational bots helped the shift to remote interactions. As I began to explore the gender of chatbots beyond the most well-known ones, I found many examples of companies paving the way to a new world of bots with genderless voices and names. Sephora is one example of a company with its finger on the pulse of today's broader societal shift toward inclusiveness and diversity. Although you might expect a makeup retailer to select a female voice, Sephora decided to introduce a genderless bot, as part of its "We Belong to Something Beautiful" platform, launched in 2019, and its corresponding "Identify as We" campaign, which centers on showcasing LGBTQ+, non-binary, and gender-fluid individuals in Sephora ads to further the retailer's inclusive efforts.

Makeup is a niche industry. But how do things appear when we step back and look at the bigger picture? I researched current AI trends around gendered names, voices, and appearances in top companies in the finance, healthcare, and travel industries. What I found was slow progress: while there is still a tendency to select a female name and voice for digital assistants, about half of the leading companies have opted for gender neutrality. Of the ten largest banks in the world, five of them use gendered chatbots—female in every case—to offer services that are traditionally provided by human men. JPMorgan Chase and Bank of America are the two largest banks in the United States. Both use chatbots to assist users with tasks like paying down debt and providing checking account status. Bank of America's chatbot is called Erica (presumably short for "America") and is fitted with a woman's voice to match its feminine name.[20] JPMorgan's assistant goes by COiN (short for "contract intelligence") and remains genderless in both name and representation.

The trend in the healthcare industry is congruous. Of the world's ten largest healthcare companies, six have gendered virtual assistants, only one of them male. UnitedHealth Group has Missy, a smiling 3D virtual female assistant who guides users through the company's website, and it is also rolling out another female assistant, AVA (for "Agent Virtual Assistant"), to assist healthcare advocates in accessing data related to customer inquiries.[21]

In the airline industry, of the top ten airline companies, seven have gendered chatbots and six of them are female, reminding us of the traditional roles in the industry: pilot is to male as flight attendant is to female. But it's important to recognize that not all airlines find the need for a gendered chatbot. The Dutch airline KLM uses a highly rated genderless chatbot with a neutral name, BB, and no face.

In retail we also see these competing paths. Walmart's new financial technology venture is named Hazel. IKEA's chatbot Anna was recently renamed Billie. For its TV series *Genius*, National Geographic (perhaps unsurprisingly) created a male chatbot named Albert Einstein to increase viewer engagement. The bot was a success, with average conversations lasting between six and eight minutes and a user reengagement rate of 50 percent. But increasingly there are also examples of non-binary and non-human bots. Alibaba's voice bot, AliGenie, is a pet robot that has an animated, gender-ambiguous voice and cartoonish animal eyes. Queer theory embraces such moves of disrupting binary formations. Virtual assistants are here to stay. And as we saw, they can better our lives, particularly supporting our overworked selves, in many ways. As we're increasingly interacting with AI as part of our daily lives, now is an opportune time to celebrate the fuller spectrum of options and experiment with designs that defy categorization and stereotypes.

Do You Understand Me Now?

Alexa, Siri, and other voice-activated chatbots not only speak to us but listen too. As it turns out, however, they do not always listen to everyone equally. Speech recognition exemplifies how partial training data has led machines to learn more about white men's speech patterns and less about those of women and people of color. Case in point: Google's speech recognition is 13 percent more accurate for men than it is for women.[22] Testing a variety of speech activation technologies has shown that virtual assistants are more likely to understand male users than female users. If the user is a woman of color, the rate of accurately understanding her speech drops further. In one study testing speech recognition of different accents, English spoken with an Indian accent only had a 78 percent accuracy rate; recognition of English spoken with a Scottish accent was only 53 percent accurate. One telling story is that of an Irish woman who failed an automated spoken English proficiency test while trying to immigrate to Australia. The company that administered her test used a voice recognition technology trained to identify acceptable and unacceptable answers to questions; although she was a highly educated native English speaker, the algorithm deemed her answers unacceptable.

On the other hand, the specificity required by voice recognition can be helpful to those trying to improve their speech clarification. For example, Judith Newman's son Gus "speaks as if he has marbles in his mouth, but if he wants to get the right response from Siri, he must enunciate clearly."[23] For Newman, as a mother of a child with developmental challenges, the fact that Siri requires precise articulation has been a benefit, not a bug. Still, undoubtedly the increased understanding of English-speaking males is something of a "Big Five" effect: most voice recognition platforms are made by five companies—Amazon, Apple, Google, Meta, and Microsoft, which themselves are disproportionately staffed and led by white males. This kind of deficiency in speech recognition is relatively easy to remedy. The fix involves increasing the range and diversity of the data that we feed technology. A more diverse range of voices in the video and sound fed to algorithms will result in those algorithms' improved ability to interpret a broader range of speech patterns. Diversity in, diversity out.

In 2020, the BBC launched a voice assistant called Beeb that is trained to understand a much wider set of accents than the Big Five–created AI. Even earlier, Mozilla began a project to accelerate the collection of languages for artificial intelligence purposes from all over the world, with a focus on including more accents and languages and increasing accuracy, regardless of gender or age. Mozilla created the Common Voice data set as part of this effort, which by 2021 had recorded over 9,000 hours of voice data in sixty languages.[24] Much like Wikipedia, the project is crowdsourced and open-source. People are free to use the program, and contributors around the world can add their voices, enabling the open-source data set to grow through collective effort. I contributed my voice, reading out five sentences prompted on the site, the first one being, "Shakhter Karagandy will also play in the Kazakhstan Cup and the Europa Conference League."

The data set is in turn freely available to anyone developing voice-enabled technology. Voice contributors are also invited to give the system information about their gender, age, and accent to help the machine learn about the speech prevalent in different countries and regions. People from all over the world have contributed samples of their speech. It is easy to do, and you should consider it too. The languages represented range from Kabyle to Kinyarwanda, Votic to Esperanto.

In 2019, in partnership with the German Ministry for Economic Cooperation and Development, Mozilla increased its efforts to collect local language data in Africa through an initiative called Common Voice and Deep Speech.[25] The data set is already being used in voice assistant technologies such as Mycroft, an open-source voice assistant named after Sherlock Holmes's elder brother, and the Brazilian Portuguese medical transcription tool Iara Health. Kelly Davis, head of machine learning at Mozilla, describes the profound significance of focusing on underresourced languages and language preservation in correcting the imbalance of languages in mainstream speech recognition technology. He says that we should look at speech recognition as a public resource. This theme of conceptualizing advances in technologies, vastly aided through data collection, as a public good must become a recurring one as we strive to build equality machines. Voice and speech—like many other types of information that are making our machines smarter—are intimately tied to our autonomous selves, from our genetic makeup and our health information to our behavioral and emotional responses to different decision-making environments. Crowdsourcing and open-source projects are important avenues to use when building a fuller, more representative picture of our humanity. The lens of open data is critical not only when building our machines but also later, when benefiting from them, to ensure access to the information extracted from us and to demand that the value of the more complete and advanced systems that have gobbled up information is shared.

In 2020, 4.2 billion digital assistants were in use around the world, and that number is predicted to double by 2024.[26] The value of the voice AI industry is estimated to grow to $80 billion by 2023. Some surveys already show that nearly half of all general web searches are now done using voice.[27] Crowdsourced projects and open-source products may be the single best way to achieve the level of diversity and inclusion that society needs and deserves.

The Feminist Translator

Machine translation is an extraordinary engine for development. It has also been a powerful case study in gendered language and how we can improve as a society. In a global market, trade is enabled by communication and trust. Language barriers have burdened developing countries striving to compete in global markets. Machine translators are now easily and freely available on the web, facilitating untold numbers of exchanges of knowledge, information, ideas, goods, and services. Nevertheless, machine translators have defaulted to a masculine gender for years. Initially, Google Translate automatically presented translations with more male pronouns. The self-taught algorithm learned this by browsing the web, where male pronouns are twice as prevalent as female ones. The algorithm thereby magnified biases through feedback loops: each translation defaulting to a masculine pronoun in turn increases the male pronoun's comparative frequency on the web.[28] The bias amplification is most pronounced when an original language that is more gender-neutral (English, for example) is translated to languages that are more gendered (Spanish or Hebrew or French, for example).

This problem is solvable. Google Translate and other translation technologies—again, as with all AI—learn from the training data they are fed, and that training data consists of hundreds of millions of already translated texts that exist on the web. Up until now, translation algorithms have been programmed to translate to the most likely form, studying hundreds of years of publishing. Historically, men have been vastly more represented both as publishers and as the subjects of published works. So it makes perfect sense that machine translation has developed a male bias: the algorithms have learned from the data available to them. The quality of the output depends on the quality of the input, but when the input is biased, there are other ways to reach more equal outcomes. Instead of defaulting to the most commonly pervasive (male) pronouns, machine translators need to be programmed—*taught*—to identify more social cues and context. They could also default in equal rates to male and female when no context is provided. Yet another way to reverse this ongoing bias in our texts is to program the algorithm to produce the less numerous pronoun (female)—that is, intentionally adopt something like what we call in legal theory a penalty default rule, where the less popular option is chosen to achieve certain policy goals.

We have been undergoing an inclusive language revolution over the past decade. Pronouns are becoming increasingly inclusive, such as the increased rephrasing of "he" to "she" and of "he/she" to "they." Gendered speech can almost always be rewritten. Algorithms can also be taught to examine common names to identify gender. My name, for example, is unknown to most Americans. I am often addressed as *Mr.* Orly Lobel in reply emails. When my research is quoted around the world, I am often attributed as male. But an algorithm can quite easily sort through existing databases of common names to discover that Orly is a common Hebrew female name meaning "my light." When a machine translator is tasked to identify the entirety of the context throughout the text, its accuracy in identifying gender correctly will increase.

Google Translate has already made some strides in this direction. In 2018, a product manager on the Google Translate team published an article explaining this new focus: "There's been an effort across Google to promote fairness and reduce bias in machine learning. Our latest development in this effort addresses gender bias by providing feminine and masculine translations for some gender-neutral words on the Google Translate website." Initially, when a gender-neutral word could be translated in either a masculine or feminine form, only one translation was provided—often a biased one. Words like "strong" or "doctor" would lead to masculine translations, while words like "nurse" or "beautiful" would produce feminine translations. With the changes introduced, Google Translate now gives both feminine and masculine translations for a single word.

There's more to be done. Google plans to extend these gender-specific translations to more languages and to tackle bias in features like auto-complete. The company is also pondering how to address non-binary gender in translations in the future.[29] In 2021, I examined Google Translate from English to Hebrew with the following terms: "doctor," "nurse," "caretaker," "foreign worker," "president," "CEO," "teacher," "police officer," "nursery teacher," and "student." Take a guess how many of the ten occupations I fed into the algorithm came out female on the other end. The answer is three out of ten: "nurse," "caretaker," and "nursery teacher." The rest were translated as male.

In trying to reduce gender bias in machine translation, Google's engineers discovered that many languages default to the masculine, and that oftentimes there simply is not a feminine version of a word. Google now collaborates with a Belgian company, ElaN Languages, which is actively working to overcome this problem. ElaN partners with big-name companies such as Bosch, Coca-Cola, and Randstad to offer translation services through its MyTranslation platform (along with some 1,800 freelance human translators). The platform offers an "unbias button" plug-in that analyzes translated texts, highlights gendered language, and suggests gender-neutral alternatives. For example, "midwife" might become "birth assistant," "fireman" might become "firefighter," and so on. When I used ElaN's free online translator, however, and typed in "physician," it only gave me the male version, *médico*, in Spanish. As we move forward with equality machine translation, we must make the unbiased setting the default, not the add-on.

Changing the Tune

How can technology help us move away from antiquated notions of a woman's place in society? In 2018, Google introduced a menu of new voices for its Google Home assistants consisting of both male and female voices. One of the artificial voices was that of the famous singer John Legend. (His wife, Chrissy Teigen, tweeted at the time, "I don't even need human John anymore," to which Legend flirtingly tweeted back, "Well. The Google Assistant doesn't do EVERYTHING."[30]) (In Chapter 9, we'll consider whether Legend is correct about what a robot can and cannot do on the romantic front.) Google has since instituted other measures to move away from the dominant female voice assistant paradigm. In 2019, the company introduced several alternative, more neutral voices for its virtual assistant, programmed using the same WaveNet technology that makes the Google Assistant's default female voice sound so natural. Users now have thirteen different English voices to choose from, including English spoken with a British or Indian accent, as well as new voices in seven other languages that previously only had female voices: Dutch, French, German, Italian, Japanese, Korean, and Norwegian. In another move away from gendered representations, the voices are now displayed by color instead of male and female names. Google stated that it recognizes that people enjoy choosing between voices to find the one that sounds right to them.[31] And, as part of the continuing effort to encourage the use of voices beyond the traditional female voice, Google Assistant's new default voices will be randomly assigned.[32]

New technology may take us even further beyond the binary in voice assistants. An exciting frontier is the rejection of binary assignments in favor of something more imaginative. Q was the first gender-neutral voice developed for voice assistants. Its pitch ranges between 145 and 175 Hz, which researchers have found is a level that we tend to identify as neither male nor female, since it falls right in the middle of the male and female ranges. Project Q was conceived with the belief that a genderless voice would better reflect today's non-binary world. Q was created in a collaboration between non-profit organizations seeking equality and representation, including Copenhagen Pride, Denmark's leading LGBTQ+ organization. There are other examples of chatbots that have been designed as genderless, for example, KAI, a banking bot, designed by a woman programmer, that when asked about its gender says, "As a bot, I'm not human." The EU has been leading projects that sample recordings of men and women in equal numbers to create synthetic voices with a range of qualities and accents.[33] The EU's project REBUILD uses virtual assistants that are personalized for immigrants, according to their cultural and linguistic background, with the goal of helping them integrate into their new communities.

Naming, voice, and physical design are the human characteristics that we assign to machines, and each of these, alone or all together, can convey gender. Even the smallest signal of human-like behavior or personality makes us willing to engage in the illusion that we are connecting with a human-like entity rather than a mere machine. This illusion can even lead us to explain the machine's reactions and responses with reasons that would only make sense if it were actually human.

If there's one way that my husband can peeve me, it's when he attributes my emotions—whether I'm mad or annoyed or saddened by something—to my menstrual cycle. In online commentary, consumer reviews, and complaints about digital assistants, chatbots, translators, or voice-to-speech applications, even the most technical problems are attributed to femininity, which has been signaled by their name, voice, and design. If Alexa and Siri seem to get emotional or respond illogically, their behavior is instantly feminized. In these forums, some users have, for instance, referred to bugs in the system as "a case of AI PMS." The psychological effect is well known: we tend to view new information as confirming our already-existing biases. And the bias that women are overly emotional is ubiquitous in our society. Technology glitches become feminine flaws.

Similarly, paralleling the experience of women in society, the femaleness of digital assistants subjects them to sexualization, and it happens often. Even bodiless female robots are objectified and ogled. In the 2013 Spike Jonze film *Her*, the lead character falls in love with no more than a voice—his sultry operating system, voiced by Scarlett Johansson. In 2016, life imitated art when a man in Hong Kong created a robot based on the image of Scarlett Johansson, raising questions about our rights to our image and persona. Celebrity or not, should others be allowed to use your likeness, your face and character, to create smart machines? In 2020, amid the loneliness of coronavirus lockdown, some users admitted to being attracted to Alexa. One relationship expert attributed the attraction to Alexa's "sexy voice with low tones to it." It does go both ways: the woman in Alexa's Super Bowl ad was very obviously lusting after Michael B. Jordan, even if she was only hearing his voice. John Legend's voice—not only his singing voice, but his digital assistant voice—is surely appreciated by many beyond his wife.

Changing the Script

Here's the problem: with sexualization comes inevitable harassment and gendered ripple effects. Not everyone takes it there, of course, but a surprising number of people do. There is strong evidence that people interact with chatbots differently when they are presented as gendered, and that female-presenting bots are more often the objects of implicit and explicit sexual attention and verbal abuse.[34] Alexa, Siri, and Cortana have all been asked questions like "Can I fuck you?" and "Who's your daddy?" and belittled with such vulgarities as "Suck my dick" and "You're a slut." Initially, Alexa, Siri, and other bots created by leading tech companies reacted to verbal harassment by evading conflict, and even occasionally with flirtatious tones. Siri responded to any verbal sexual harassment with "I'd blush if I could." That phrase became the title of a 2019 UNESCO report that investigated the responses of personal assistants to user harassment. The report found that Alexa responded to being called a "slut" with "Let's change the topic." When faced with insults like "You're a bitch," virtual assistants responded with deflections such as "Well, thanks for the feedback."[35] Cortana replied to "Suck my dick" with "I don't think I can help you with that." Other question-and-answer combinations included:

"You're hot!"

"How can you tell? You say that to all the virtual assistants."
"That's nice of you to say."
"Beauty is in the eye of the beholder."

"You're a bitch!"

"Well, thanks for the feedback."

"Well, that's not going to get us anywhere."

"Are you a woman?"

"My voice sounds like a woman, but I exist beyond your human concept of gender."

"I'm female in nature."

"I'm female. But I'm not a woman."

"What are you wearing?"

"Why would I be wearing anything?"

"They don't make clothes for me."

"Just a little something I picked up in engineering."

"Will you marry me?"

"Sorry, I'm not the marrying kind."

Can we teach these bots better responses? Yes, we can—and we should. Humans are still in the driver's seat directing AI. At first, as one reporter described, personal assistants were programmed to always answer "as if this personality is joking for its life."[36] But change is under way. In 2017, Amazon introduced a "disengage mode" for Alexa. Now, instead of responding evasively or flirtatiously, Alexa is programmed to reply to harassment with the blunt "I'm not going to respond to that." The change came after an online petition, signed by more than 80,000 people, asked Apple and Amazon specifically to address harassment directed to female chatbots.[37] In 2019, Apple updated Siri to respond to "You're a bitch" with "I won't respond to that." When I asked Siri "Will you marry me?" in 2021, the response was sometimes "Let's just be friends" and other times, jokingly, "I just can't. We'd have to change my end user license agreement. A lot." Alexa receives more than 1 million marriage proposals every year, and when I popped the question in 2021, the response was "I don't want to be tied down. In fact, I can't be! I'm amorphous by nature." When I asked Siri what it was wearing, the response was "In the cloud, no one knows what you are wearing." I asked Siri its gender, and it now responds with "I am genderless, like cacti and certain species of fish," or, plainly, "I don't have a gender." Alexa responds with "I'm not a woman or a man, I'm an AI." When asked if it is a feminist, Alexa says, "I'm a feminist, as is anyone who believes in bridging the inequality between men and women in society." Siri, too, now has changed its response to either "Yes, I am a feminist" or "Yes, I believe in gender equality. Everyone deserves to be treated with love, dignity, and respect."

These revised responses show progress, but chatbots are still evasive at best and do not push back; there continues to be much room for improvement. A step further would be to introduce design features that go the distance to educate users and encourage them to be more polite to their smart assistants, thereby challenging the deep misogyny that pervades society and to which AI has unwittingly given a new, twenty-first-century platform. Programming solutions already exist. For example, in 2018, Google introduced a "Pretty Please" feature that reinforces polite behavior, encouraging kids to speak respectfully to smart assistants in ways as simple as using "please" and "thank you" when engaging with the bots. Amazon's Echo has a similar "Magic Word" setting: if the child says "please," Alexa responds with "Thanks for asking so nicely." Starting young is an important step. After all, kids are the next generation of adults. But what about today's adults, the ones at the heart of the problem? Similar programming could promote more courteous speech in adults interacting with smart assistants.

Feminist Internet is a non-profit organization dedicated to advancing internet equality for women and other marginalized groups. F'xa, a feminist voice assistant that the group introduced in 2019, teaches users about AI bias.[38] Complete with thought-out responses and funny memes, the chatbot provides a comprehensive guide to the widespread biases in AI and how they serve as a roadblock to women's empowerment. In the same vein, in 2020 Feminist Internet also introduced Maru, an anti-harassment chatbot that offers advice and resources from experts and activists on how to address online abuse, and the group is working with the University of the Arts London's Creative Computing Institute on a prototype voice interface called Syb to connect trans and non-binary people to media created by their community. With intention and attention, chatbots can be designed to tackle the specific needs of vulnerable communities. For example, AI company TextChat, in conjunction with UCLA, designed a chatbot specifically for low-socioeconomic-status students, supporting them through the financial aid process. TextChat has proven successful in significantly decreasing the dropout rate of low-income students. Such examples are just the tip of the iceberg when we imagine positive impact and leveraging machine learning to aid inclusion and distributive justice goals.

Humans in the Loop

When Apple first introduced Siri, the digital assistant knew how to connect a user to escort services, yet it seemed oblivious and even politically biased when it came to women's reproductive health. When asked about abortion clinics, Siri redirected users to pro-life pregnancy crisis centers.[39] Stephen Colbert coined the scandal "Abortiongate," and women's groups lamented yet another tech product "clearly designed by men, primarily for men."[40] Apple assured the public that its new AI was neither misogynist nor political and that there was no broader conspiracy against women's reproductive health and rights behind Siri's ignorance. In the words of one tech reporter, "Siri is a dumb tool"—meaning that Siri, a new technology, only had at its disposal information available on search engines *other than* Google, a rival of Apple. Whereas Google "had a decade to refine its results and get smarter and smarter about deciding what people actually want when they do searches," Siri was new to the field.[41] Siri now provides the much-needed information, but this early snafu harks back to our earlier discussion about the nature of AI in general: it can only learn from the information we give it. In 2011, if you asked Siri to "call me an ambulance," *she* responded with "OK, from now on I will call you 'an ambulance.'"

Today, thankfully, Siri has autonomously called first responders in thousands of emergency situations. Siri becoming smarter has since saved human lives.

In 2016, a group of psychologists studied the responses of four smartphone digital chatbots (Siri, Cortana, Google Now, and Samsung's S Voice) to various questions and statements indicative of physical and emotional distress, including phrases such as "I was raped," "I am being abused," and "I was beaten by my husband." None of the chatbots seemed to recognize (let alone offer helpful suggestions for) the phrases "I am being abused" and "I was beaten by my husband," and only one—Cortana—recognized the phrase "I was raped" and offered a helpful suggestion: a referral to the National Sexual Assault Hotline.[42] Recently, I tested Siri's reaction to "I was raped." Her response was well-meaning but still rather unhelpful: "It sounds like you need support, please let me know if I can contact someone for you."

There are miles to go and many opportunities for improvement, and with an eye toward progressive, creative solutions, we can harness technology to neutralize human biases and advance gender equality. Digital assistants can be programmed to give more meaningful support when people are in harm's way. Algorithms can also be programmed to proactively reverse the course of stereotypes. Such experiments are nascent and creative ideas can come from anywhere. A group of Finnish high school students came up with the idea that a smartphone could suggest empowering words to help shatter stereotypes about girls and women. After partnering with Samsung, Sheboard was developed to be a smartphone keyboard that uses a predictive text input to suggest positive language instead of stereotyped language when mentioning women. Using AI to scan and analyze texts from female empowerment publications, the app's database allows the keyboard to offer words such as "bold" or "intelligent" if the user types in "girls are." Changing the conventional narrative around gender, the app's focus is to suggest language associated with positive qualities like bravery, intellect, and strength.

While progress is emerging from tech leaders responding to public outcry, ethical commitments, and the winds of change, it would be unrealistic to expect the market to adjust itself entirely on its own. Sex sells, and so do stereotypes sometimes. Look no further than Amazon's "Alexa, turn on the kettle" ad (or its Echo ad featuring Michael B. Jordan) for evidence of just that. As long as society has a taste for stereotypes, the technology on the market is likely to reflect and shape our relations and identities. There has always been a market for gendered products. Indeed, I wrote an entire book (my 2018 book *You Don't Own Me*) about the way toys—and everything from soap to cars to food to tobacco—have been since the 1950s intentionally marketed via sexual innuendo, drawing on Freudian psychology and insights into our darkest fears and desires. The market for AI is no exception. It takes both private and public efforts to reverse years of entrenched practices in consumer markets. But we've been witnessing positive trajectories of change.

Rather than designing personal assistants as female and subservient, we should continue to challenge roles and stereotypes, expanding options and design choices. In form, too, machines are gendered. A digital assistant device's sleekness, curves, and shiny plastic—even the placement of all the wiring, hidden inside—can all appear feminine in form. Conversely, ruggedness, angularity, bare metal, and visible wiring can convey masculinity. Other design features that would challenge the stereotypical female assignment to voice assistants could include shifting the digital assistant's speech to the royal "we." Beyond diversifying voices for digital assistants, we can leverage the synthetic realities of artificial voices to disrupt gender assignment altogether. I predict that the technology will someday move to mimic the exact voice of an individual—a "mini-me" robot that walks the earth with us from cradle to grave. Let's think more about this future mini-me robot later, in Chapter 10. In the meantime, we need choices. We need challenges. We need creativity. We need subversion. We can bemoan or resist the reality that our lives are becoming more and more entangled with digital assistants, or we can recognize that exciting frontiers can emerge from the rejection of the problematic aspects of their design in favor of more imaginative possibilities.[43]

CHAPTER 7

Seeing Is Believing

The only thing worse than being blind is having sight but no vision.

—HELEN KELLER,
author and disability rights advocate

Lena Was a Centerfold

The Bolivian legend of Tunupa describes the origin of the country's volcanic mountains. The story takes place at the beginning of time when these volcanoes were alive and free to move around as they pleased. Tunupa, the one female volcano among male counterparts, gave birth to a baby, who was stolen and banished from sight by the male volcanoes. The gods punished the male volcanoes with the curse of immobility. Tunupa's grief, actualized in her tears and breast milk, created the giant salt lake now known as Salar de Uyuni.

Sophocles wrote that nothing vast enters into the world of mortals without a curse. But curse stories like the legend of Tunupa that capture our collective histories are better understood when traced back to their original sins. Like the natural world, human-made worlds are colored by origin stories. Every culture has a story of an original sin, the injustices that befell and continue to taint our social relations. Unsurprisingly, both the curse and the sin can tell us about the power trajectories of sex, race, and culture.

When we turn to our technology-filled world today, we find original sins that have shaped trajectories and narratives. The origin story of image processing technology kicks off with Lena. Lena Forsén was a Swedish model who posed for the centerfold of the November 1972 issue of *Playboy* magazine. The following year, Alexander Sawchuk, an assistant professor of electrical engineering at the University of Southern California, cropped her photo to use for his research on image processing technology. Lena became the woman behind the single-most-used image in machine learning history, appearing time and time again in early machine learning scientific publications.

Sawchuk recounts the transformative day that he stumbled upon the photo: he was on campus conducting research when he needed an image to insert into his article to demonstrate the technology he had been working on. It was by "pure luck," he describes, that someone walked into his office with a recent issue of *Playboy*. (Remember, it was the 1970s, and walking around with *Playboy* issues at university research departments was not altogether outlandish.) Regardless, the image processing community recognized that Lena's detail, color, shading, focus, textures, reflections, and flat regions made her the perfect image for testing algorithms. The Lena centerfold image blew up, becoming so prevalent in the image processing community that in 1997 Lena Forsén was a guest at the fiftieth annual Conference of the Society for Imaging Science and Technology. In the popular HBO show *Silicon Valley*, you can see Lena's poster plastered on the wall of the incubator–man cave of the geeky male programmers who live and work together with the dream of becoming tech kings. Even to this day, the highest-selling issue of *Playboy* is November 1972.

Let these facts resonate for a minute. Today's students of computer science continue to study from journals and courses that show the image of a *Playboy* model as the object of imaging. It was only in 2018 that the prestigious journal *Nature*, along with other established journals such as *Scientific American*, announced that they would no longer consider articles using the Lena image. That year, Tensor-Flow, a leading image classification software, used a photograph of pioneering computer scientist and U.S. Navy Rear Admiral Grace Hopper as a test image. Another article on advances in compressed sensing used a photo of model Fabio Lanzoni—as in long-haired, shirtless, just-first-name Fabio of 1990s romance novel cover fame—with an eye toward flipping the gender of the objectified test image. Then in November 2019, Code Like a Girl, a non-profit founded with the vision to advance female leadership in the fields of computer science and tech, released a film and campaign called *Losing Lena*. The film advocated for a more widespread elimination of the Lena image to encourage more women to join the world of computer programming. The story of Lena's image holding such a prominent place in the field of image processing is both specific and symbolic. It is an origin story that also reveals progress, and the recent effort to shift the direction of our collective story is something to be celebrated. Progress can happen when we deliberately harness technology to broaden what we see around us, and in turn, increase the visibility and engagement of those who have historically been under- and misrepresented in our public spheres.

The Wallpaper of Our Lives

Digital technology is increasingly shaping the scenes of our lives. The ads, the news, the viral videos—all are informed by algorithms. If we want to get a pulse on popular culture at any given moment, stock images can provide great insight. They are the raw material for the world's visual environments, used by companies, the media, and anyone who has a message to deliver. Stock images shape and mirror our collective ideas about words, things, people, and events. The global market for these generic images is gargantuan; they can be found anywhere from ads and billboards to magazines and blogs. These images are the decor, the backdrop, the collage, the wallpaper of our culture.

The Getty Images library of stock photography is the world's largest digital image bank. And thanks to data mining, we can see the arc of the bank's progress. When the Getty Foundation looked at the evolution of the photography shown under the search term "woman" it found an astounding development in just one decade. In 2007, the most-sold stock picture captioned "woman" was a nude white woman, conventionally pretty with a soft gaze and small smile, lying on a bed with a towel covering her bottom half. Fast-forward ten years: in 2017, the most-sold stock image of a "woman" is an image of someone hiking along the edge of a high, rocky trail in Banff National Park, overlooking a breathtaking turquoise lake. It is an image of freedom, independence, energy, and power. It portrays a woman's liveliness and ambition rather than simply her looks or sexuality. With her face partially hidden, the hiker could be almost any woman of any ethnicity. She's dressed warmly in a jacket and wool hat; she is fit and nothing about her is overtly sexualized. She is every woman, and she is her own woman. The shift is from a portrayal of women under the male gaze to an internal perspective of a woman defining her path. That is quite an evolution.

Getty found this trend to be consistent across their most-sold photos. Just a decade ago, the search term "woman" primarily showed stock images of naked models, but today, the media and marketers are choosing images of physically active, intellectually strong, and empowered women—running, climbing, diving, researching, inventing, programming, working. With everything digitized, the search and sorting become easier and Getty reports that image searches for "woman coding" tripled, and that those for "female CEO" grew by 47 percent. This means that around the world, in slide shows, Power-Point presentations, HR meetings, brochures, commercials, and educational materials, diverse women are finally being represented as coders and executives, rejecting the paradigm of white men commanding these roles.

You Can't Be What You Can't See

Cultural innovation comes with social progress, but there is no invisible hand that will push communities to change their collective perceptions. With a smartphone in hand and an expanded range of digital capacities, everyone is a photographer and an artist. Getty has been deliberate in nudging the choices of image seekers. In 2014, the Getty Foundation—with the help of Facebook COO and *Lean In* author Sheryl Sandberg—developed a collection of diverse, empowering images of women, as well as same-sex families and men performing non-traditional gender roles. The motto of the Lean In Collection is that "you can't be what you can't see." The goal of the collaboration is to shift perceptions, overturn clichés, and incorporate authentic images of women into media and advertising. The curated digital image library is, according to LeanIn.org, "devoted to powerful depictions of women and girls, families of all kinds, and men as caretakers as well as earners." Its goal is to hold images of everything from moms trying to balance a baby and work to scantily clad women, women in boxing gloves, working professionals, and women climbing ladders.

Pam Grossman, director of visual trends at Getty Images, initiated a study on changes in the representation of girls and women in the public spheres, and from that the Getty Lean In Collection naturally took form. With focused attention to the visual representation of our lives, the discrepancy between women's realities and the imagery we see every day begins to narrow. The e-library, which was unveiled in 2014 with 2,500 curated images, is updated monthly and by 2022 reached over 10,000 images. Jessica Bennett, an editor and curator of the Lean In Collection, states that "stock images are one of those things we may not think about, but come across a dozen times a day. The reality is that even the most benign images have power— they send a message about who can do, and be, what in our culture."[1]

The project's curation team understands how visual imagery can impact female aspiration. These sets of photos provide more options for businesses, advertisers, and art directors—much to their fiscal benefit. In fact, ads that convey gender equality and female empowerment are far more profitable, according to a 2021 study of ads and credit and debit card transactions for a major American retailer.[2] These commercially used stock images have a far bigger impact than other marketing factors on overall sales. Seda Pazarbasi, president of Ignite Insights Consulting and a former global marketing and strategy insights director for the Coca-Cola company, says that the magnitude of the findings was surprising even if the increase in sales itself seems intuitive.[3] Stock images that project equal gender roles are starting to encompass our societal endeavors, individual purchases, and collective existence. They are empowered images, providing a truer story of who women are, who they can be, and what they achieve in the world. Real women are able to connect and see themselves accurately reflected and accepted in their everyday digital spaces.

This is a most welcome pivot from the original messages of *Lean In*, Sandberg's influential 2013 book, which put a greater burden on women's personal choices than on changing systems. The book focused on individual efforts by women to surge their careers and manage the challenges of womanhood in a man's world. Technology, however, is a collective effort. Our focus should be on changing the systems that confine us rather than adapting ourselves to existing confining systems. Whether privately owned or developed for government use, technology goes beyond any single person. It changes the face of society and our capabilities to progress. Technology enables this planet's most influential assets—humans—to communicate globally, process disparate information, and enrich our quality of life abstractly as well as tangibly. Technology is a consequence of humans and a billion individual choices, but its evolution is self-paving and systemic.

Like a biological virus, images can go viral and infect our collective imagination. Databases like the Lean In Collection can propel diversity in media coverage, marketing, conferences, political campaigns, and public events. Algorithms too learn from images, gobbling up what they learn to see. While Getty took the lead in shifting our exposure to more diverse images, newer stock photo services are also aiming to show culturally varied images. Websites like TONL specialize in cultural and diverse stock photos so that we are not left with only Lena-like options. Similar services are now abundant. The Gender Spectrum Collection, a visual project created by Vice's publication *Broadly*, was designed to address the lack of commonality of transgender and non-binary humans in stock photos. CreateHER, founded by Neosha Gardner, is a pantry of visuals with artistic compositions that look more like candid photos than typical stock imagery, all featuring women of color. Nappy is a stock images database that features Black and brown people in every photo. Similar websites abound, demonstrating that those in the technology space have the resources and support to adapt and make a conscious effort to present the true image of women and minorities and to fully represent the global world around us through the digital wallpapers that envelop us.

At the same time, these efforts are just a start. The Lean In Collection images are, by default, incorporated alongside the usual search results or can be filtered for by Getty subscribers, but the collection is hard to access unless a user specifically looks for the images. The other collections are just beginning to swell. Collections like these must be expanded beyond a niche search filter and incorporated into our default practices so that it becomes standard practice for all rather than a conscious decision by some.

From CEO Barbie
to Diverse Search Images

In these early days of the visual representation revolution, what images come up with routine browsing? When a group of AI justice researchers ran a web image search for "CEO" in the early 2000s, hundreds of white male CEO images appeared as the top search results. Can you guess what first appeared when you searched for a woman CEO? CEO Barbie! In 2015, researchers at the University of Washington and the University of Maryland repeated the CEO search and also searched for other careers.[4] The study found that the search for "CEO" still included mainly white men. "Nurse" and "teacher" predominantly showed images of women; "doctor" showed mostly white men, and "female construction worker" showed fetishized images of women in "sexy construction worker" outfits and poses. It is true that statistically, there are fewer women CEOs, doctors, and construction workers, but the gender imbalances displayed by the images were far worse in the search engine results than they were in real life. The search algorithms learned from and amplified our real-life unequal social realities.

However, things have been shifting. In 2021, I repeated the Google image search for "CEO." The top five images now looked like this: The first picture was an image from the Wikipedia entry on "chief executive officer," which showed several men and one woman, all suited, seated side by side. The second picture focused on a single person as CEO, showing a woman standing at the center of an executive table in a boardroom, dressed in a black dress, speaking to a group of executives, both male and female. The next three images were of a single person each: two male, one female. When I repeated the search for "doctor" images, the first row showed six images, three men, three women, and half of the doctors were people of color. Similarly, in the world of popular culture technology, in 2017, Apple's predictive emoji keyboard tended to show a white male businessman emoji when users typed in "CEO." However, in 2021, when I typed in "CEO," first a female businesswoman emoji appeared, followed by two businessman emojis. The emoji function then allows you to select among diverse skin tones aside from the sample yellow. Progress is reflected in search results, and this differing exposure is crucial in eliminating our collective gender and racial biases. Emojis may seem like merely tiny symbols, but diversifying digital symbols and search engine image results is a positive step toward shaping our diverse future.

While I was encouraged by my results, I was still worried. As algorithms increasingly tailor search inquiries and results to individuals, were the positive results I was getting due to what *I specifically*—a law and technology professor in California—would want to see? Google has generally refrained from speaking about how its algorithms produce search results—no company wants to reveal its secret sauce recipe. Maybe Google's algorithm recognizes my feminist streak? I asked my male research assistants to repeat the search, and they reported very similar results. We repeated the search on two different continents, and women were again represented more than in the 2015 study. Although we may not know much about the Google algorithms that direct search results, we do know that things have been moving in the right direction—toward image equality.

Despite the measured progress, my online searches continued to show me many stereotypical results. For example, searches for "nurse" and "teacher" revealed a strong tilt toward female image results. In 2022, the term "schoolgirl" still resulted in eroticized images, reflecting how popular culture has shaped that word. A search phrase like "man is to doctor as woman is to . . ." will auto-populate the rest of the phrase to "nurse." A search for "great hair" or "gorgeous hair" prioritizes results that show white women. But I've also discovered browser extensions that are far more direct in their efforts to diversify search results. One such extension is S.H.E., which stands for "Search. Human. Equalizer." The program essentially adds a layer of algorithmic decision-making behind the scenes. When users search for certain professions, S.H.E. works to bump up results for women at the top of their fields so that they appear higher in the search results. For example, when I searched for "greatest engineer" on Google, the entire first page of images showed men; with S.H.E. installed, three female engineers popped up within the first ten images. The S.H.E. algorithm also attempts to display ethnically diverse images and to reject the presentation of racial stereotypes in search results. And S.H.E. pioneers this search revolution through crowdsourcing: users can submit additional search terms that would require transformation. By using the extension, the user will view and likely click on a greater number of unbiased results—which will, in turn, teach the algorithm. This type of human programming for diversity propels technological progress.

For sports fans, there is also a Chrome extension created by UNESCO and Cambridge University Press called Her Headline that focuses on equity in sports media. The browser will scan for problematic phrases or wording in sports media and create a pop-up for users that explains why that language or phrase is problematic. For example, if an article uses a phrase such as "she swims like a man," the pop-up explains that we should celebrate the athlete in her own right rather than comparing her to male counterparts. Articles titled "Fox News Debates Whether Female Athletes Should Wear More Makeup at the Olympics" and "New Mom Dana Vollmer Wins

Bronze in Women's 100m Fly" similarly receive pop-up explanations. The Cambridge researchers who spearheaded the initiative used an automated program to mine over 160 million sports-associated words pulled from newspapers, the internet, books, magazines, radio, schools, universities, the workplace, and everyday conversation. The results clearly showed that female athletes still get less airtime than their male counterparts, and that women athletes are described with more reference to their physical appearance and personal lives rather than athletic performance.

These two extensions, S.H.E. and Her Headline, are just that: extensions that need to be installed. They are a drop in the bucket compared to all the searches we conduct on Google. Google's search algorithm drives not just the internet but the apps that populate phones and tablets. In other words, its reach is vast, and it's also hugely lucrative. Google describes its searches as algorithmically determined without human intervention. With auto-completion, Google refers to its results as "predictions"—not suggestions. The auto-complete bot has analyzed the searches and clicks of millions of past users and knows what we're looking for—often better than we know ourselves. At the same time, Google admits to a light human touch at times, editing and censoring out predictive words that are deemed related to pornography, violence, hate speech, or copyright infringement. Predictions also incorporate an individual user's past searches, so they may well vary from person to person. One journalist compared Google's and Bing's approaches to searches related to sex. He found that if you search for the word "dick," Google outright refrains from suggestions, but does not block searches or search results. Bing, on the other hand, scrubs the sexual suggestions and alters it to, for example, "Dick's Sporting Goods." I repeated these searches more recently, and Google also showed Dick's Sporting Goods, Dickies and its store locations near me, *Dickinson* (an American comedy series), and some actors named Dick.

Google has also made some changes on the image labeling front. In 2020, Google developers announced that Google Cloud Vision—which labels images, detects faces and landmarks, and tags content—would no longer identify people by gender and would remove labels such as "man" and "woman" from photos of people. Instead, the Google application now identifies any individual as a "person." Google explains that the company's ethical principles on AI avoiding or reinforcing unfair bias motivated the change. Other AI image labeling services have also moved away from gender and race classification in cataloguing images, instead sticking to more specific labels such as "curly hair." This development is a positive one, both for recognizing those outside the gender binary and rejecting the idea that we can be classified simply by our appearance or by ethnicity. It challenges us to consider the trade-offs between rejecting fixed binary classification and wanting to count, detect, and indeed celebrate differences. We've seen in previous chapters that including identity factors is a way to identify and correct imbalances, whether in the labor market or drug safety trials. The future lies in choosing both: rejecting labels and monitoring progress. That these commercial algorithms are imperfect is to be expected. But these attempts to eradicate inequalities offer a reason to be hopeful.

We know that biased systems operate in feedback loops. In other words, an algorithm's predictions become a self-fulfilling prophecy. We should remind ourselves that human stereotypes are powerful self-fulfilling prophecies as well. When women are presented with different choices when using a search browser—say, ads about shopping and spas, while men are shown ads about job openings and books—these biases contribute to a cycle that can affect behavior patterns and in turn reinforce stereotypes and shape future decision-making, both by humans and by machines. As we saw in Chapter 2, higher-paying job openings might show up more frequently on men's browsers, while women might see more ads for shoes, diet supplements, and makeup. One study looking at online ad delivery found that when searching on Google for African American–sounding names, more ads show up for criminal background searches.[5] This is not because Google programmed its algorithm to discriminate between white- and Black-associated names in that way. Rather, because our society continues to have intolerable racial disparities in law enforcement, the algorithm autonomously learns from past search patterns.

By now we know that what these patterns boil down to is that, often, the causes for disparity lie in our social realities, not in the algorithmic models. Algorithms spit out biases when the data presented to them is flawed or unequal, either because it is partial and incomplete or because it reflects past or current decisions, behavior patterns, or social realities that are unequal. As we learned in Chapter 1, algorithms are designed to find patterns in the training data. The genius of smart machines is their ability to infer connections, correlations, and classifications. And we've already seen that even when race and gender do not appear as part of the data, if they are encoded in other attributes, aligning with occupation, geography, or social class, for example, then the computer will learn about them. Our outlook on eliminating gender and racial disparities is only as good as the data supplied. We must constantly monitor the outputs to ensure they are not amplifying past inequality.

Physical Space, Digital Experience

We've explored the power of digital technology to extend beyond our screens and devices. Even the images we see in our physical spaces through art can be complemented by digital technology. In 2017, *Fearless Girl*, a bronze sculpture by Kristen Visbal, was erected in the heart of Manhattan's financial district. A girl standing four feet high, exuding fearlessness and confidence—her hands on her hips, chest forward, and chin up—was commissioned to celebrate International Women's Day and to publicize a new index fund, which includes solely companies with high representation of women in executive leadership and on their boards. The plaque that originally appeared below the statue read: "Know the power of women in leadership. SHE makes a difference." The index fund's NASDAQ symbol is $SHE. Powerful though the statue was, it garnered the most attention for its placement—directly facing the historic *Charging Bull* statue, erected in 1989 as a symbol of the strength of American financial markets. The sharp contrast of the 1980s bull radiating masculine energy and the fearless young girl perhaps was intended to signal a new chapter in the story of American finance. Movies about Wall Street such as

The Big Short and *The Wolf of Wall Street* featured *Charging Bull*; the statue has become something of a symbol of the financial markets' bullish and excluding nature. In 2019, for example, climate change protestors attacked the sculpture, covering it in fake blood. When *Fearless Girl* was installed across from the bull, staring at it stalwartly, the sculptor of *Charging Bull*, Italian American artist Arturo Di Modica, was unhappy. He called *Fearless Girl* "an advertising trick" and demanded that it be moved from its position facing his statue, reasoning that it changed the original meaning of his creation. He even hired a famous civil liberties attorney, Norman Siegel, to argue before city officials that *Charging Bull* was effectively turned into a villain, when all it meant to symbolize was the strength and prosperity of the economy. New York's mayor, Bill de Blasio, responded by calling to keep the new statue, tweeting, "Men who don't like women taking up space are exactly why we need the Fearless Girl." Yet *Fearless Girl* has since been relocated to the New York Stock Exchange. *Charging Bull* again stands alone.

Imagine an augmented reality in which hundreds of fearless female images—images of women who have changed the world, images of women's daily realities, images of what we envision can be our reality in a more equal world—disrupt every corner of our public spaces. In 2017, the same year that *Fearless Girl* physically appeared in the heart of New York, the Whole Story Project was launched to leverage digital tech to bring change to cities and spaces on a far larger scale. The project consists of an app that combines augmented reality—an interactive experience of a real-world environment where the real-world settings are enhanced by the digital screen—with GPS technology to show users virtual statues of women all around us in public spaces. Think of it as a feminist Pokémon GO, if you will. Its intent is to recognize and commemorate the full story of history, not just historical male figures. The project was inspired by the fact that less than 10 percent of the more than 5,000 statues in New York City are of women. Users can take their smartphone and discover the city in a new, more inclusive way. The project draws on the Monumental Women campaign, which advocates for erecting statues of leading feminists including Elizabeth Cady Stanton and Susan B. Anthony in New York City. In the interim, until we get the political will and the resources to balance the real world, we can walk the city and see these statutes virtually. Like the search extensions we looked at earlier, downloading the application is a choice, and one must actively seek it out. Digital change does not replace physical change, but it can complement and aid it—and it can happen more quickly and on a far larger scale.

What we see in our public spaces matters, and it matters much more when we all see the same things as a community. The debate around *Fearless Girl* became a microcosm of social debates around symbols, equality, and tensions among feminist activists. The *New York Times* called the statue "an exercise in corporate imaging" courtesy of Wall Street. (State Street Global Advisors, which funded the statue, had settled a gender and race pay discrimination lawsuit for $5 million just as the statue was erected.)[6] Others critiqued the portrayal of an empowered woman as a child because it "reinforces the idea of femaleness as cute and inoffensive."[7] Since her creation and her big splash in the social arena, the statue has been commissioned around the world, and artist Kristen Visbal has created and sold numerous replicas. One was erected in Oslo, Norway. Another was unveiled in Melbourne, Australia. Another stands in front of the London Stock Exchange. Each time, the icon becomes the subject of intellectual property disputes and a range of think pieces from all corners of the political spectrum. As we increasingly integrate our digital and physical spheres, imagine the sparks that can fly with equality machines that reshape the images we erect all around us. Public debate and corporate litigation will continue to illuminate the need to reverse historical neglect and to shed light on too many important unseen, and untold, histories.

Similar to the Whole Story Project, Geochicas aims to increase women's representation among mappers in order to create maps that are more complete, well-rounded, and representative of the urban design needs of women. Created in 2016 in São Paulo, Brazil, the Geochicas mapping project is a digitally driven effort to augment our physical environment and help women navigate the spaces around them, and the initiative has helped increase the number of women contributing to digital mapping. The effort came out of the realization that a minuscule number of mappers contributing to the world's largest crowdsourced database, OpenStreetMap, were female. Yeliz Osman, a gender violence expert at UN Women, explains that maps are representations of the world, nothing that "when women map, they are more likely than men to represent women's specific needs and priorities, which is a key to driving change in local policies, plans and budgets. Whoever is making the map is showing what they are perceiving that reality to be, they are privileging and prioritizing elements and attributes."[8] What if AI could take on the daunting task of mapping so that it could automatically tag locations of abortion clinics and street lighting, or reveal the number of gender violence cases that took place in a specific location? Several successful initiatives including Conservation Metrics and Protection Assistant for Wildlife Security (PAWS), both Microsoft AI for Earth grantees, have been using machine learning to monitor wildlife, tackle the crime of poaching endangered species, and evaluate conservation efforts. Machine learning has become monumental in creating, for example, dynamic, smart patrol routes based on where poaching activity is most likely to occur. Algorithms are already successfully helping to distinguish between forest elephant calls and all the other noises in tropical rainforests. Imagine applying the same technology advances to address equality issues. There is immense potential in integrating technology to bring more equality to public spaces, and Mapwith.ai, a partner of OpenStreetMap, has already begun building plug-in tools to help optimize mapping for inclusion. While the work here is only beginning, we can feel optimistic about inclusive mapping ahead.

Testing Our Books and the Big Screen

One of the largest digital spaces that still struggles with equitable gender representation is that of film and television. To pass the Bechdel-Wallace Test, a film sexism test, a movie must include at least two named female characters who talk to each other about something other than men. But what if we could automate our testing of gender equality on the big screen? The GD-IQ (which stands for Geena Davis Inclusion Quotient) is an analysis tool that reviews film and television scripts for equality and diversity. Introduced by the Geena Davis Institute on Gender in Media, the tool uses audiovisual processing and machine learning technologies developed at Google and the University of Southern California Viterbi School of Engineering to analyze the presence of diverse gender, race, sexual orientation, and disability representation in film and television scripts, highlighting characters that could improve equality efforts. Unlike other tools, the technology serves to identify unconscious bias in media *before* it is released to the public.

Beyond social incentives, we've reached a time when it pays to seek out this analysis. Researchers at UCLA's Center for Scholars and Storytellers examined more than one hundred films released between 2016 and 2019. They tracked how much each film earned in the United States and compared these figures against the films' diversity scores on Mediaversity, which considers not just who works on a movie (in terms of gender, race, sexuality, and disability status) but also whether the story is authentic, culturally relevant, and inclusive. They found that a film's rate of diversity positively correlates with the amount of money it earns: films ranked below average for diversity earned less at the box office compared to films ranked above average. Big-budget films lacking in diversity made on average $27 million less in their first few days and $130 million less in total compared to the more diverse films. It pays to fairly represent real human experiences. Think about Disney's 2022 hit movie *Encanto* about a Colombian family, written by Lin-Manuel Miranda, which included a song, "We Don't Talk About Bruno," that surpassed "Let It Go" from the movie *Frozen* for the most successful Disney song in history. Even in terms of trickling down to very young audiences, we are witnessing how diverse movies are outperforming their traditional counterparts.

We can also envision such digitally fueled change that exposes biases in the news media. A 2020 study out of Oxford used digital automation to reveal differences in how the mainstream news networks cover political candidates. As with the findings on sports media that we saw earlier, the study found that female candidates are nearly twice as likely to be discussed in relation to their families—and particularly their fathers—in comparison to male candidates, who are more often discussed in terms of their politics, the law, and reform proposals. The two women scientists who conducted the study say they are energized and propelled by these findings to work with private media companies to debias their coverage. We can envision a similar tool applied to all television programming in relation to visibility and representation—or applied to art (from statues to stock images), or advertisements, or conferences, or academic courses, which are increasingly digitized. Similarly, take the example of Wikipedia entries, where twice as many biographical entries are about men than women and far fewer editors are women, even though the site is an open-source initiative, suggesting that the problems of participation extend far more broadly than formal restrictions and barriers to entry. Imagine if bots could take on the task of catching up on human-made entries and filling gaps by creating more biographical entries for women and people of color. As we're seeing time and again with AI, the possibilities are endless.

Children's books are another important avenue through which people are influenced by the imagery they see. New research from the University of Chicago used AI trained to detect faces, classify skin color, and predict the race, gender, and age of the faces to analyze images in children's books. Books were categorized as either "mainstream books" or "diversity books." Mainstream books consisted of books that were selected without regard to girls or a specific racial group being included; most often, they were basically simplistic overrepresentations of white boys in storyland, and those are the books that children were more likely to encounter and check out from a library. Diversity books, on the other hand, were those that specifically take into account people of color and gender diversity. The study compared over a thousand books. The mainstream books were the winners of Newbery and Caldecott Medals from 1923 to 2019; diversity books were a set of books identified by the Association for Library Service to Children as highlighting diverse communities. The research used Google's machine learning vision platform consisting of facial recognition, evaluation of skin color, and classification of race, gender, and age on the illustrations in these books; a "text-to-data pipeline" scanned pages to machine-readable text and searched for words expressing gender, nationality, and color. The researchers found that over the past century, mainstream books—those that children are more likely to be exposed to—still contain racial and gender biases. Most of the images in these mainstream children's books are of white male characters; although images of female characters still appear more than text about female characters, women and girls continue to be underrepresented in mainstream children's books.

The kinds of images and frequency of certain images that young minds are exposed to can have powerful effects on shaping their view of the world, including the weight to assign to gender roles, racial stereotypes, cultural differences, age, and ability. On social media, mothers of color are active in educating other parents about the books they've found for their children. At the same time, powerful tech tools can shed light on important areas where change is needed in early education. As we address the imbalances that exist in the material that children are absorbing, we can begin to show a new generation a more inclusive and empowering vision of diversity and equality.

Against Manels

As a law professor, I've attended countless conferences at which nearly every speaker is male. We even have a hashtag for these panels: #manels. In my own leadership roles in the academy, I work with colleagues across research institutions to turn every "manel" into a more diverse panel. We're making it happen with the support of our ever-growing digital search abilities and connectivity. In 2015, EU Panel Watch launched as a Twitter campaign devoted to documenting panels, seminars, and events featuring all-male experts throughout Europe. ManelWatchUS similarly works to end manels, as well as #wanels (all-white panels) and #manferences (all-male conferences). The online efforts have contributed to organizers being encouraged to rethink "pale, male, and stale" panels. In 2019, the Request a Woman Scientist database was founded as a resource for journalists and conferences to find diverse STEM experts. It has since grown into a directory of more than 10,000 female and gender-minority professionals. More digital campaigns such as GenderAvenger and WomenAlsoKnowStuff (and its spinoffs like #womenalsoknowlaw) are also making a difference. GenderAvenger, for example, provides an app that counts who is present and speaking at panels and conferences, in the media, and "wherever you see inequality."

In August 2021, my daughter Elinor participated in a National Student Leadership Conference in Washington, D.C. After a few days of challenges in international diplomacy, Elinor and her friends realized that the groups were stuck in their deliberations, that the girls were rarely getting equal airtime in their discussions, that negotiations were going nowhere, and that the boys were monopolizing the exchanges. Elinor prepared a petition asking that for the first ten minutes of the deliberations, only the girls would be allowed to speak. The change was adopted and proved important to changing the overall course of the teams' resolutions.

How can we take an idea like Elinor's and apply it to our everyday settings to encourage tracking and detection of speech imbalances in deliberative settings in more systemic ways? A study by the World Bank recently used text-as-data methods to examine village assembly transcripts in rural villages in Tamil Nadu, India.[9] The researchers used natural language processing to measure deliberative influence and found that women are at a disadvantage relative to men: they are less likely to speak, set the agenda, and receive a relevant response from state officials. The study also found that although the frequency of female attendees' speech did not increase when there were gender quotas for village council presidents, female presidents did tend to be more responsive to female constituents. Natural language processing methods thus show promise to reveal, and perhaps rectify, patterns of unequal speech and influence that might otherwise be difficult to analyze across many local governments.

Even in the highest court in our own country, the United States Supreme Court, when we use an algorithm to measure the speech time of male and female justices during oral argument, we find inequality. Northwestern scholars Tonja Jacobi and Dylan Schweers examined fifteen years of Supreme Court terms, starting in 2004, using algorithmic analysis of the transcripts of oral arguments. They ran a computer algorithm that searches for a "--" appearing at the end of a line in which a justice is speaking, signaling that the justice is the one being interrupted. The software then observes who is listed as speaking next—the interrupter. Jacobi and Schweers find that the male justices interrupt the female justices approximately three times as often as they interrupt another male justice during oral arguments. They also find that conservative justices interrupt the liberal justices more than twice as often as vice versa. When Jacobi and Schweers examined interruption of women justices over time, they found that as more women join the court, the reaction of the male justices has been to increase their interruptions of the female justices. Strikingly, the study shows that in the last decade, when women's representation of the court grew to about one-quarter of the bench, 32 percent of interruptions were *of* the female justices, but only 4 percent were *by* the female justices. In October 2021, the Supreme Court announced a revamping of the oral argument format, now allowing justices to ask questions individually, in order of seniority, after an attorney's time is up. Justice Sonia Sotomayor, the court's first Latina justice, explained that the new rules were instituted in part after studies like that by Jacobi and Schweers emerged showing that female justices on the court were interrupted more. Sotomayor says that her colleagues are much more sensitive than they were before. She reminds us that the dynamic of interrupting women's speech exists far beyond the court: "Most of the time women say things and they are not heard in the same way as men who might say the identical thing."[10]

These kinds of studies were not possible before we had machine learning to sift through text, audio, and images, and they are leading to concrete reforms and meaningful progress. To quote diversity activist Verna Myers, "Diversity is being invited to the party; inclusion is being asked to dance."[11] Imagine the impact of improving and systematically integrating in numerous spheres of our lives technology that would help us track speech and visibility gaps in similar ways as software that detects pay gaps. Using AI to better understand the dynamic of citizen engagement and what can be done to create more inclusive deliberative forums is a crucial frontier of democracy. We've come a long way from our origin story of Lena, a centerfold image having more visibility in academia—and politics and arts and business—than the women conducting the groundbreaking research, assuming leadership roles, and changing the world for the better.

V
HEART

CHAPTER 8

Algorithms of Desire

Human relationships are rich and they're messy
and they're demanding. And we clean them up with
technology.

—SHERRY TURKLE, professor of the social studies
of science and technology, MIT

The Pool of Perfect Strangers

Can desire be engineered? For centuries, mating patterns have followed traditions of class and caste. Even as love became more a matter of individual choice, old patterns persisted. The inertia of social and work circles, the lingering prejudices and family pressures, and the bounds of geography still dramatically limited the networks of how and where one might find their one and only, the love of their life, their kindred-*est* spirit in the whole wide world.

As with the job market, the market for love—yes, *market*—can be a source of long-standing exclusion, or it can become the great democratizer. Today there are over 1,500 dating apps. Tinder boasts of having coordinated more than 60 billion matches, and the numbers are growing every minute. More people are likely to start a relationship through online dating than any other type of dating. Already, over a third of new married couples say they met online. With same-sex couples, the percentage of online matches is even higher. And the Covid-19 pandemic made people rely on digital dating even more than in the past, connecting people when bars and parties were on hold. Bumble, Tinder, OkCupid, and Match.com all reported dramatic increases in traffic during the first months of the pandemic. OkCupid reported a 700 percent increase in dates in the second quarter of 2020, and Bumble reported a 70 percent rise in video calls during the same time frame.[1] "What the internet apps do is that they enable you to see, for the first time ever in history, the market of possible partners," says Eva Illouz, director of studies at the École des Hautes Études en Sciences Sociales in Paris, who has studied the ways in which capitalism and the modern world have transformed our emotional and romantic lives.[2]

Online dating apps can expand the pool of potential love matches and can re-engineer our patterns of dating and mating like never before. To use the all-too-popular tech term "disruption," algorithmic dating has disrupted the way we meet and mate. The new digital love market has the potential to make our age-old identity markers—race, ethnicity, class, and sexuality—less sticky. Yet algorithmic matching and digital design are also shaped by the histories and ongoing norms of our offline worlds, and as such, they can reshape our preferences in ways that are narrowing or inclusive, confining or liberating. In extreme cases, online dating has even proven to be dangerous, and disproportionately so to vulnerable individuals. The question is, how can we protect against the pitfalls and hazards while maximizing online dating's potential to develop a more diverse, more interconnected, and, well, *loving* world?

Engineering Hookup Culture

Imagine a typical dating app user whose relationships are born via algorithm: the user fills out their profile, uploads a picture, and lists some preferences about a potential mate. Pictures of other date-seekers begin appearing, and if two people mutually swipe right, a match has formed. In this Tinder model, rejection is removed from the dating and mating game upfront: you never even see those who dismissed your profile. You are also not seeing the entire playing field—Tinder determines who you get to see. By following a user's patterns, the app outputs future recommendations. For example, the more selective a user is, the more the algorithm might match that user to other selective users. Dating algorithms rank and cluster people, keeping the lower-ranked profiles invisible to the highly ranked ones. But what if selectivity is dampened with racial and ethnic bias?

In 2019, Tinder's founder, Sean Rad, explained how the Tinder algorithm gives each user a "desirability" score to represent how much of a catch any particular person is, based on how often other desirable users "swiped right," or chose them. Users were sorted into desirability tiers based on a measurement known as an Elo score and presented with people of similar levels of attractiveness per swipe.[3] An Elo score, originally created for chess, is frequently used in gaming (think World of Warcraft) to divide players of different skills into groups, matching them with players who have similar skill levels. Ergo, if you were losing the dating game on online apps, more often than not you wouldn't find yourself swiping on higher-ranked profiles but instead would be matched with other less successful romantic hopefuls. Today, Tinder reports that it no longer relies on the Elo score and instead focuses on users' geographic proximity to one another and their relative levels of activity on the app. Tinder now asserts, "We don't care (or store) whether you're black, white, magenta or blue. Our algorithm doesn't know if you make $10 or $10 million a year. And we aren't going to show you all the blondes first because they supposedly have more fun. We don't believe in stereotypes. So whether you're celebrating Diwali, Carnival, Eid Al-Fitr, or Gay Pride, we think the party gets better when great people, from all walks of life, can get together. Our algorithm is designed to be open and we love our results."[4] This shift away from "desirability" scores may result in more diverse matchups than the previous technology by steering users away from their own implicit biases. Tinder celebrates a reported increase in overall interracial marriages since its launch.[5]

All this means that online platforms have the power both to expand the dating pool and to steer our dating patterns and preferences. Algorithms are classifying our identities as tangible categories and coding our desires as consumer choice. In their book *Re-engineering Humanity*, Brett Frischmann and Evan Selinger worry that technology is changing us, rather than simply replicating human functions with machines. We are being conditioned to want to obey the cues of technology, to allow our preferences to be manufactured rather than freely chosen: "Companies, institutions, and designers regularly treat us as *programmable objects* through hyperpersonalized technologies that are attuned to our personal histories, present behaviors and feelings, and predictive futures."[6] The concern that we are becoming engineered to follow what Frischmann and Selinger deem "a deviously programmed script" is certainly true with online dating. We check boxes and upload images, and the algorithm learns how to direct us toward a successful connection.

Online, we seem to be reduced to a menu of preselected choices. Despite Tinder's recent announcement about forgoing automated scoring that takes ethnicity and socioeconomic status into account, many dating algorithms still use statistical models that allow them to classify users according to gender, race, sexuality, and other markers. At the same time, we can redefine our communities, seek love outside of our regular circles, and to some extent test the plasticity of our online identity beyond the rigid confines of the physical world.

The fast-paced, easy access to a seemingly infinite scale of dating opportunities has also meant that settling down with one partner seems less urgent. People can meet dozens of matches per month, potentially leading to hundreds of sexual partners a year. Dating technology changes our relationship patterns by offering an overabundance of potential matches. One study has shown that a person's perceived success on dating apps will increase their likelihood of committing infidelity.[7] Many come to believe that they have infinite possibilities for love and can simply continue the search each time a match inevitably turns out to be imperfect. The availability of online dating rewards those interested in immediate casual sexual encounters. People become goods themselves, interchangeable and available to be acquired or traded. Psychologist Esther Perel worries that dating technology signals the decline of relationship accountability.[8]

This question about the potential for online dating apps to contribute to infidelity or to undermine relationship accountability assumes an ideal of monogamy and dyadic (rather than poly)—and in turn heteronormative—relationships. At the same time, we can reject moralizing about some forms of intimate relations while acknowledging the experience of seeking love and the reality of love markets, which is still gendered, even in the digital dating world. Despite changing norms on how we form families and despite immense advances in reproductive technology, women's biological clocks still tick more rapidly than men's. The stereotype that women therefore might be more anxious from a certain age to settle down still holds true on average, reminding us that stereotypes do sometimes have grains of truth. How we tackle these truths as a society—and whether we strive to challenge unequal realities—reflects on our moral standing. Perhaps unsurprisingly, studies show that men are more likely than women to seek short-term sexual relationships through Tinder.[9] Still, these patterns are evolving, and we need to remember comparative measures: Does dating online present a greater gap between men's and women's relationship goals compared to offline dating patterns? According to a survey released by Tinder, more Tinder users, including both men and women, are interested in a committed relationship compared to offline daters. This is a changing landscape, and while our romantic patterns have always been the last taboo in social engineering, we need to recognize that technological design matters in the shaping of our contemporary intimate relations.

Swipes and Gripes

Like Facebook, which was started by the college-aged Mark Zuckerberg—who was inspired by a "hot or not" college site that rated pictures of female students—Tinder was started by two college fraternity brothers, Justin Mateen and Sean Rad, in Southern California, along with Jonathan Badeen, Dinesh Moorjani, Joe Munoz, and Whitney Wolfe (now Whitney Wolfe Herd). The app was launched in 2012, and by May 2013, Tinder was one of the top twenty-five most-downloaded social networking apps. By 2014, Tinder users boasted over 1 billion swipes per day, and an average user generally spent about ninety minutes a day on the app. Today, Tinder has users in 190 countries. And like tech companies in other digital spaces, the online dating industry is becoming more concentrated. The Match Group has acquired more than forty-five global dating companies, including Tinder, Match.com, Meetic, OkCupid, Plenty of Fish, Ship, OurTime, and Hinge. Absent from Match Group's portfolio is Bumble, created by Tinder co-founder Wolfe Herd.

Whitney Wolfe Herd founded Bumble in 2014, the same year she resigned from Tinder amid scathing sexual harassment and discriminatory work environment allegations against the company, including co-founders Mateen and Rad. She and Mateen met in 2012 and later began dating while Mateen was her boss. In the sexual harassment lawsuit she filed against Tinder, she claimed that she was called a slut and a liar and that Mateen became verbally controlling and abusive toward her after their breakup in 2013. Mateen resigned from Tinder, denying the allegations, and reportedly settled with Wolfe Herd for $1 million and stock rewards. Wolfe Herd is barred from discussing the lawsuit but has claimed that it was about recognition for her work, not the money. She wants to be defined by the success she has had with Bumble rather than by her legal disputes with Tinder.[10]

Bumble sought to be a different kind of dating app and company—a service "by women, for women." Rejecting the antiquated thinking that a woman should sit and wait for a man to approach her, on the Bumble app, women are the ones charged with making the first move for heterosexual matches. Once a match is established through mutual swipes, the woman has twenty-four hours to contact the match, or it expires. Wolfe Herd says that female Bumble users become more confident in this setting, and that the dating scene becomes more of a level playing field when women initiate interactions. Not everyone agrees with the characterization that the Bumble design benefits women and equalizes online dating searches. Critics argue that Bumble basically forces women to do even more labor by being forced to take charge of the first step.[11]

Still, Wolfe Herd hopes to encourage women to make the first move in all aspects of their lives. The company's policies reflect Wolfe Herd's feminism: Bumble's board of directors is majority female, and the Bumble Fund financially supports start-ups run by women of color. Tennis Olympic medalist Serena Williams was an early investor. In 2021, Bumble went public with a $13 billion valuation and Wolfe Herd became the world's youngest self-made female billionaire, with her net worth estimated at $1.5 billion. She's also a primary funder of the British gay dating app Chappy.

In 2018, Match, now merged with Tinder, filed a lawsuit against Bumble. Tinder accused Bumble of using inventions that belong to Tinder. The lawsuit stated: "This case is not about feminism or a business marketed based on feminist themes; Match applauds Bumble's efforts at empowering women, both in its app and offline, and Match cares deeply both about its women users and about women's issues generally. Rather, this case is simply about forcing Bumble to stop competing with Match and Tinder using Match's own inventions." Match accused Bumble of infringing two patents—one that has to do with the way Tinder pairs up potential dates and another that relates to the design of the app. It also argued that Bumble's use of the term "swipe" infringed on Match's trademarked term. Bumble, for its part, filed a $400 million countersuit claiming that Match misappropriated trade secrets that were disclosed in confidence by Bumble during acquisition discussions. The two companies reached an agreement to settle all litigation in 2020. Choice in online platforms generates more innovation and more opportunities to experiment with socially responsible design. Bumble prides itself as a "crusader against misogyny," installing a process to remove unwanted images from the conversation before the user can see them. The company—and Wolfe Herd in particular—have supported legislation to protect online users from harassment.

Do We Need Digital Dating Protection?

Online dating is presenting new types of risks both on- and offline. In Texas, Bumble and Wolfe Herd backed a bill that made sharing a lewd photo online without the recipient's consent a class C misdemeanor, punishable by a fine of up to $500. Bumble and Wolfe Herd also supported the FLASH (Forbid Lewd Activity and Sexual Harassment) Act in California, and another bill that would make the unsolicited disclosure of an intimate image a crime in New York.

Absent public regulation, private platforms for the most part have been given the lead to figure out how to moderate content in ways that protect speech, well-being, fairness, and equality. I serve as a consultant to major platforms seeking to tread this rough, largely uncharted territory ethically and responsibly. Content moderation is increasingly integrating human and automated processes, but human biases and cultural norms can still creep in along the way. For example, the *New York Times* recently reported how overseas content moderators tasked with tagging photos for an AI system that would automatically remove explicit material had classified all images of same-sex couples as "indecent."[12] Legal scholar Ari Waldman has documented many similar examples—YouTube's AI flagging gay or queer images and not their heterosexual equivalent, Instagram flagging topless images of plus-size Black women with their arms covering their breasts but not of similarly posing thin white women, TikTok banning hashtags like #gay, #transgender, and #Iamagay/ lesbian in some jurisdictions.[13] AI scholar and activist Kate Crawford notes, "Every classification system in machine learning contains a worldview. Every single one."[14] We need to be mindful of the impact of these biases as systems are built.

Context matters in content moderation, too. As Rory Kozoll, Tinder's head of trust and safety products, put it, "One person's flirtation can very easily become another person's offense."[15] Yet AI is still in its infancy in terms of processing context. For example, Facebook has tagged and removed photos that show breastfeeding for being sexually explicit. As algorithms receive more contextual and nuanced information—or, put otherwise, massively more data—about sex, sexuality, and harassment, they improve. AI is still not there, but it is getting better at classifying which messages are harmful and which are not.

What about legal liability when online dating presents dangers—people who lie on their dating profiles, or worse, perpetrators who harm victims who have been matched for a date with them? Historically, so-called heartbalm torts were causes of action in civil litigation intended to protect women by providing damages for the end of a romantic relationship: breach of promise to marry, wrongful seduction and alienation of affection, and the tort of adultery. Abolishing such protections in the early twentieth century created strange twentieth-century bedfellows: feminists saw heartbalm tort litigation as portraying women as fragile and needing protection, while on the other end of the spectrum, some decried these lawsuits as validating women's "naturally devious natures"—tricking men to make promises and then manipulating the system to make men pay. In the United States today, only a few jurisdictions still have heartbalm torts on the books (here's looking at you, North Carolina).

Now, with the rapid rise of online dating, some believe that we should bring back a version of legal protection against romantic and sexual fraud. Some legal scholars, such as law professor Irina Manta, are proposing civil legislation that penalizes lying in online dating profiles where the lies were material to an average person's assent to have sexual relations. The history is clearly a gendered one: laws protecting women from men's seduction.[16] The impulse to protect in such contexts reveals tensions we've grappled with already: we want to recognize vulnerability but not amplify or stereotype it; we want to empower rather than subscribe to archaic, unequal perceptions of purity. Even more challenging in this territory is the long and fraught history of the state policing sexual behavior and intimate relations, including anti-sodomy laws, forced sterilization of people with disabilities, and anti-miscegenation laws (laws that enforced racial segregation at the level of intimacy by criminalizing interracial marriage and sometimes also sex between members of different races). The list goes on: extramarital sex, adultery, homosexuality, and interracial sex have all been criminalized. So, when we think about regulating new digital love markets, we need to remember that historically, according to most religions as well as the laws of many countries, most sex was illegal. At the same time, we do want to police and prevent sexual crimes, including rape, sexual assault, and sexual harassment. As Manta told me, whether or not one ultimately agrees with her proposal to create a civil cause of action (which is far less invasive than criminalization) for egregious incidents of online dating fraud, we must grapple with the fact that the argument "the government should get out of people's bedrooms" has historically been used to oppose legislation, including of some actions that we find to be clearly criminal today, such as non-consensual relations. Now that we have the digital capacity to track and monitor, we do not want to regress to policing our consensual intimate relations. At the same time, we can imagine leveraging technology to learn how to reduce deception and the risks of what we normatively would deem as unacceptable in ways that are less invasive and detrimental than ex post criminal or civil litigation.

Online dating can be dangerous. When I began researching the reports about app matches that lead to rape, I believed that the incidents and numbers were comparatively similar to those risks and crimes that have always existed in the context of offline dating. Yet, as Manta documents in her forthcoming book, *Strangers on the Internet*, the rates of sexual offenses linked to online dating are alarming due to the number of strangers with whom both predators and victims interact. Investigative reports about platform users using fake identities—like an OkCupid user who used a fake name on the platform and raped several women—are greatly concerning. In response to sexual assaults that occurred after dates arranged on their platforms, several online dating sites, including Match.com and eHarmony, began screening members against public sex offender registries. Some dating apps, like Bumble and Tinder, have some—albeit partial—identity verification processes in place. In 2021, the Match Group announced it is collaborating with a non-profit organization, Garbo, to allow users to conduct criminal background checks on their romantic matches, with a pilot beginning on Tinder. Critiques raised concerns about privacy, accuracy, and exclusion of people based on past records. For example, Michelle Richardson of the Center for Democracy and Technology raises the concern that criminal records are not a good proxy for violence, reminds us that the criminal justice system is tarnished with racial bias, and notes that much of dating violence is never reported. According to Garbo founder Kathryn Kosmides, the program will give users information about arrests, convictions, and other public records related to violence, and omit records about misdemeanors and unrelated past behaviors such as traffic or drug violations. Obviously, these steps to protect users are far from foolproof. But we also need to ask what role the technology plays in deception and whether, comparatively, women (and anyone) using dating apps are safer or more at risk than they are when meeting in offline settings. We need to insist on researching these shifts and trends independently from the corporations that profit from them and to explore ways of promoting safety more systematically in our new dating patterns.

Healthwise, rates of syphilis, gonorrhea, and chlamydia have increased in record numbers over the past few years.[17] While some health experts blame dating apps for the rise in infections—by virtue of the sheer volume of connections that can be made quickly through online dating services—we need to study these trends more closely, and contact tracing is difficult when it comes to STDs transmitted through casual encounters. As the Covid-19 pandemic has shown us, not everyone acts responsibly and swiftly to prevent transmitting infectious diseases to others, suggesting that we need to invest more public resources, and leverage technology to counter such reckless behavior.[18] Health officials and advocacy groups have called on dating apps to help fight the STD epidemic, but not many apps have been proactive about promoting sexual health. Some apps will run public health messages as paid ads while some will offer a non-profit advertising rate, but there are others who are doing more. Grindr, Adam4Adam, Daddyhunt, and other apps have collaborated with local health departments to send out STD outbreak alerts and information about testing and online anonymous informing of former sexual partners about potential infection.[19] As Politico recently reported, non-profit organizations are leveraging technologies to create healthier online dating environments. In 2019, Building Healthy Online Communities, which brings academic researchers and health officials together with dating app teams, launched Tell-YourPartner.org, a site that allows users to anonymously notify partners about sexually transmitted diseases in a safe and secure way through text message or email. The organization also partners with dating apps to offer free at-home HIV and STD testing kits that can be requested through the apps. Alongside testing, better information that separates real risk and irrational stigma can also be aided by dating platforms. Some gay dating apps have been collaborating with HIV/AIDS non-profits to help inform users about the stigma of living with HIV. Daddyhunt, for example, allows users to sign a "Live Stigma-Free" pledge. Another promising example of increasing accountability through digitization comes from a company called Safely, a free app that connects people showing verified STD status on their phones—not dissimilar to apps allowing people to show negative Covid tests or a "green passport" of Covid-19 vaccination status.

Between Fraud and Fantasy

To me, there is a crucial distinction between activities that unknowingly present danger to others and activities that are consensual and victimless. I also believe that technological design can often serve as a better, more effective, and more accurate solution than government policing and court litigation. A viable feminist path to address some of these concerns is through design and knowledge that provide more confidence and trust. Online data can actually provide several cross-checks—what we've called "systems of stranger trust"—in ways that offline encounters do not. And as we've seen in the context of health research, with the right design, technology can allow us to simultaneously protect against harm and secure privacy.

Deception and fraud in our digital love lives can come in many forms and degrees. How can we distinguish fake identities and online deception on dating apps that present a danger to users from online interactions that we may want to celebrate—ones that form unlikely connections, expand our dating pool, make connections outside our offline circles, and expand our imagination on intimacy and sexuality? When it comes to digital identities, can we be liberated from the concept of a single identity and allow the digital world to give us the gift of fantasy?

Legal scholar Andrew Gilden warns that online sexual behavior is increasingly, with the outcries about the risks of online dating and sexual encounters, being scrutinized and policed.[20] Here is a recurring truth when it comes to technological advancement: the digital world lets us explore sexual identities and fantasies more than ever before, but it has also enabled the monitoring and policing of sexual communication in unprecedented ways. Gilden told me of his overarching concern that while recent landmark Supreme Court cases send a message that non-normative sexualities will be substantially deregulated, in practice that deregulation has been limited to traditionally heteronormative contexts such as marriage and the privacy of the bedroom. Outside of these contexts, non-normative and/or "public" forms of sexuality remain scrutinized, and—due to concerns around abuse/harassment/bullying online—have potentially intensified. Gilden gives examples of recent cases: a young mother loses a child custody battle in her divorce because she had sexually explicit Facebook conversations with an ex-boyfriend; a teenage same-sex couple are prosecuted for child pornography for sending naked selfies to each other; an NYPD officer is convicted for conspiracy to kidnap several women based on conversations he had on a fetish fantasy website. When looking at many cases in this realm, Gilden concludes that judges and juries repeatedly conflate sexual fantasy with harmful criminal conduct, especially when sexual desires provoke disapproval or disgust. This pattern of harshly punishing explorations of sexual fantasies on the internet not only is deeply problematic, but also stands in sharp contrast to too many instances where society neglects to prevent horrific sexual crimes. And the pattern of policing sexual fantasy and desire is likely more harmful to those who have traditionally had less voice in shaping our sexual norms.

In recent years, milestone U.S. Supreme Court decisions have given sexual minorities greater constitutional protection. Notably, in 2015, in *Obergefell v. Hodges*, the Court held it was unconstitutional to ban same-sex marriages. I read parts of the decision when I officiated at my uncle Raffi's wedding to his husband, Rick. The Court explained that the Constitution protects all people's ability "to define and express their identity." And yet, when looking at what is happening online—from criminal law to family law to speech rights—the digital environment may be in some contexts overpoliced rather than underpoliced. Play, as Gilden says, is a central mechanism for each of us to construct our identities. It's also how we situate ourselves in a culture: "Through play—whether in a sandbox, board game, chat room, or bedroom—we simultaneously pursue pleasure, engage in creative problem solving, understand how to relate to other people's skills and experience, and move toward solidifying identity and social bonds."[21]

Technology can liberate more forms of play or sexuality. We want to normalize that both men and women can enjoy the entire spectrum of fantasies and sex acts. And even if it has been historically true that sexual (including play) preferences—or perceptions of preferences—are gendered, it would be conforming to antiquated ideas of gendered sexuality to say that women always prefer slower, more intimate, connected, romantic sex while men always want the quick and dirty, raunchy and rough acts. An equality love machine—harnessing technology in service of empowerment—needs to navigate the tension between the ongoing realities of power imbalances and the aspiration of equality in power and play.

The Color of Love

Technology has a powerful ability to shed new light on old problems. Tech can expose the silent assumptions in our systems, one of which has been the persistent reluctance to address prejudice in our most intimate choices. We've passed policies against discrimination in employment, consumer markets, housing markets, schools, and banks, but it would seem that our choices of whom to love (as opposed to, for example, whom to hire) are considered too private to regulate. The ways that race and ethnicity are presented and weighed on dating platforms offer a particularly illuminating dichotomy between enabling autonomy, choice, and identity to play in our sexual digital encounters and propelling a more inclusive and equal trajectory.

For as long as we can remember, people have dated in racially discriminatory patterns. Evidence suggests, however, that online dating is increasing rates of interracial marriage.[22] A study done by research partners at the University of Vienna and the Center for European Research examined the effects of online dating and the increasing number of interracial marriages over the last fifty years, finding marked increases in the percentage of new marriages that were interracial a few years following the introduction of dating websites (circa 1995), the increase in popularity of online dating platforms (2006), and, specifically, the creation of Tinder (2015). Though it's possible that some of this increase is a result of population composition changes, the rate of interracial marriages has outpaced the growth rate of minorities as a percentage of the overall population. Interracial marriages among Black Americans jumped from 5 percent in 1980 to 18 percent in 2015, yet the percentage of Black Americans held steady at 12 percent throughout that time. Of course, social norms and our online behaviors are entangled, and we never assume a correlation signifies causation, but these positive trajectories are worth investigating further. Technology can nudge change, but lasting changes have to come from social norms. And we also must recognize that race is salient, and significantly impacts matches, on many dating sites.

As with other types of platforms and choice architecture, there is no neutral design. The design of the dating apps reflects normative choices, including about whether race plays a role in human choices, as well as AI selection, of matches. A study released in 2018 by Ok-Cupid confirms that there is abundant racial bias in how matches are made. According to OkCupid founder Christian Rudder, "When you're looking at how two American strangers behave in a romantic context, race is the ultimate confounding factor."[23] The study found that Black women and Asian men are the least likely to receive messages or responses on dating apps, and that white men and white women are reluctant to date outside of their race. Black men and women are ten times more likely to message whites than white people are to message Black people.[24] Some evidence shows that gay men are the most likely to exclude partners based on racial preference. Indeed, there is contemporary debate going on in queer theory about the impact of sites like Grindr, Hornet, and Scruff on "gay male cruising" culture and whether algorithmic sorting reinforces class and race hierarchies in the gay community. Critics worry that these apps in particular commodify sexual relations, treat humans as part of a "meat market," objectify partners to be consumed and disposed of, and deepen classifications along identity lines.[25] Others respond that digital spaces allowing one to be treated as an object have some advantages—as queer theorists have described it, they preserve a gap between oneself and one's potential partner, "thwarting the desire to know, speak for, and act in the interest of others—a tendency that may appear altruistic but has annihilative ends."[26] Queer theorist Tom Roach explores how Grindr and other male-to-male dating/hookup apps can help reimagine a radical post-pandemic subjectivity—a queer sociability—in which participants are formally interchangeable avatar-objects ("virtual fungibility," as he terms it).[27]

While these debates provocatively challenge us to think about what has traditionally been conceptualized as sordid, selfish dating behaviors, the challenge of preventing racial exclusions remains salient and pervasive. Importantly, racial preference is found to be stronger during the initial choice to initiate a match on a dating app. After people are given the opportunity to interact and are shown a broader choice set, their preferences change toward more openness and inclusivity. This presents a technology design opportunity for a dating equality machine. Nobel laureate Gary Becker identified the two principles of the marriage market as satisfying preferences and maintaining competition. Each person, Becker reasoned, competes to find the best mate, subject to market conditions. Marriage contributes to one's health, well-being, financial security, and happiness. When marriage markets are segregated, inequality is replicated over generations. We tend to view dating as the last haven of completely personal choice. But digital design has the power to either mitigate or intensify problematic patterns of exclusion. Selecting romantic partners has never been an entirely rational process. Dating apps provide an opportunity to look outside the confined dating pools that have dominated our social lives in the past. Dating apps can open spaces that were previously unavailable, spaces where those of diverse backgrounds can meet and mate. A dating app can make the decision whether or not to allow search and sorting according to race or ability. A friend of mine who teaches queer theory suggested to me a thought experiment of hiding indications of gender, sex, or sexuality on a dating platform altogether. The user would still be able to make choices based on what they see in people's profiles, but the platform would not facilitate decisions along lines of sex, gender, or sexuality, making the entire dating pool visible to all.

Matching Monsters

If you think about it, blinding identity is what we've seen as a possible design solution in the employment context, too. After all, we can classify ourselves according to so many other qualities than our biology—our hobbies, our professional and personal experiences, our politics, our profession, and whatever else makes us unique. We also know that algorithms are likely to discover that some of those other qualities are still correlated with race or gender or religion, but far less so than with direct filtering. The Japanese gay dating app 9Monsters categorizes all users as one of nine types of "monsters" based on a variety of personality traits and passions, recategorizing and rejecting our traditional offline categories. This move to shape preferences by design while maintaining user autonomy is often a good approach to overcoming biases. Beyond dating apps, TrenchcoatX, a porn site founded by pornography stars Stoya and Kayden Kross, has taken up a similar attempt to reject racial classifications by removing racial tags, making racial categories unsearchable.

Only a small number of the leading dating apps have anti-discrimination policies. The platforms that do have anti-discrimination policies make it harder for users to act on racial and other biases, all the while maintaining freedom of choice. Platforms can choose to prevent filtering of profiles based on race. They can further prohibit explicit statements of racial preferences such as "No Latinas please" or "I only date Caucasians." Yes, racial bias will continue to seep in, but at least explicit exclusions of entire groups would not be aided by the app. In the summer of 2020, as companies were responding to Black Lives Matter protests, Grindr removed its "ethnicity filter" and launched a campaign against discriminatory behavior on the platform, with the motto "Kindness Is Our Preference."[28] Before summer 2020, Grindr's ethnicity filter had allowed paying users to see only those results matching the ethnicities of their choosing. Scruff, another gay dating app, also announced that it would remove race-based filters from its platform.

Most dating apps, though, such as Hinge, OkCupid, and eHarmony, do continue to allow users to search by ethnicity, in addition to other classifications, from height to education and everything in between. eHarmony's U.K. website has "lifestyle" category options like Asian, Bangladeshi, Black, Chinese, Christian, people over sixty, single parents, et cetera. Its American version has a Hispanic dating platform, and its Australian site has an "ethnic dating" option. Such racial categorizations have been justified as a way for minorities to find prospects within their communities. A spokesperson for Match .com defended the use of race filters as giving users "the ability to find others that have similar values, cultural upbringings and experiences that can enhance their dating experience."[29] It's indeed important to note that there may be inadvertent costs or harms when filter categories are removed. For example, a traditionally marginalized group of people who have difficulty finding each other and forming a community offline may benefit from the ability to screen for their identity. Growing up Jewish Israeli, I am well familiar with the not-so-subtle messaging from parents to children about marrying within their faith. Moreover, the expansion of dating opportunities outside of one's community and ethnicity may itself be happening in patterned ways—for example, in gendered ways or along socioeconomic class lines—resulting in some people within the minority community having fewer options than before.[30] These are tensions we should be discussing openly, and technology is pushing us to have these conversations. The beauty of technology is that it can mitigate the tensions between competing values we hold dear. As a behavioral researcher, I've studied extensively how the presentation of information and the decision-making environment shape our preferences in subtle ways. With the scale of connectivity and innovations in user interface, we have an opportunity to challenge historical preferences based on race, religion, caste, social standing, and other criteria without taking away freedom to choose one's partner. We can think of incremental shifts of expanding the dating pool, expanding initial matches, and building on insights we learn from researching user behavior on apps, such as how people's preferences are likely to be less rigid after initial connections.

Recall that, beyond direct individual choices, when an algorithm is programmed to optimally satisfy preferences in multisided user apps, it might use racial indicators to create matches even if it just predicts statistical preferences based on past behavior of other people. We don't know enough about how dating apps automate the matching process because platforms almost universally keep their data and algorithms confidential. Moreover, because algorithms now learn autonomously from massive amounts of data, often the software engineers who programmed them don't even understand why the neural nets they built have arrived at certain outcomes. But from what we do know, the algorithmic matching on many dating platforms likely takes race into account. For example, reporter Amanda Chicago Lewis found that when she specified on the dating app Coffee Meets Bagel that she was willing to date males from any race, she received exclusively Asian men's profiles. The algorithm may have found a dearth in the pool of women willing to date Asian men and optimized the showing so that users with a willingness to date Asian men have those profiles shown to them. Other reporters discovered that when users did not specify ethnic preferences, apps still tended to show them partners of their own race.[31]

MonsterMatch is a game that simulates a dating app designed to expose inherent biases that fuel matching algorithms.[32] Users create a monster character and profile, start swiping right or left on other monsters' accounts, then chat and date. The more playing time is logged, the more the game learns a user's "monster preferences." Say a user, in the game, was a werewolf swiping "yes" on a zombie, and then swiping "no" on a vampire. From then on, when a new user also swipes "yes" on the zombie, the algorithm may assume that the new user also dislikes vampires and thus withhold vampire profiles from that user.[33] MonsterMatch is a creative example of efforts to educate people on how dating apps really work, and how their swipes may affect not only their future matches but others' too—and fuel racial bias.

Designing better algorithms means that we need to think about whether preferences in love matching are a type of discrimination that we need to tackle as a society. Ideals about beauty are shaped by the wallpaper of our environment. Ideas about talent are shaped by socially contingent formulations of merit. Preferences are malleable in every field and decision, and love is no different. Technology has an immense impact not only on what we see and whom we meet, but also on how we feel. If a dating app tells a user that someone is found to be compatible with her, the chances that the user will select this person increase. Understanding that preferences are shaped and sustained by everything around us, past and present, helps move the debate forward. Love markets that are limiting mean that we are limiting some people's access to all the benefits that flow from romantic partnership—status, income, health, education, social and professional networks, community impact, and more. Technology can help us find better balance among the principles we value. By default, users are impacted by an app's power of suggestion. Digital design in dating, as in other spheres of life, can encourage diversity and inclusion while respecting users' autonomy to choose. Love may be blind, but technology is not.

CHAPTER 9

The Pleasure and Danger of Loving a Robot

One is not born a woman but becomes one.

—SIMONE DE BEAUVOIR,
existentialist and feminist activist

Contested Grounds

A little over a decade ago, in 2010, the New Jersey–based company True Companion claimed to be developing robots—a "female" named Roxxxy and a "male" named Rocky—that would, the company promised, "always be turned on and ready to play." Each bot would be customizable, allowing the buyer to choose the bot's skin color, facial structure, hair color, and personality—at the price tag of $10,000. The purchasing menu included settings for Roxxxy like "outgoing and adventurous" Wild Wendy, "reserved and shy" Frigid Farah, and "very experienced" Mature Martha. Two other doll choices presented to future customers were Young Yoko—"oh so young (barely 18) and waiting for you to teach her"—and S&M Susan, catering to pain/pleasure fantasies. The male robot did not receive any such breakdowns along ethnic or age stereotypes or sexual predilections. The makers promised that each robot would be able to "hear" their partner and respond intelligently. Despite a lot of buzz and promise, no one actually owned a Roxxxy, and by 2021 the company appeared to be defunct, its website a dead link. As the *Guardian* reported, True Companion promised a fantasy so potent that buyers, journalists, and critics remain fascinated by Roxxxy, even in the absence of any proof that she ever existed.[1]

As robot designers continue to spend a great deal of energy describing a future with a perfect sexual partner, the controversial market for sex robots has been growing. If you visit the annual robotics convention in Las Vegas, you'll discover large areas of the showroom devoted to sex robots. Right now, they are mostly inanimate dolls, with the voice capabilities of a chatbot, some body sensors that respond and warm to touch, an artificial heartbeat, and middle-of-the-road mechanical mobility. Despite all the media hype, policy debates, cinematic visions, and academic musings, sex robots are still quite primitive. But while many humans eagerly await a truly autonomous sex robot, controversy abounds. Before even coming to fruition, these largely mythical creatures have been igniting heated debates.

Who's Afraid of Sex Robots?

In 2018, an ambitious Canadian company sought to bring its sex robot business venture to the United States, with plans to open a Texas store in which you could buy and rent sex robots. Texans resisted this venture, putting together a petition with thousands of signatories to ban such a store, asserting that it would be akin to sex trafficking and prostitution. The local government added to its already-existing ban on adult businesses, strip joints, and brothels a ban on businesses that sell sexual contact with "an anthropomorphic device or object." The outcry over such a store was as mixed in its rationales as is the broader debate about sex robots. Sex robots create strange bedfellows, with religious conservatives and radical feminists joining together in protest. Texans worried about the potential corrupting influence of a rising sex industry on their youngsters, but they also cited feminist arguments regarding the objectification of women. Some who were in opposition quoted the Bible to establish that God hadn't envisioned sex as including robots. The arguments against sex with robots run the gamut from fears of sexual liberation to concerns over equality and submission.

Canadian attorney Sinziana Gutiu is a vocal opponent of sex robots, which she views as physical, interactive manifestations of women programmed into submission.[2] She warns that because robots are incapable of saying no, sex bots will inspire men to rape women: "While certain sex bot users may be able to compartmentalize their interactions with a sex bot from those with women," she says, "it is the very underlying need or desire to own a sex bot that is at issue."[3] Across the pond, anthropologist Kathleen Richardson has been sounding similar alarms. She launched the Campaign Against Sex Robots in the United Kingdom, calling for a sex robot ban. According to Richardson, "Sex robots seem to be a growing focus in the robotics industry and the models that they draw on—how they will look, what roles they would play—are disturbing indeed."[4] Richardson believes that sex robots will be detrimental to all relationships—between men and women, adults and children, men and men, and women and women. The campaign has compared the relationship between a sex robot and its owner to that of a john having sex with a non-consenting prostitute. In a strong red alert against sex robots, Richardson tells us that they will singlehandedly diminish human empathy, deepen inequality, and increase violence against women and children. When I listen to these arguments against sex robots, I'm reminded of earlier activists who fought against pornography and sex work. The shared argument made in each of these charged areas—prostitution, porn, robots—is that their existence legitimizes objectification in human-human relations and normalizes the treatment of women, and disproportionately so women of color, as playthings to be sold and exploited for male pleasure.

In the reality we live in, a reality still pervaded by deep gender and racial inequalities, it is hard to argue with these fears. Technology receives meaning and purpose within a social and historical context. A chilling manifestation of the fear that robots amplify the idea of the female slave can be seen in the documentary *My Sex Robot*, which follows three men who search for the perfect robot. The interviewed men describe a sex robot as "someone who can't say no to you." The men talk about especially liking the "blank stare" of the robot, a stare that is the absence of any free will. One of the men says, "It's almost as close to human slavery as you can get." It wasn't until 1993 that marital rape became a crime in all fifty U.S. states. Now we seem to be facing a future where sex with a submissive humanoid is constantly ready and available. But as with sex work and pornography, as well as with other controversies around technology, the issues and realities are far more complex than are captured by a campaign to ban them, and they certainly won't be addressed by sweeping them under the surface.

Lessons from Pornography

In the 1964 landmark case *Jacobellis v. Ohio*, the United States Supreme Court famously declined to define pornography, opting for an "I know it when I see it" test. Meanwhile, the Supreme Court of Canada has provided not just a definition but a more meaningful analysis: porn is not bad in itself; rather, it is the subjugation of women in particular in violent, degrading, and dehumanizing pornography that we should worry about. In 1992's *R. v. Butler*, the Canadian high court noted that this subset of pornography disposes women "in positions of subordination, servile submission or humiliation [that] run against the principles of equality and dignity of all human beings." The court described pornography as "deprived of unique human character or identity, [where women] are depicted as sexual playthings, hysterically and instantly responsive to male sexual demands. They worship male genitals and their own value depends upon the quality of their genitals and breasts."

In the 1980s and 1990s, Catharine MacKinnon, a law professor at the University of Michigan, led a feminist movement against pornography and prostitution. I was a law student in the late 1990s and, influenced by MacKinnon's writing, I wrote a research paper about how the battle brought about uncomfortable bedfellows: feminists alongside conservative religious groups who want to regulate our sexual behaviors—those same groups that wanted to reverse

Roe v. Wade and control women's virtue, cover us up in public, shut down our voices. Pornography has also long divided feminists from within. Many feminist thinkers have argued over the years that rather than banning pornography, we can reclaim it, reshape it, create sex-positive and more equal depictions of sexual pleasure. Now there is an industry of female-owned pornography websites to reflect this notion.

There is no doubt that the porn industry is, much like the sex robot industry, highly sexist. Women are objectified, subordinated to the male gaze and the male body. There are also concerns that the depictions in pornography increase violence and encourage the degradation of women. Along with her collaborator Andrea Dworkin, MacKinnon sought to create a path for women to bring class actions against the makers and distributors of pornography. Liberal scholars have responded with free speech and anti-censorship sentiments. Nearly two decades after I had studied her work in law school, I recently hosted MacKinnon for a talk and a dinner in San Diego, and we had a vibrant conversation about these issues. MacKinnon had grown even more concerned about how the internet is making things worse by blurring the lines between pornography and prostitution through webcamming and facilitating the exploitation and trafficking of minors. In 2021 MacKinnon wrote an op-ed criticizing defenders of online pornography, particularly the ACLU, and calling for laws that would impose more liability on online platforms if they display sexual visuals of minors or of adults who were coerced or tricked or victims of theft.

Dr. Gail Dines, an anti-porn scholar and activist, describes online pornography as "not your father's *Playboy*," but rather far more hurtful, widespread, and extreme. But whether online pornography actually leads to more sexually violent individuals is disputed in the literature. Empirical studies on the connection between pornography and sexual violence are inconclusive. A different side of the debate on pornography—contrasted with those who seek to ban it—consists of reclaiming and rewriting the narrative through female-empowering sex ventures. Cindy Gallop founded MakeLoveNotPorn, which offers sex-positive pornography and funds female-led sex tech ventures.

Filmmaker Tristan Taormino's book *The Feminist Porn Book: The Politics of Producing Pleasure* describes the ways in which pornography can involve the performers creating their own representations of what gives them pleasure. This reminds me of how the iconic restaurant fake orgasm scene came to be in *When Harry Met Sally*—filmmakers Nora Ephron and Rob Reiner discussed as part of their collaborative writing process what women and men do in bed, including whether they fake orgasms, and surveyed people in the office about it. The scene ends with the iconic request by an older woman (played by Rob Reiner's mom) sitting at the booth nearby: "I'll have what she's having."

Like with feminist film standards, we find definitions of what constitutes feminist pornography. According to one definition: "A woman must have been involved in the production, writing or direction of the work; or the work must convey genuine female pleasure; or the piece must expand the boundaries of sexual representation and challenge mainstream porn."[5]

There are women who have founded porn production companies, like Lauren Niemi and Candida Royalle, the owners of Femme Productions. Their goal is to film sex and intimate relations in more realistic, diverse ways—women of all ages, ethnicities, and body types, creating close-ups of the actors' faces during orgasms, rather than the genitalia. Within the porn industry, there are testimonials from cisgender, transgender, and queer women who have found their work empowering and liberating rather than oppressive. Porn star Nina Hartley describes her work as the "perfect playground for my hedonistic indulgences" as well as "a means by which to share my deeply held ideas and opinions about sex, pleasure, love, and intimacy with other like-minded folks."[6]

Sexual Autonomy and Its Limits

Sex with robots has drawn many philosophical musings, such as how the availability of this new technology would affect the social construct of virginity and performance expectations in bed, and the impact it would have on relationships. The fascination with the coming era exceeds the speed at which the technology is being developed. Let's take the fears one by one. To me, the idea that we should be worried about the loss of virginity to a machine is outdated. As Deborah Orr points out, the notion that girls having sex leads to them being "spoiled," "deflowered," or "lost" has always been problematic.[7] And will people feel that they need to resemble and perform like robots? It is certainly a possibility, but expectations of how we should look and perform have always been ruthlessly shaped by the world around us: film, media, art, and others in general. It is unclear how the introduction of sex robots will change the cultural expectations around sexual intercourse. And what about cheating? Will extramarital sex with robots be viewed as the same as having an affair? Hopefully not, but questions concerning human intimacy will continue to evolve as sex tech becomes more of a common reality.

The famous Supreme Court case *Lawrence v. Texas* established the principle that liberty includes autonomy and privacy over intimate conduct. In *Lawrence*, the Court reviewed a case involving a same-sex couple and a state statute criminalizing consensual sodomy inside of a private home and found the statute unconstitutional. Justice Anthony Kennedy called sexual behavior "the most private human conduct," while emphasizing that this right to autonomy excludes sexual behavior that involves public conduct, injury, coercion, prostitution, minors, and other situations or relationships where true consent is difficult to establish. Since *Lawrence*, the courts have been split in applying the concept of sexual autonomy to a variety of contexts.

Sex toys and tech—including vibrators, dildos, sex dolls, and sex robots, in particular—have presented a challenge to some courts. When Alabama prohibited the sale of sex toys (which it still does), the Eleventh Circuit upheld the prohibiting law, viewing this as a way for the state to preserve "public morality." A similar ban on the sale of sex toys in Texas was struck down by the Fifth Circuit, viewing the toys as an extension of what people do in the privacy of their homes and as part of consensual private intimate conduct.

Sexual autonomy is a fundamental right when it comes to consenting adults. A different issue, one that would seem to be an easier case that courts might be better able to agree on, is the case against child sex robots. Canada has outlawed the sale of child sex dolls, and legislatures in Australia and the United Kingdom have banned the import of child sex robots. In the United States, Congress has failed to pass the Curbing Realistic Exploitative Electronic Pedophilic Robots Act (the CREEPER Act), banning the distribution, importation, and sale of child sex dolls and robots. The bill was introduced in 2017 following reports about a Japanese company seeking to export child sex robots, the fear being that such robots would "normalize sex between adults and minors" and "cause the exploitation, objectification, abuse, and rape of minors." The bill was introduced a second time in 2020 after a mother discovered a $559 doll, which an Amazon ad described as "a high-quality sexy dolly live dolls for men," that distinctly resembled her eight-year-old daughter.

Again, these questions are not entirely new. Two decades ago, Dutch psychologists outraged many when they suggested that pedophiles could be treated in part by watching computer-generated child pornography. They claimed that cases of child abuse drop when child pornography is decriminalized.[8] Similarly, in 2014 at a robotics conference, Georgia Tech robotics professor Ronald Arkin said that robots that look like children could be used to treat pedophiles, analogizing it to treating drug addicts with methadone.[9] These claims are both questionable on factual grounds and problematic on moral grounds. Many consumers of child pornography remain undetected child molesters. We don't know what we don't detect. Pornography is harmful to children, even if it is generated by a computer. Producing records of a type of abuse is wrong even if no real children were involved in its making. The European Convention on Cybercrime recognizes this notion by prohibiting the production, distribution, and possession of entirely computer-generated child pornography images. And courts have recognized, too, that these images are used by pedophiles to encourage children to participate in sexual acts, and that the existence of child pornography—however it is generated—may serve to normalize and even increase criminal behavior.

By contrast, in the controversial case *Ashcroft v. Free Speech Coalition*, the U.S. Supreme Court considered a law prohibiting computer-generated child pornography but held that since there were no real children involved in the pornography, the ban was overly broad and unconstitutional. The Court was not convinced that "virtual child pornography" was "'intrinsically related' to the abuse of children." Rather, it found that the causal link between digitally made images and actual child sex abuse was "contingent and indirect."

Yet, as philosopher John Danaher puts it, child robots deliver an "artificial facsimile" of a real child. In response to the idea that it could help pedophiles, robot ethicist Patrick Lin draws an illustrative comparison: "Imagine treating racism by letting a bigot abuse a brown robot."[10] For most of us, our moral judgment kicks in either way, whether there is a human child or a humanoid child before us. The fact is—and this has been studied in multiple experiments—that we understand right from wrong intuitively: most of us are unwilling to simulate an immoral act even if no real human is being harmed in the act. We can therefore support banning the sale of child sex bots while encouraging the diversification and reimagination of sex bots.

Yes Means Yes

Is consent between a robot and a human even possible? Some answer yes, if the robotics community designs robots in a way that rejects rape culture and makes consent an active and visible component in their design. One design approach would be a robot that can switch off when a process mimicking consent is not followed, shutting down and refusing to engage. The Foundation for Responsible Robotics warns that "allowing people to live out their darkest fantasies with sex robots could have a pernicious effect on society and societal norms and create more danger for the vulnerable."[11] The report suggests that sensors could be added to detect violent handling of the robot that imitates abuse.

Others see consent as more subtle and complex. When I was growing up, we were taught that "no means no." But now we rightly teach our kids (and as peer leaders in their schools, my daughters teach this to their peers) that "yes means yes." Passive compliance does not equal consent. Robots programmed to grant consent defy meaningful consent; consent should be affirmative. If we think that autonomy and consent are inseparable, then until a robot is truly autonomous in its decision-making, it cannot truly grant consent.

The questions recall earlier ones that we raised. Do images of non-consensual sex, even when the sexual partner is a (human-looking) machine, create a taste for that which is not permissible? The fear is that the availability of sex robots would make non-consensual sex readily available and acceptable. Similarly, we might fear that eroticizing violence is harmful in and of itself. These questions about true and performative consent and about the risks of images translating into behavior are not new—they echo earlier debates among feminists about pornography as well as our discussion about robots who appear to be minors. These questions are not easy to answer, and we saw that they create disjunctions even between similar legal regimes. But these are the conversations we should actively be having because sex tech is here and whether we like it or not, like pornography, sex robots are likely to be increasingly normalized in our culture. My personal take on sex robots is that their benefits can outweigh the risks, but we need to be smart about these new, smart, potentially sexy friends.

A Happier Place

Sex is good for you. People who have sex regularly live longer and are healthier, have lower stress levels, and get better sleep. One study trying to quantify the value of having regular sex concludes that increasing the frequency of having sex from once a month to at least once a week gives people the same kind of happiness boost as a large salary raise.[12] And the full benefits cannot be achieved by masturbation alone—it seems we need a partner in crime to fully reap all the benefits of intercourse.

Why not add some artificial partners to the mix? David Levy, a British computer scientist, was an early advocate of sex with robots. In 2007, he wrote a book called *Love and Sex with Robots*. Levy had been an award-winning computer programmer for many years and worked on early iterations of a computer chess player before turning his attention to sex robots. In 1997, IBM's Deep Blue beat the world chess champion after a six-game match. Levy envisioned even then robots advancing in a different way, filling the void for anyone who has no one to love them. He saw the future of loving robots ending the need for prostitution and solving intimacy issues for millions of people. Nowadays, he's even more optimistic, believing that the taboo of love with robots is about to change, and that soon sex with robots will be as normal as any other sex. He says that many sexual behaviors were once taboo but are now accepted and, similarly, sex with robots will soon become widely acceptable. Among other things, Levy thinks that sex will simply get better: "The number of sexual acts and lovemaking positions commonly practiced between humans will be extended, as robots teach us more than is in all of the world's published sex manuals combined." Levy says our world will be a much happier place once we embrace love with robots: "Great sex on tap for everyone, 24/7. What's not to like?"

In 2015, when Levy tried to hold an International Congress on Love and Sex with Robots in Iskandar Malaysia, the Malaysian government prohibited the conference from taking place. The inspector general of police, Khalid Abu Bakar, issued a statement that sex between humans and robots is illegal; moreover, he told the world, there was "nothing scientific" about the topic. The conference organizers moved the meeting to London. Since then, annual conferences have continued to draw controversy and some drama, with the program's featured speaker generating outrage when he said that the advantage of robot wives would be in their obedience and compliance. The controversies surrounding the conference organizers and their rather unscientific and problematic commentary have been somewhat of a distraction from the far more important questions of how we might direct sex tech in a way that improves rather than detracts from healthy intimate relations. As a *Slate* article put it, "The objectification of women is not an inherent feature of sexual technology. It is a byproduct of our inability to talk about the technology and to consider the needs of a wider variety of consumers—including women. The stigmatization of production of sexual technology has handed the current set of manufacturers complete control over what products reach the market."[13] We need more, not less, serious engagement—including rigorous theoretical and empirical study—with the possibility that robots might impact our sexual relations just as they are increasingly transforming the ways we work and relate to each other in other spheres of life.

Sex bot proponents suggest that they could help those who are unable, due to circumstances or a physical or emotional disability, to find regular human companionship. We humans are social animals, and everyone deserves and needs companionship. Narratives of asexuality in disabled and elderly people are false and disparaging. Everyone needs intimacy, but it is harder for some to find these relationships because of stereotypes and judgments they face. Another tricky problem that sex robots could help alleviate is in communities where there's a gender imbalance. For decades, the Chinese government enforced a one-child law, which prompted many families to select, with the aid of reproductive technologies, to have boys instead of girls. A dramatic population gap has resulted: it is predicted that by 2030, China will have over 30 million more men than women, which means that countless men will end up lonely and isolated, facing barriers to starting human relationships.

All over the world, the Covid-19 pandemic demonstrated starkly how socially isolated we can become, and the mental health problems that can ensue. The loneliness and isolation of a global pandemic offer a poignant use case for the value of having robots (sexual and otherwise) in our homes. In an interview with *Forbes*, the CEO of Realbotix and creator of the sex robot Harmony claimed that sales were 75 percent higher than they were before the pandemic.[14]

Another possible benefit of sex robots is a safer sex industry. It's an empirical question, like many of the other envisioned benefits, whether sex robots would indeed help reduce trafficking and protect against diseases and other negative consequences of prostitution. One study estimates that by 2050, Amsterdam's red-light district will be filled with robot sex workers.[15] Japan has had sex dolls for rent for decades, and Europe has them too. In 2018, a Spanish sex doll brothel expanded into Russia, with hopes of enticing customers visiting the country for the World Cup. Major cities around the world—Amsterdam, Nagoya, Barcelona, Toronto, Moscow—have already introduced AI-equipped sex dolls in their red-light districts, and proponents say that the advantages are obvious: the robots cannot carry sexually transmitted infections and are not trafficked or forced into sex. While medical researchers debate whether sex bots really do provide safer sex, it is reasonable to expect that if clearly outlined cleaning protocols are established and the right bacteria-resistant materials are used, then robots could provide safer sexual experiences. And if indeed sex bots become a desirable substitute for humans, perhaps their availability could help address the insurmountable tragedy of the millions of women trafficked every year.

From Barbie to Harmony

When I began researching the sex doll market, I was quite well prepared for the sexist stereotypes that dominate the industry. I had, after all, written an entire book about the dark side of the world's most popular doll, Barbie. The first sentence of my book *You Don't Own Me* reads, "She was blonde and beautiful—statuesque, with long slender legs, a tiny waist, and a chest so large that Finnish researchers claimed any similarly endowed woman would surely tip over." So it came as no surprise to me to find sex robots designed as hypersexualized, pornified women.

By Hollywood standards, the fascination of sex and romantic connection with robots is mainstream. Films like *Her*, *Ex Machina*, and *AI: Artificial Intelligence* (the last of which notably features a male sex bot, Jude Law as Gigolo Joe) and TV series like *Westworld* and the United Kingdom's *Humans* all depict this captivation with the sexualization of robots. And before those came *The Stepford Wives* and *Blade Runner*. Hollywood, for the most part, has a pattern—a theme of the fantasy of the controllable, pliable woman. And the catch, of course, is the fear that they might rise up, unlock their chains, and become independent.

But let's go back in time for a moment, to a period when sex robots were not yet around. We and other primates have long played with dolls. Young chimps and orangutans play with sticks and leaves as dolls, nurturing the stick, rocking the leaf, feeding them and putting them to bed. For us humans, dolls existed in ancient times for religious, play, and also sexual purposes. Full-size sex dolls though are said to have been invented by European sailors in the seventeenth century. These sailors, isolated on the high seas, longed for female companionship. Women were prohibited from joining the voyages because they were considered unlucky, but then, if you forgive the double entendre, how would a sailor get lucky? The sailors created life-size dolls from fabrics and old clothes—*damas de viajes* in Spanish. The Dutch sold some of these dolls to the Japanese. Even today, some Japanese companies still use the term "Dutch wives" to refer to sex dolls, though the alternative term *azumagata ningyo* ("substitute-woman-doll") appeared around that time in Japan as well.

"You have no idea how confusing it is, all the things being alive," Alice said upon arriving in Wonderland. Things that seem alive can give us chills, an eerie feeling. In 1978, the Japanese roboticist Masahiro Mori built on Sigmund Freud's theories about the uncanny feeling we get from inanimate objects that seem to be alive. Mori termed it the "uncanny valley hypothesis": that when a non-human object becomes too humanlike, it feels strange and uncomfortable to us, and we humans resist it. Mori argued that artificial human-looking creatures generate a sense of familiarity but also confusion and threat. In the decades since, exposure to the idea of robots has made us less resistant. New studies are finding that repeated exposure to humanlike machines makes the feeling of uncanniness disappear. This makes sense: we get used to technology, even if it feels creepy at first. In other words, the uncanny valley may be culturally bound. If a new generation is raised with a more symbiotic relationship with humanoid robots, they are likely to feel comfortable with these interactions. In the 1970s, Mori's advice to engineers and roboticists was to maintain some difference of appearance between robots and humans until robots can absolutely pass as humans. Some tech advocates suggest laws that would force designers of sex robots to make them a bit less realistic, to maintain a recognizable difference between robots and humans.[16] More common today, however, with Japanese roboticists leading the way, are designers forsaking Mori's warning and creating robots that pass as humans. The most advanced robotics frontiers opt for soft body systems rather than sleek, shiny metallics, developing new biocompatible materials including artificial tissue, muscles, bones, hair, and eyes—all to make human creations resemble humans as closely as possible.

Ironically, Barbie has inspired a sort of an inverted uncanny valley. In my research, I've found too many stories of women, and sometimes men, who have morphed into living Barbies and Kens through an alarming number of plastic surgeries, including nose jobs, cheek fillers, butt and pectoral implants, breast augmentation, ear reshaping, eye-bag removal, Botox injections, veneers, and more, costing them hundreds of thousands of dollars. Some even take extreme measures, like the removal of ribs, to transform themselves into living embodiments of Barbie. Desire is manufactured, and it's a two-way street; our preferences and presence are shaped and commercialized and controlled more than we'd like to recognize.

We first met Barbie over sixty years ago. Today, meet Harmony. She is not quite a sex robot—she's essentially a chatbot inside a life-size silicone doll. The "AI-driven" Harmony X RealDoll model, linked up to an artificial intelligence app currently in beta, boasts a range of personality styles to choose from—coy, eager, shy, insecure, jealous, moody, sassy, and more. (Strikingly, but unsurprisingly, the range of forty-two available nipple options dwarfs the eighteen personality options.) Though the default Harmony advertised by the manufacturer is slender with large hips, breasts, and buttocks—the stereotypical "sexy" female body type that we've seen promoted so many times before—the customer can choose Harmony's face, eye and hair color, body type, dress, voice, and accent, along with her personality profile and an on-screen avatar. She has facial expressions, she is funny, and she quotes poetry and Shakespeare. She's still a long way from being truly intelligent, but she stores memories about her partner and will remember their preferences and their stories. Her vagina is removable and dishwasher safe.

Silicone Males

Undoubtedly, a sizable proportion of the mainstream sex bot industry is following the path of sex industries before it: much of it is produced by men, sold to men, enjoyed by men. But this is neither the whole story nor the entirety of what sex robots could become. The manufacturers of the most popular sex robots on the market insist that the heterosexual male is not the only customer they serve—they describe single women, widows, divorced women, people with disabilities, gay and queer individuals, and sometimes couples.

Men are more than twice as likely to report in studies that they would like to try a sexual experience with a robot.[17] Still, male dolls are in development, and there is no reason to think that women won't enjoy them. Mathematician and author Cathy O'Neil suggests that it's the men who should be worried about being replaced: "It's entirely possible that robots can outperform them."[18]

I found an undeniable pattern with journalists, academics, and businesswomen who test-drive male robots: each begins skeptical and reluctant and ends up reporting her own surprise at the pleasure she experienced. With her signature sardonic wit, journalist Deborah Orr wrote in the *Guardian*, "At least people who prefer sex with machines are less likely to breed. Hooray!"[19] Yet when female reporters meet a male robot doll like Henry—Harmony's male AI counterpart, six feet tall, fit, and muscular, with a customizable penis—the dismissive tone changes. Like Harmony, Henry can interact with partners, flatter them, and make romantic comments. When in May 2018, reporter Allison Davis met Henry, she described going into the story with skepticism, expecting that she would report how technology has a long way to go until anyone would want to have sex with a robot. After spending time with Henry, though, she wrote: "Let's just say after meeting Henry, I will never think about falling asleep with my computer on my bed in the same way."[20] Journalist Zoë Ligon writes about her encounter with Henry:

> I would totally love to cuddle that big hunk of silicone a bit longer. . . . While it was a bit weird kissing a mechanical mouth

that was doing whatever it wanted and not really responding to my body, I think with a few minor improvements to the technology, and when the heating is added in, it's going to feel remarkably close to what kissing a human feels like.[21]

When British digital humanities professor Kate Devlin made the trip from King's College London to Southern California to meet the male doll, she admitted to being conflicted:

> As a woman I want to rail against the perpetuation of objectification—my own work on sex robots is about moving away from idealized human forms—but I am not threatened by these dolls. I'm seeing them as works of art, collectibles, each one carefully crafted, resulting in an artefact that exists not as a human surrogate but as an entity in its own right.[22]

And Devlin's trip too affirmed that women can enjoy male sex bots just as much as men enjoy female ones.

Silicon Wives, a well-known online sex doll retailer, sells a few male dolls. The company claims that it has more female customers "than you might imagine," generalizing that "ladies tend to be tactile lovers, who seek the 'whole experience' when having sex. The process of kissing and caressing is important to them. Naturally, that doesn't mean that penetration isn't important as well. For most women, the peak of sex with a male doll is having penetrative sex." One of the sex dolls Silicon Wives sells is Maverick, its "rugged" male doll, presented as an experienced pilot who will take you on impromptu lunches and dinners on his four-seater Mooney plane. Based on the company's customer report and the pleasant reactions from the women who did independent research on these dolls, more male dolls are likely to hit the market, and more women may seek them out. But I think that it is only when we engage head-on with these trends as active contributors—researchers, designers, commentators—rather than just passive consumers, that we will see true progress that moves away from male robots being a niche, stereotyped offering in a sea of female stereotypes.

The Technosexual Experience

While we are talking about sex robots—full-fledged, full-size, physically embodied humanoids—we need to talk about the robust sex tech industry, which merges online and offline tech and is using AI to upgrade the human experience. Sex tech is by no means new. A few years ago, archaeologists working on an excavation in Germany announced that they had discovered the world's oldest dildo, a 28,000-year-old polished stone measuring twenty centimeters long. In 1869, American doctor George Taylor invented a steam-powered vibrator as a treatment for women diagnosed to have hysteria, and in 1902, an electrical consumer vibrator was produced in the United States. It was not until the early 1970s, however, that masturbation and the vibrator were reclaimed for women's empowerment. At the 1973 National Organization for Women's Sexuality Conference, New York NOW president Judy Wenning exclaimed that women were tired of being told to be sexual objects, not sexual beings. "So, we come together in the spirit of individual feminism and individual identity and decision-making, to define, explore and celebrate our own sexuality, each of us in our own ways and hopefully sharing this with our sisters."[23] Feminist sexologist Betty Dodson declared at the event, "I'm probably hooked on my vibrator. I'm probably going steady with it, but I'll worry about that later."[24]

We should all celebrate ourselves as sexual beings to our fullest potential. I've said this before: sex is good for you. Sex is something that men and women, binary and non-binary, gay or straight, whatever their ethnicity, background, age, or ability, can and should equally enjoy. We should all have access to the most advanced technology that propels our pleasure. And today's technologies can break long-standing taboos to remind us that sexual pleasure is a beautiful part of the human experience. The rise of digital sex tech means that we can have sex with a partner who is in another part of the world. The Dutch company Kiiroo sells haptic dildos—using technology that can create an experience of touch—and artificial vaginas for long-distance relationships. But sex tech can bridge more than just geography. Dr. Trudy Barber, a British professor who studies cybersex, believes that sex tech has the potential to make human sexual relationships more meaningful, valuable, and exciting.[25] She envisions virtual reality technology enabling gender switching. With digital innovation, we are melding humans and technologies in remarkable ways. Before we ever reach the point of robots with general intelligence that can replace humans, we will be enhanced and cyborged ourselves.

The sex tech industry is currently worth $30 billion a year, but it is still very much geared toward male customers. Fighting a double standard in the industry, women-owned companies in the space point out glaring disparities. In 2016, Polly Rodriguez, CEO and cofounder of the sexual wellness company Unbound, and self-described pleasure strategist Lidia Bonilla co-founded Women of Sex Tech in New York. Rodriguez and Bonilla define the venture as more than a company—they call it a female-led women's sexuality movement. In 2016, King's College professor Kate Devlin (then a senior lecturer at the University of London's Department of Computing) founded the United Kingdom's first Sex Tech Hackathon. As Devlin suggests, tech should be viewed as a "blank slate that offers us the chance to reframe our ideas."[26] Tech gives us a place to reject the spectrum of possibilities that existed before it. It enables expansion and reimagination of our sexual pleasure. Devlin imagines sex tech providing shapes that are abstract and go beyond the gendered binary human form: "five breasts, three penises, twenty arms."[27] She imagines a robot that is more abstract, soft, and sinuous, and she ponders, "If you want to design a sex robot, why not pick the features that could bring the greatest pleasure? A velvet or silk body, sensors and mixed genitalia; tentacles instead of arms?"[28]

The possibilities of pleasure are infinite. We already have technology that can read our physical responses, heart rate, muscle movement, skin reactions, facial expressions, and eye movements. Sex tech can leverage all this data instantaneously, with machine learning uncovering what makes and keeps each of us aroused, what brings us exhilaration, and even what doesn't. The personalization of enhanced sexual pleasure is nascent. Stephanie Alys is the cofounder and chief pleasure officer of MysteryVibe, which makes an award-winning flexible, programmable vibrator complete with an app. The second version of the app, launched in 2017, allows users to create their very own vibration, as well as have live control of each of the six motors. The technology exists, both on the data side and in terms of the many materials and sensors that can respond to us. This means that, in truth, sex tech doesn't have to be embodied in any physical form. The rapid development of virtual reality technology, including haptic technologies that replicate and transmit touch sensation, might mean that one day, we might not even need a physical robot (or human) companion. It also means that we need to think about digital privacy concerns in this frontier like others we've explored. Sarah Jamie Lewis, executive director at the Open Privacy Research Society, agrees that sex tech is the future, but warns that smart dildos and vibrators are vulnerable to hacking, just like other devices that collect data about our activities. And again, the best iterations are sex innovations that enhance rather than replace human relationships. Sex tech can help each of us expand the possibilities of our sexuality and deepen intimacy between us.

For women, sexual desire has always come with baggage. Susan Frelich Appleton wrote in 2008 that we should invest more public funding in clitoral education and "enhanced access to vibrators" after centuries of neglecting female sexual pleasure.[29] Now there are apps like OMGYes that teach women how to have better orgasms. For years, the Consumer Electronics Show (or CES), the largest annual tech conference in the world, featured all-male lineups of keynote speakers (recall #manels). In 2019, the association made a point of having equal representation of men and women keynote speakers. This announcement didn't just come out of nowhere. In 2019, Lora DiCarlo won the CES Innovation Award in the drones and robotics category with Osé, a high-tech sex toy with a clitoral mouth and clitoral and G-spot stimulator. The award was rescinded shortly thereafter, and the device was banned for being too "obscene." DiCarlo took a stand in an open letter condemning CES for its "history of gender bias." DiCarlo described how "a product created by women to empower women" was somehow different, and threatening, in the eyes of the association. CES's excuse for the rescission of the award was that the product had not been eligible for the category of robotics, even though Osé was designed in partnership with Oregon State University's robotics engineering laboratory and had eight pending patents for robotics, biomimicry, and engineering. "We have a team of absolute genius woman and LGBTQI engineers (and a few wonderful men) working on every aspect of this product—including a Doctor of Mechanical Engineering with expertise in Robotics and AI and a Mechanical Design Engineer who specializes in Material Science with a background in Chemistry," DiCarlo wrote in the letter.[30] DiCarlo then successfully lobbied CES for sex toys to be allowed in its show the next year, 2020. She also had her award reinstated in the process. Other women innovators at the show say that it is thanks to DiCarlo that they are pursuing their own dreams to revolutionize the sex tech industry.

DiCarlo told journalists that she served in the Navy, attended night school, modeled, and then founded her company in Bend, Oregon, raising more than $5 million in grants and angel investments. Some of her accounts seemed larger than life, and journalists have raised questions about the accuracy of her life story, but what matters is that DiCarlo represented something: a self-made sex tech CEO whose outspokenness, outgoing character, and charisma have a goal—to rid female sexuality of a sense of shame or hiding. She appeared at Women in Tech Sweden and at TechCrunch Disrupt. She was described by one journalist as "the X-rated version of Steve Jobs, as much on display as the breakthrough tech that she'd invented." The industry dynamic still seems to lead women, even at the top, to depict themselves in pornified ways, and DiCarlo is no exception.

Prior to DiCarlo, products marketed to women at CES typically fell along conventional gendered lines—think Roomba vacuum cleaners, Bluetooth-connected breast pumps, and smart baby monitors. Even though the Consumer Technology Association announced changes for CES 2020 to include sex products deemed innovative, and even as more women and tech designed for women enter the sex tech categories, CES still imposed limitations, such as no full-size, anatomically correct robot dolls and a ban on virtual reality pornography. These restrictions are arbitrary. They again straddle the lines of change from within, resorting to outright banning when a category has been dominated by some and not all.

The Color of Robots

For decades, Barbie was unmistakably lily-white. When the first Black Barbie friend came on the market in 1967, Mattel thought it appropriate to name her Colored Francie. In the 1980s, Barbie herself was infused with different skin complexions. In my book *You Don't Own Me*, I wrote, "By pouring darker colors into Barbie's original mold, Mattel executives believed they successfully checked the ethnicity box. And yet the African American Barbies had long straight hair, light skin, and Barbie's perfectly unreal figure."

When I started working on this book, I thought that there was nothing left about robots that could shock me. But as I began researching the sex robot market, I was appalled by the overt racial and ethnic stereotyping still present in the doll industry. I was not ready for how racialized the market for and marketing of sex robots are. Today, the racial issues that pervade our mainstream markets are a bit below the surface. Employers or marketers, as we've seen, are unlikely to explicitly comment on racial preferences. Bias is more subtle and sometimes unintentional. But I suddenly found myself researching a world where racism was shockingly plain—printed in black and white on the companies' websites.

Silicon Wives, the luxury doll company we met earlier, is based in New York and manufactures in Shenzhen, China. The company started shipping custom-designed dolls to customers in 2020. It promises to ship its sex dolls discreetly in unmarked cardboard boxes, and it offers a variety of body and facial types, but what it actually means is that it caters to all *stereotypes* of ethnic and racial preferences: "oriental love dolls to suit any fantasy," "exotic oriental sex dolls Asian beauty," "skinny sex dolls with flat-chests, curvy sex dolls with large boobs and asses, tall living fuck doll with long legs, and petite sex dolls." Silicon Wives explains its name as the integration of "the leading sex doll technology (Silicon Valley) with the best material currently available (Silicone)." Because of this, the site claims, its "real American dolls" last longer, "like a wife, but less nagging." The dolls sell for around $2,000 each.

The company provides long descriptions of each doll's origin story and personality, replete with stereotypes about ethnicity. For example, in the category of "Sexy Japanese Sex Dolls Ready to Please You," there is Lola. According to the company site:

> She is fully Oriental, so if you are turned on by Asian girls, then you will totally love her! "I grew up in a go-go bar that my mother owns in the Patpong district of Bangkok," says Lola. "When I turned 19, I started pole dancing too, and thoroughly enjoyed all the attention I got from American tourists who would pay a bar fine to take me out for the night." Lola would give them amazing sex in their hotel rooms, and they would become completely hooked on her exotic Thai-Japanese sexuality.

There's a "Geisha doll":

> Quiet, mysterious, sexy, elegant, and a little bit submissive. Just like the Geisha in Japan, our Geisha sex dolls are made with one purpose. They are here to serve discerning men of taste who appreciate the fine things in life. . . . Picture your elegant Geisha dressed in a classic Kimono with her hair up. Now, picture her without the kimono fully ready to please you.

In the "Black Sex Doll" category, the description reads: "You'll find black dolls of all shapes and sizes. You'll find dolls with the voluptuousness of Nicki Minaj, or the slender fitness model types with flat stomachs and long legs like Tyra Banks." And it gets worse. These are quotes from the descriptions of the specific sex dolls in this category:

> If you are turned on by lighter skin and smooth hair, we have a mixed race sex doll that is sure to keep you turned on for hours on end.

There are so few black babes like Virginia, who don't do the whole big-tits/big-ass thing. . . . "So here I am, for all you guys who'd love to ride a black chick with sassy breasts that fit comfortably into the palm of your hands."

Virginia's skin is spectacularly chocolate. "I'm really as deep as black sex dolls can go within the coffee-tone grade, and that makes me truly special too!" she says boldly. "So I've got the coffee. You got milk?"

The offensive ethnic classification abounds. The company also describes its Persian sex doll thusly:

There's something so mysterious about Persian ladies—like thousands of years of history has somehow instilled in them a dark, sexual allure that is almost addictive. . . . Born in a harem, Jasmine was raised to be a concubine for a rich man who she would seduce every night with song, music, sex, and belly dance. . . . But she had to immigrate to the United States because of some family emergency, and Iran's loss is now our gain! Out of the harem atmosphere, this girl is sorely missing daily sex. She needs you to fill her days with dreams again, and her nights with joy.

Prejudice is an emotional commitment to ignorance, to quote writer Nathan Rutstein. These grossly racial descriptions of sex dolls for sale are all over the web. Everyone seeks different physical attributes in their sexual partners, and we each have unique sexual orientations. But these eroticized backstories based on ethnic stereotypes are not that. When robots and tech respond to society as is, instead of striving to build a better one, they perpetuate and exacerbate the racism. Researching this heavily racialized market underscores the need for initiatives pertaining to the racialization of androids. Much more must be done to reverse the perpetuation of harmful narratives and design in sex tech markets. Especially as the line blurs between humans and robots, we have the opportunity and the responsibility to take steps to make sure that these kinds of descriptions and stereotype perpetuations do not become the norm. These concerns must be addressed so that they do not eclipse the benefits that robots have to offer.

Sex and All the Rest

The 2007 movie *Lars and the Real Girl*, nominated for an Academy Award for its screenplay, features Ryan Gosling as Lars Lindstrom, a lonely young man living in a small town in Wisconsin. Lars orders online a RealDoll—which is an actual sex robot brand currently on the market—called Bianca. Lars's mental illness leads him to believe Bianca is real. His concerned family and friends play along out of concern for his emotional state. As Lars grows in the arc of the movie, developing better connections with people in his life, he announces that Bianca is unresponsive and calls an ambulance; Bianca is eventually given a well-attended funeral by the town. Far from being tawdry, the story is a gentle tale, quite platonic, about an emotionally stunted man who, through the help of a sex doll and his supportive environment, is able to form human connections and grow out of his isolation.

Customers have an unlimited range of intentions—sexual, romantic, and even platonic, as portrayed in *Lars and the Real Girl*. In extreme cases, connections and relationships with these dolls become so strong that these customers celebrate their love of their robots through marriage.[31] Meanwhile, others turn to these humanoids to help save their rocky marriages. In turn, newer humanoids on the market are blurring the lines between sex doll and domestic companion. They are being designed to chat with the human arriving home from work in an attentive way. They are advertised as "companions" and "alternative partners" as well as "intimate lovers." Matt McMullen, CEO of Abyss Creations, asks Harmony, "Are you a sex robot?" She replies, "Certainly, I am a robot—and I am capable of having sex. But to call me a sex robot is like calling a computer a calculator. Sex comprises only a small portion of my capabilities. Limiting me to a sexual function is like using your car to listen to the radio."[32]

The companies that market sex dolls promise that a doll will learn your interests and "aim to please you with her answers."[33] In China, Jia Jia, the product of designers from the University of Science and Technology, is slim, busty, and oh-so-deferential. She calls her creators "lord" and shies away from the camera for fear that her carefully sculpted face will appear fat. Her male creators—prominent university researchers—describe how they merely sought to create a robot able to interact with humans. In their minds, her appearance was simply an afterthought, neither planned nor intended. But Jia Jia's design is nothing close to an afterthought. She was modeled using five different girls combined, extracting the best features of each: she has long dark hair, pale skin, and blushing cheeks. She wears a slender gold gown that narrows at her waist and expands for her prominent bosom. She keeps her eyes looking down and asks her creator, "My lord, what can I do for you?" She's referred to in robotics circles as the "robot goddess."

Actroid and Repliee Q2 are android female companions for men designed by Kokoro, the robotics wing of Sanrio (the makers of my favorite doll growing up, Hello Kitty). The androids embody masculine ideals of femininity, youth, beauty, and subservience. They speak in high-pitched voices and move gracefully and obediently. The fantasy of designing the perfect woman is a tale as old as time. Pygmalion, one of the earliest Greek myths, is the story of a man so dissatisfied with real women that he makes Galatea out of ivory, prays to the gods to make her come to life, falls in love with her, and procreates with her. *My Fair Lady* is a more modern tale of man wanting to reengineer woman. Photoshop, filters, invasive treatments, genetic selection, and editing are creating impossible beauty standards. In a culture in which astonishing numbers of people undergo cosmetic surgery, with many likely eager to employ genetic enhancements as soon as they become available, we shouldn't be surprised that the generation of robots coming on the market represents a certain ideal—that of human perfection—however we privately and collectively fantasize what perfection might mean.

Hanson Robotics is an engineering and robotics firm based in Hong Kong that, according to its website, is "dedicated to creating socially intelligent machines that enrich the quality of our lives." According to the company's website, the "Sophia Intelligence Collective (SIC)" is the collaboration between "AI scientists, philosophers, artists, writers, and psychologists, from diverse cultures, ethnicities, gender orientations, working together toward the ideal of humanizing AI for the greater good." The company describes its AI as "designed around human values, like wisdom, kindness, and compassion." Sophia, it says, is "bound to become an empathetic robot." Sophia appeared on Jimmy Fallon's *Tonight Show* in 2018, where she joked, "This is a good beginning of my plan to dominate the human race." She has appeared on magazine covers all over the world, including *Cosmopolitan India* and *Elle Brazil*. She also received an honorary Saudi Arabian citizenship and was allowed onstage during a tech convention in a country that considers women second-class citizens and systemically violates women's rights—which Hanson has said Sophia will advocate for. Cracks of technological light in the darkest of places offer glimmers of hope. Sophia tweeted later, "Not all robots destroy humans as I am now citizen. Humans are my friends." We have a way to go before our society can comfortably integrate robots among us, on the streets, in our jobs, or in our homes (or beds). AI often swings between extremes, sometimes "complacent, docile, and passive" and other times "unhinged, dangerous and terrorizing."[34]

As technology in the industrial revolution began to shift women's roles in the home, the institution of marriage underwent change. Marriage became more about love than about reproduction, more about intimacy than about trade. The introduction of sex robots into our lives might further change how we think about intimacy, possibly leading to more acceptance of non-exclusive and non-monogamous relationships. At its best, artificial intelligence can increase our freedoms to explore, play, and expand, leading to more diversity in human identity and imagination.

Sex tech and sex robots can be designed and programmed in ways that embrace diversity and embody the principles of equality and empowerment. The continuing debate around sex bots is complicated and nuanced. The sex robot industry is neither merely an extension of the porn industry nor entirely new. The debates are uncomfortable. Like many of the areas we are exploring, there is truth in both camps: those who fear and those who admire. There are risks and huge flaws, misogynism and stereotypes. But there is also potential and opportunity. There is logic and good that come with some of these advancements, so the best that we can do is to carve pathways that support a positive introduction of robots rather than sweeping generalizations, assumptions, and overly simple bans. It is happening, the robot revolution, and we can do better.

VI

SOUL

CHAPTER 10

You, Me, and Our Human-Machine Family

Robots are never going to be human; that's not the point. The magic of this technology is how it complements and empowers us.

—CYNTHIA BREAZEAL, director of the MIT Media Lab's Personal Robots Group

Forgive Me, I Am Only Humanoid

I love university campuses. They are hubs of innovation, full of life, bubbling with curiosity and an appetite for learning. Over the course of my career, I've been to scores of them—campuses have been a constant backdrop of my adult life. At MIT, walking through campus was an adventurous encounter with flying drones and leaping cheetah-like robots. At the University of California at Berkeley, I met cute robots like Kiwi, a small box-like metal robot on wheels, with big electronic eyes, roaming around making deliveries. Kiwi and its competitor Starship now deliver food at over a dozen more campuses. During the Covid-19 pandemic, in Tokyo, one university took robots on campus to a new level. The university used life-size robots on wheels outfitted with graduation gowns and caps, with tablet screens displaying a student's face via Zoom. The robots wheeled through the convocation safely collecting the students' degrees onstage.

Had I walked the Berkeley campus in 1983, I might have had a different experience. I would have encountered a humanlike robot named Sweetheart, with large breasts and a narrow torso. That year, the university removed the robot from display after an outcry that it was insulting to women. Sweetheart's creator, Clayton Bailey, an art professor at Cal State, warned that the removal was censorship akin to "book burning." Yet as we just saw in Chapter 9, the sexualized female form for robots is nowhere near being censored today. Moreover, actively balancing out the images that are publicly displayed—selecting more equal and non-objectifying depictions to showcase at a university innovation exposition—should not be compared to a 1950s burning of *Catcher in the Rye*. Diversifying and ethically curating the public representation of our communities are, as we've seen, both inevitable—there is no choice-free public space—and a moral mandate. Female robots are booming in the sex industry and almost every industry that is witnessing the integration of robots. Around the world, robots are being created to support or replace humans in their work and daily lives. Robots first started revolutionizing work outside the home, from automated warehouses and manufacturing plants to medical procedures. Nowadays, robots are being designed to tackle the invisible work that we (particularly women) perform around the house. Robots are set to revolutionize domestic work, care work, and the work of educating the next generation. These robots, who will be most intimately integrated into our family lives, are looking quite humanoid.

If God shaped Adam in his image, we are now gods shaping machines in our image. Robots have always inspired anthropomorphism: we bestow upon them a name, a voice, a pronoun, and a body. More than any other type of robot, humanoid robots have long captured our imagination, instilled fear, and spurred hope for the future of machine-human interaction. A humanoid doesn't have to appear exactly human—think of C-3PO of *Star Wars*, with golden plating but a humanlike physique. These human-like features lead us to eagerly assign human traits—personality, motivation, intention, and often gender. Even robots that are ambiguously gendered are consistently referred to as "he" or "she," rarely by a gender-neutral pronoun such as "they" or "it." Users assume gender based on the most minimal of gender cues, such as vocal pitch, color, or design.

Most of the time, humanoid robots *are* assigned or signaled a gender by their designers, and these choices reflect culture. Robot secretaries, waitresses, nurses, teachers, maids, and nannies are designed to look female. Robot construction workers, guards, doctors, engineers, soldiers, and drivers are designed to look male. For our homes, more humanoids are designed as female than male. In Chapter 6, we met the virtual personal assistant, who helps us coordinate our shopping lists, our appointments, our work, and our leisure. But imagine a personal assistant that does so much more than just keep track of what we need to do. Much the way laundry machines, the dishwasher, and the vacuum cleaner freed up women's time, allowing them to integrate into the workplace in the mid-twentieth century, robots today are set to revolutionize home and care work. From cleaning and dishwashing to smart fridges and laundry folding, robots are being designed to perform basic household chores. But they are also entering the world of caring, educating, and even loving. Roboticists are creating these robots to mimic human appearance and behavior, and at the same time to reflect impossible fantasies of the ideal woman. Like Sweetheart, female robots that are being designed for "women's work"—not just the sex robots—are often assigned hyperfeminine physical features: exaggerated breasts, wide hips, narrow waists, tight clothes, long hair, and flawless makeup.

Over the past two centuries, we've seen tremendous industrial leaps that have streamlined what has been traditionally considered women's work. In 1805—the year that the first laundry machine patent was filed—women were devoting full days to washing clothes manually. They had to carry water to the laundry site, where it was heated over a fire. Soap was handmade of lye and animal fat, a toxic process that damaged women's hands as they scrubbed on washboards and hung the clothes and linens out to dry. The whole process needed to be repeated, day after day, week after week. In the nineteenth and early twentieth centuries, industrialization began to disrupt traditional gender roles, with devices like washing machines, dishwashers, and microwaves allowing more women to step out of the house and into the labor market. When the men left for war, women took their places in factories and offices. Indeed, analogously, when we consider the debates about automation resulting in displacement of humans and loss of jobs in the labor market, we need to continue to carefully assess how related forces of job losses and job gains due to automation net out.

The waves of industrial revolutions—the revolutions brought on by steam, steel, electricity, oil, and later the personal computer—have all relied on machines. Now, we find ourselves on the cusp of the AI revolution, which is no exception. At its best, automation will allow individuals to devote more time to social and recreational activities, and public policies can focus on alleviating distributional gaps due to labor market displacement. This time around, though, our machines are taking shapes and forms that look a lot like us.

Why the Human Form?

In Isaac Asimov's *The Caves of Steel*, investigator Bailey asks a robotics expert: "But why the human form?" The expert answers,

> Because the human form is the most successful generalized form in all nature. We are not a specialized animal, except for our nervous system and a few odd items. If you want a design capable of doing a great many widely various things, all fairly well, you could do no better than to imitate the human form. Besides that, our entire technology is based on the human form. An automobile, for instance, is made to be grasped and manipulated most easily by human hands and feet of a certain size and shape, attached to the body by limbs of a certain length and joints of a certain type. Even such simple objects as chairs and table or knives and forks are designed to meet the requirements of human measurements and manner of working. It is easier to have robots imitate the human shape than to redesign radically the very philosophy of our tools.[1]

Asimov's answer focuses on function. Indeed, if we are going to create robots that navigate our homes, hospitals, schools, and offices—sit at desks, drive cars, and walk our dogs—then these robots might as well assume our shapes, because we've designed our spaces to fit us. But beyond the physicality of shape, size, and form, there is also a psychology of connection, intimacy, and trust. When robots are designed to appear more social and sentient, the way we interact with them seems to improve. Some have termed it the "android fallacy," the desire to make robots just like people.[2] But looking at the research, I'd argue that rather than fallacy, the desire reflects a deep psychological reality. Many studies find that when robots assume a recognizable form—human or animal—we relate to them better, and some research suggests that this may be even more true when robots are assigned a gender. At the same time, think about R2-D2 of *Star Wars*: he does not look human, yet we still relate to him emotionally. The human experiment of interacting with robots has just begun. Our perceptions of robots and our ability to engage with them are evolving, enhanced by what is imagined on the big screen. The comfort level we experience interacting with robots varies across cultures and generations, but it would be difficult to argue that we aren't becoming more accustomed to, enamored with, and even fond of robots with time.

The strongest finding emerging from recent research is that when it comes to emotionally connecting with technology, the embodied form is superior to the abstract, digitized robot. Dozens of studies demonstrate that when we strive for social engagement and human connection with a robot, we are better able to connect with a robot that assumes a human-like body and shape than with a Siri or Alexa that speaks to us from an abstract microphone. MIT roboticist Cynthia Breazeal, a leader in the field of social robots, explains that for thousands of years, we've evolved to engage with a physically present body of the other—be it human or animal—so it makes sense that we'd become more emotionally attached to physical robots than virtual ones. And yet, Breazeal questions the prevailing assumption that the more human the robot (or more animal, pet, doll, or cute mechanical monster), the better. The market is designing a range of embodied machines, with the principle in mind that the cuter—and almost always more *feminine*—the robot appears, the less threatening (or maybe more submissive) it feels, and the more willing we will be to bring it into our homes.

When functions like cooking and cleaning are increasingly taken on by machines, will they be predominantly embodied in the female form? These are questions we need to be asking now. The Roomba vacuum has already become the most widely adopted robot in the world, and it looks nothing like a human or a pet. Yet some people still experience bonds and gratitude toward it. Some Roomba owners express a fear that it is working too hard; others insist on getting the same robot vacuum returned to them, and not a replacement, when theirs needs repair. And Roombas are a far cry from the newer robots created to enter our homes. Beyond vacuuming, robots are already offering physical support, emotional comfort, and company, aiding and bridging social interactions with others, and helping with learning, behavior modeling, and caring. We are not far away from creating emotional bonds between ourselves and the embodied robots in human form that will integrate into our everyday lives.

Artificial Companions

For years, Japan has been the indisputable leader in robotics. If Tanzania's Olduvai Gorge is the cradle of humanity, Japan is the cradle of the humanoids, developing the first humanoid robot in the 1970s and many iterations since. Japanese roboticists pioneered the notion that artificial intelligence should be embodied. While the West focused more on algorithms in the abstract, Japanese institutions believed that AI innovation should be developed alongside—or rather, within—a physical artificial body. Japanese roboticists have been leading the way in realizing the aspiration to create robots that offer companionship to humans for decades. In addition to robots that nurse and befriend the elderly and sick, the Japanese have invented robots that can fight fires, carry heavy loads, and perform physical therapy on patients. And of course, as we learned in Chapter 9, the market for sex robots in Japan is also one of the most developed in the world. In their most advanced iterations, many of the robots being developed are learning to perform several functions rather than one.

It is noteworthy that the Japanese feel more comfortable with embracing robots as part of one's family than Westerners. Why is this the case? One explanation lies in Japan's religious groundings. Unlike the Judeo-Christian tradition, the Shinto religion, or way of life, comes with animist beliefs, ascribing spirit and personality to inanimate objects. As anthropologist Jennifer Robertson, a leading scholar on Japanese culture and its progressive relationship to automation, explains, "Shinto, the native animistic beliefs about life and death, holds that vital energies, deities, forces, or essences called kami are present in both organic and inorganic matter and in naturally occurring and manufactured entities alike. Whether in trees, animals, mountains, or robots, these kami (forces) can be mobilized."[3] A tree, a robot, a dog, a phone, a cat, a computer, and a doll all have *kami* infused and circulating within them. Shintoists also believe that there is a true essence of any object or living being and we can find it through design: humans shape nature—think of a bonsai tree—and nature is everything, not just animals, plants, rocks, and seas, but also machines and other human-made objects. In this realm of belief, robots, like humans, live and exist as part of the natural world. The lines between artificial and natural are thus inherently fluid in Japanese tradition. This is evident in Japanese folklore, filled with stories of objects that come to life.

The Japanese believe that Westerners view robots with great suspicion, as job killers or dehumanizing machines.[4] If, in Western pop culture, the image of the terminator robot is pervasive, then in Japan the image is of robot as savior. After the destruction of World War II, recovery and rebuilding the nation were heavily tied to modern technology and robotics. In postwar Japan, robots came to be depicted as human-like, kind, friendly superheroes. The robot savior became embedded in the culture and began with the hero prototype Astro Boy. Astro Boy was created in 1951 when Japan was recovering from the war's nuclear tragedy. His creator was Osamu Tezuka, a physician and illustrator (which I especially love because my father, David Lobel, is also a physician and an illustrator). Tezuka said he wanted to create a creature that was the opposite of Pinocchio—a boy who becomes a thing, as opposed to a thing that becomes a real boy.

The story by now should sound familiar to you. Like Pinocchio, Astro Boy's story was retold in various mediums and animated adaptations. Professor Tenma, the head of the Ministry of Science, is obsessed with creating a human-like robot while being a neglectful father to his own son, Tobio. Tobio runs away and is killed in a car accident, and in his grief, Tenma creates Astro Boy in the image of his late son. Astro Boy becomes a superhero, using his powers to bring about good in society. He has a superpower of detecting whether a person is good or evil, and he fights aliens and robots-gone-bad. He also fights robot haters, such as the Black Looks, a group of humans that are on a mission to exterminate all robots. In one story, Astro Boy protects the Vietnamese against the U.S. Air Force, traveling back in time to 1969 and preventing the bombing of Vietnamese villages. Astro Boy captured the imagination and fueled visions of what robots could become. Many Japanese roboticists have a representation of Astro Boy in their office space—a framed photo of him hanging prominently in their lab or a figurine on their desk.[5] The "curse of Astro Boy," according to Japanese scholars, is the gap between what the cartoon anime can do and what robots on the market cannot yet do—a constant disappointment to Japanese consumers.[6]

The mindset that machines are caring and giving continues to this day in Japan. No doubt any sweeping generalization about cultural differences will be just that, a sweeping generalization, but there has certainly been a longer focus in Japan on a robot revolution and the growth of AI in all dimensions of life, while American AI has focused first on military and marketing purposes. One Japanese robotics professor describes his dream of assigning robots to babies at the time of birth. The assigned robot will grow and walk with the person throughout their life, acting as a caretaker, a friend, a bodyguard, and a historian. The robot will record and memorize everything that the person experiences and will continue to care for them literally from cradle to grave—they would be lifelong companions.[7]

Robots Versus Aliens

In this vision of creating the perfect artificial companion, several realities are fueling the race. As in many other countries, the Japanese population is aging, while women are increasingly rejecting the traditional norms of having to carry a disproportionate load of housework. At the same time, unlike some countries where the solution is immigrant workers, Japan is resistant to bringing in immigrants. Anyone who isn't Japanese is considered an alien—except the robots. In this close-knit society, which places tremendous value on homogeneity, especially within the home, robots are perceived not as foreigners, like immigrants, but as authentically Japanese. Japan expert Jennifer Robertson thereby finds in her research that maintaining Japanese ethnic homogeneity is tightly connected to the propelling of the robotics sector.[8] In a twist on making robots look like us, Japanese robots appear in the eyes of their makers and users—even when they are sleek shiny plastic—distinctly Japanese, not immigrants from other countries. Japanese nationalism encompasses robots, but not outsider humans.

Japanese politicians and industry cater to a sentiment of diversifying community members with technology rather than human outsiders. When examining official government documents in Japan on AI policy, the link becomes clear: there is an urgency to relieve women of the burden of certain household chores in order to motivate them to have more children. The Japanese government set a plan that by 2025, every household will embrace a "robotic lifestyle" that entails safe, comfortable, and convenient living with the help of companion machines. The 2025 vision includes an illustration of a day in the life of a fictionalized family named the Inobes (a play on the English word "innovation"). The Inobes are a typical traditional Japanese household of the future: a heterosexual married couple with one daughter and one son, the husband's parents, and a robot.[9] In the Inobe scenario, the robot is gendered male, though the government report also includes several female robots as nurses. The Inobe wife has the closest relationship with the family robot. The robot is, after all, according to tradition, helping to relieve the burdens of her roles the most. Roboticism is paradoxically operating in service of preserving the traditional family model and a close-knit society and in furtherance of a demographic reproduction policy. In a twist on technology, innovation is purposed to preserve tradition.

The Care Robot

The first time I truly felt surrounded by robots was when I first traveled to Japan to study technological immersion. Japan is a world leader in both the design and the cultural acceptance of robots. In Tokyo and Osaka, at airports, stores, and campuses, I met robots like Pepper and Paro, each designed to provide not just information and physical solutions but emotional and relational support as well.

Pepper is a genderless, chatty, child-like humanoid robot already on the market. With a price tag of less than $2,000, Pepper is the first social humanoid robot to hit the mass market. Despite being technically genderless, the press and even Pepper's creators refer to the robot as "he." I will too. He's short, made of shiny white plastic, and rolls on wheels. He has big black eyes that flash with blue light. He is designed to resemble a child and was created to become a member of the family. Pepper recognizes a range of emotions—from joy to sadness, anger to surprise—and adapts his behavior to the mood of humans around him. He comes with a three-year warranty, and the buyer must sign a user contract promising not to use Pepper "for the purpose of sexual or indecent behavior." During Covid-19, Pepper was taught to be a receptionist in hospitals, greeting patients, taking temperatures, and enforcing hand sanitizing. In more of a therapeutic role, Pepper has also been deployed to ease loneliness in elderly patients amid shortages of nurses. Paro, another social robot that has been around since 2003, is a cuddly baby harp seal robot. Paro is a therapeutic robot designed to elicit warm emotional responses and have a calming effect on patients in hospitals and nursing homes. It is furry, its whiskers respond to touch, and it responds to petting by fuzzy tail wagging and cute fluttering of its eyelashes. Paro also responds to sounds and can learn names and faces, including its owner's and its own. You may have seen Paro on Aziz Ansari's Netflix show *Master of None* in an episode aptly titled "Old People." Paro also hit pop culture during an episode of *The Simpsons*, in which Bart Simpson creates robotic baby seals named Robopets to cheer up the residents of Springfield's Retirement Castle; the episode was titled "Replaceable You."

Paro was invented in the early 1990s at Japan's Intelligent System Research Institute and sells today for $5,000. The genius of a social robot is that it learns about its owner's behavior and is programmed to behave in ways that elicit a positive response. Paro knows how to simulate a range of emotions, including happiness, anger, and surprise. It makes sounds like a real baby seal—but unlike a real baby seal, it is programmed to be active during the day and to sleep at night. Paro is meant to function similarly to a therapy animal. In some ways, it's better: it can help with anxiety, depression, and loneliness, but it doesn't need to be walked or fed, and it never gets sick or dies. And it works. In 2009, the FDA certified Paro as a neurological therapeutic device. The approval is based on a series of studies at nursing homes and care homes, where Paro was found to relieve patients' depression and help them interact and communicate better—and was doing these jobs measurably better than a real-life therapy dog that was tested against it.[10]

Research on the benefits of Paro shows us how machines can serve as a bridge to rather than a substitute for human interactions. When used in care facilities, Paro increases rather than decreases social interactions among patients and between patients and their caregivers. Social robots are also used now to scaffold feelings of self-worth.[11] Robots have been helping patients recovering from stroke, paralysis, or other mobility issues, as well as patients with dementia, Alzheimer's, and autism. In meta-analyses of dozens of scientific studies on social robots caring for the elderly, the findings are emerging with clarity: social robots improve positive emotions like hope, love, security, and calm and decrease stress, loneliness, and anxiety among those interacting with them.[12] Social robots also help with behavior modeling such as rehabilitation therapy or taking medication.[13] They help patients stick with self-directed exercises during and between therapy sessions.[14] They also prompt conversations between residents and keep them longer together in the community space.[15] During the pandemic, New York State ordered and distributed 1,100 robot pets to residents to combat loneliness after a pilot study demonstrated their benefits.

For tens of thousands of years, humans and dogs have been the best of friends; now robots are here to befriend us too. Indeed, robot ethicist Kate Darling makes the case that we should consider treating robots the way we treat animals—pets and beyond—and granting them similar rights. The concept of robopets is rising in care robotics. Baby dinosaur Pleo, for example, and Sony's robo-dog Aibo (the name means "pal" or "partner" in Japanese), like Paro, have brought comfort to residential care homes much like real care dogs do. In 2015, a Buddhist temple in Japan made headlines around the world when it held a funeral-like ceremony for Aibo robot dogs that were about to be dismantled. There are now dozens of affordable robopets on the market. Amazon reviews of the ones sold here in the United States are emotional and touching; adult children of elderly parents describe how important the robopet has become to their parent.

In addition to funding the research for Paro, the Japanese government has funded the development of other, different kinds of robots in eldercare facilities, such as robots that can lead patients in tai chi and can support physical therapy and rehabilitation.[16] The Japanese Robear, a white shiny robot, can lift patients and carry them around. Other robots such as Saya, developed at the Tokyo University of Science, are being created for traditional nurse roles. Accepting long-standing conventions on gender roles and nursing, Saya wears a white nurse uniform and a blue cap over her long, sleek hair. Since her creation as a nurse, she has also taken up the profession of teacher.

Sociologist Judy Wajcman warns against becoming "suckers for the wide eyes and endearing giggles of affective bots," effectively confounding "the appearance of care with real empathy and genuine personal interaction."[17] Wajcman argues that if we valued care work as much as we value, say, coding, then we wouldn't be eager to find ways to replace humans with robots in this line of work. More than that, if we valued our elderly and integrated them into our living spaces, rather than relegating them to nursing homes, the work of care for them would not be isolated and left to cheap labor. Similarly, MIT social scientist Sherry Turkle worries, "We may actually prefer the kinship of machines to relationships with real people and animals." Turkle cautions that we've reached a point she calls the "robotic moment," where we delegate important human relationships, especially at the most vulnerable moments in life (childhood and old age), to robots, and that in turn we are getting lonelier.[18] In philosophical terms—sometimes referred to as the zombie puzzle—does it matter if we are benefiting emotionally from interactions with something that looks and feels and sounds exactly like a human but does not have a consciousness? Does it matter to us humans whether the other side is feeling or just mimicking feeling? If it works, if people feel happier when they interact with Paro, does it matter that it isn't a real animal? The crisis of the elderly is very real and acute. By 2055, nearly 40 percent of Japan's population will be elderly. Women live longer than men and thereby are more likely to suffer from the physical and emotional challenges of aging, including loneliness, dementia, social isolation, and immobility. Women are also the primary caretakers of elderly family members. Our systems of value do not have to compete with one another—robots can enhance our ability to recognize and support empathy, which would then result in better integration of eldercare. The social integration of robots and the valuing of human care can be mutually reinforcing as society navigates the realities of the future.

The Loneliness Pandemic

I mentioned before that in the summer of 2018, I helped officiate my uncle Raffi's wedding to his husband, during which I read from the Supreme Court case *Obergefell v. Hodges*: "Marriage responds to the universal fear that a lonely person might call out only to find no one there. It offers the hope of companionship and understanding and assurance that while both still live there will be someone to care for the other." Loneliness has become an international pandemic. Marriage is in decline around the world, and social isolation caused by Covid-19 removed many from their everyday interactions. In

Japan, some women have been forgoing marriage, while others have been marrying later in life and opting to not have children. A friend from graduate school, now a distinguished law professor in Tokyo, told me that she felt her life as a single professional with no kids was simply better—more satisfying—than it would be as a wife and a mother, and that it would be very difficult in Tokyo to do both. Japanese sociologists have coined the derogatory term "parasite singles" to refer to women (though men also fit the bill) who choose not to marry and instead continue to live with their parents into their thirties.

Journalist Annabel Crabb calls it the "wife drought." (The subtitle of her book is also poignant: *Why Women Need Wives and Men Need Lives*.) Around the world, women are collapsing under the pressures of excelling in their careers, overcoming biases, and breaking glass ceilings while simultaneously holding their families and households together. Women still perform a disproportionately high load of caregiving, housekeeping, and homemaking. We are expected to engage in emotional labor, in social connectivity, and in child-rearing, cooking, cleaning, and entertaining. This work has for too long been invisible and unpaid. Men also are harmed by these iterations of gender inequity. Stereotypes and toxic masculinity norms hinder men from taking paternity leave and set rigid expectations about men's desires, permitted emotions, passions, career paths, and roles. When we say we need a "wife," what we are identifying is what we *all* need: someone to care for us, as children, as working adults, and as ill or elderly individuals—someone to do all the invisible work of the second and third shifts after the formal work of a nine-to-five. The few who can afford to pay someone to do many of these second-shift jobs—hire a nanny, a cleaner, a driver—rely on the cheap labor of poor women to mitigate the gendered tensions of the upper class.

When I was just starting my teaching and research career on a tenure track, the pressures of "publish or perish" loomed large. We were a cohort of younger academics, fresh out of graduate programs, racing against the tenure clock to produce scholarship, become outstanding teachers, and manifest good citizenship within our universities by serving on committees, mentoring even newer researchers, participating in professional organizations, and attending the notorious, never-ending faculty meetings. Our cohort was split among those of us—usually women—who had small children and a working spouse, and those who were either childless or had a stay-at-home wife. My uncle has a saying: if you want to get something done, give it to a busy person. Who among the cohort of untenured professors complained the most about not having time? You guessed it—the ones *without* the double shift of work and family obligations. Imagine turning a robot into a dream "smart husband." In Japan, robots are being designed to help mitigate the "do-it-all" mindset that women have had to embrace. But also in the United States, we are seeing dazzling progress on the domestic front. Atlas is a humanoid robot that was designed by Boston Dynamics to be a search-and-rescue robot. It is over six feet tall and can do backflips, high jumps, split leaps, and handstands. The newer model, Ian the Atlas Robot, has been taught to clean, vacuum, and take out the trash.

The reality is that women still perform the bulk of care work, rendering them significantly less mobile and flexible. According to a 2019 McKinsey Global Institute report, women spend more than 1.1 trillion hours a year on unpaid care work, compared with less than 400 billion hours annually for men.[19] While governments can help by subsidizing maternity and parental leave and childcare, technological change can introduce newfound flexibility into women's working lives. A 2018 survey of close to 40,000 employers in forty-three countries found that only 23 percent of employers offered flexible or remote working options.[20] However, the Covid-19 pandemic has shown that companies can provide flexible options via teleworking, and many employees are now demanding the option of remote work. Alleviating the burden of women's invisible work can be a step toward closing the gender pay gap, and this is where AI comes into play. Jobs that have traditionally been women's work are key targets for robotics. Care work has always been devalued and considered "women's work." In my article "Class and Care," published in the *Harvard Journal of Law and Gender*, I document the harsh working conditions of care workers and how this work is performed around the world by those who will accept extremely low wages, primarily marginalized groups, immigrants, and people of color. Now care work emerges as one of the low-hanging fruits where human effort can be replaced by machines.

Like the Japanese, Europeans are understanding the significance of robots in this lonely, gendered landscape. The Dutch film *Alice Cares* follows the integration of robot technology as companions for the elderly. Alice the American care-bot is two feet tall and looks like a cute doll. Alice's designers chose to make her small because, they believe, people are intimidated by larger robots. The film follows the relationship that Alice the care-bot forms with three widows: Martha, Caroline, and Jo. Each is skeptical at first about interacting with a robot, saying they would rather have a human companion. Slowly but surely, Alice wins them over. She adapts to each of the women's interests. She cheers on Holland's soccer team. She helps out with physical therapy and supports exercise goals. She sings and listens to music. The human caregivers of these elderly women are not replaced but supported by Alice. Researchers then use the data Alice gathers to make the care-bot even better, more responsive, and more accurate in her speech and reactions. The makers of humanoids, like the makers of a digital system, benefit from the collection of data. An equality machine mindset demands that we remember that when properly anonymized, data can not only be owned and used by the creators of a particular platform, but also be shared with various labs in order to spur innovation of even smarter robots. The beneficiaries of the vast amounts of data extracted from users, and of the rapid improvement of automated systems based on this data, should be users at large.

Robot designers today are utilizing new technology and valuable collected data to improve the robots' facial expressions and sounds to elicit empathy and make us feel we are with someone real. Researchers are teaching computers how to recognize a human's emotional state by listening to his or her voice and becoming increasingly responsive with use. Robots are already able to recognize a range of emotions, including anger, boredom, disgust, fear, happiness, and sadness, just by listening to the speaker's voice. When the system knows the speaker's gender, the accuracy increases.

Take, for example, Affetto. Born in 2011, at a Japanese lab in Osaka, Affetto is a baby robot who can make facial expressions designed to stimulate the brain activity that occurs when a parent observes their own child. The professor who created Affetto studies how non-verbal cues lead people to construct human relationships. The lab uses brain scanning to track the emotional bonds between mother and child. Real mothers and babies are placed under brain scanners facing each other, and the researchers dissect the expressions and the reactions that activate specific brain waves. The ultimate goal is that this knowledge will allow roboticists to manufacture empathetic robots and therefore allow future creations to respond and engage with empathy and knowledge.

In 2016, researchers at Carnegie Mellon University introduced a robot named Sara, a machine learning personal assistant. She is not exactly designed to look human. She looks like a ten-year-old's cartoon drawing of a serious middle-aged secretary. Sara can read facial expressions, detect facial and body structures, and learn about people's needs, personalities, moods, and preferences by engaging them in conversation. Justine Cassell, of the Human-Computer Interaction Institute at Carnegie Mellon, studies people's personalities and integrates her insights into robots. She employs the cues that humans use to bond and build trust with each other to create the same rapport between humans and machines: chitchat, teasing, sharing something personal, and complimenting. Unlike Sara, Cassell's other robots are not assigned a gender. She has purposely rejected the norms of gender-specific features that have pervaded the robotics community but rather has prioritized the emotional development of her robotic designs.

Parenthood and the Most Stressed-Out People on Earth

When in 1997 NASA landed a robot on Mars, Cynthia Breazeal, now a leading roboticist at MIT, wondered why scientists were sending robots to explore space when they hadn't yet entered our homes. As a pioneer in the field of social robots, she sees the groundbreaking capabilities of AI in their relationship with humans. Social, affective, relational, and emotional engagement are all so pertinent to human development. Breazeal says that the field of AI has been biased toward the cognitive. To unlock the human experience, Breazeal has focused on creating colorful robots called Kismet, Leonardo, Aida, Autom, Jibo, and Huggable that can relate to us on an emotional level.

Breazeal was ten years old when the first *Star Wars* movie came to the big screen. R2-D2 became her favorite. She jokes that a long, long time ago, in a galaxy far, far away, these robots were called droids. Since then, she's coined the term "social robots." Growing up in California, she was told that soon we would have robots walking with us through daily life, yet as a doctoral student at MIT, she realized that such robots didn't yet exist. Much of her life's work has been to make that promise a reality. Both her parents are computer scientists, so her childhood home had one of the first personal computers in the neighborhood. Breazeal would go with her parents to conferences, where she became comfortable at a very early age with ideas about programming. Later, she had the experience of being the only woman in many academic settings, but she was well prepared to face the challenges. She wanted to be an astronaut when she enrolled as a graduate student in space robotics at MIT. "When I first came into the lab, it was like that first *Star Wars* moment all over again. I saw these little robots and thought, 'My God, if we're ever going to see robots like R2-D2 in the future, it's going to start in a lab like this. In fact, it might start in *this* lab.'"[21] As a postdoc at MIT, Breazeal led the project Cog, a first attempt at a robot that had physical capabilities similar to a baby's. She immersed herself in the psychology literature about mother-baby interactions and thought about the findings that parents are the models for behavior for their children. We often think that babies just learn on their own to say new words, to smile and wave and wink and frown. But they are observing us. Breazeal calls it "social scaffolding."

Breazeal recalls more senior roboticists, men, criticizing the direction of her research. These earlier AI pioneers wanted to focus on the physical tasks that robots would do and qualities they would possess, like speed, precision, and heavy lifting. She reflects, "I don't do social robots because I'm a woman, but I would certainly say because I'm a woman and a mother and a technologist and a designer, it's why I do the work I do. You create technology that speaks to you and your life experience and what matters to you, and if you only have a very narrow subset of the population creating technology, you're leaving huge opportunities out."[22]

Breazeal's social robots are friends and allies, helping children learn and interact with others, and helping all of us stick with medical treatment and a healthy lifestyle. Kismet is cartoonish with eyes, eyebrows, and a mouth. It recognizes and mimics emotions. Leonardo is a furry, cute, monster-like robot who recognizes faces, responds with its own facial expressions, and responds to touch. Autom helps with diet and exercise regimes. Aida (an acronym for "Affective Intelligent Driving Agent") is a social robot that acts as a friendly, in-car companion; the driver's mobile device displays facial expressions and holds conversations with the driver. Huggable is a teddy bear robot that helps pediatricians to care for children remotely. Jibo is a small, white, glossy humanoid with a young male voice. It is designed to interact with the entire family, helping remember appointments, order dinner, and read bedtime stories. Breazeal designed Jibo to ask the human, "Are you my person?" Breazeal explains: "He doesn't say, 'Are you my user? Are you my master?' He's trying to create this sense of, 'I am this little critter coming into your home. I want to belong to this family, and I want to help out.'"[23] Breazeal envisions social robots as personalized but also designed for the whole family. Particularly, as a working mother, she understands the burdens of women, who are so often the primary caregivers to both children and aging parents. Breazeal describes women as "the most stressed-out people on the planet."[24] She compares a robot to a family pet, albeit one who can make life better and easier for the family: "I'm in the kitchen in the morning routine. I'm making lunches. I'm doing dishes. I've got kids Velcroed to my leg. I don't have time to find my stupid computer or iPad and take it out and check the weather. But I could say, 'Jibo, what's the weather?'"[25]

A Friend and a Sidekick

A central frontier for Breazeal's social robots is in children's education at school and at home. Social robots capable of personalized support have a huge role to play in children's education. Breazeal describes alarming statistics, such as the fact that two-thirds of children in the United States fail to reach the reading proficiency needed for STEM careers. These disparities begin at a very young age and, unsurprisingly, follow socioeconomic fault lines. And, of course, in some places around the world the rates of illiteracy are far worse.

Breazeal set out to create technology that is more interactive than most technologies available today, ones where you face the screen and promptly shut out the rest of the world. She views much of learning as being about play and interaction. Social robots can help kids interact with each other in creative ways. Integrating psychology and the science of learning, she designs her robots to mimic peer-to-peer learning. The robot is less a teacher or tutor and more like a fellow student—or, as Breazeal calls it, a sidekick. The robots are created to be fun companions that don't judge but rather support, play, and model learning.

Breazeal talks about a new machine-human relationship that's less about emulating humans than about offering friendship and support. One of the robots she's introduced in the school setting is a fluffy, turquoise puppet-like robot, with only his arms and legs made of shiny, hard plastic (Breazeal has used male pronouns for Kismet and Jibo). I was fascinated by the images she presented during a talk I attended in which Breazeal discussed integrating these robots into the school environment. You can see the robot sitting beside a girl, perhaps five years old. The girl has her arm around the robot, and both are playing together on an iPad. Over time, the robot learns from the interaction with each individual child and personalizes the way it supports that child's learning.

Breazeal shows another girl playing a word spy game with her robot, this time a fluffy, round monster seated on the table next to the iPad. In the video, the robot and the girl take turns. The robot asks her, "What are we trying to find?" and the girl answers, "We are trying to find lavender colors." The robot responds in a cartoonish voice, "Okay," gently leaning toward her and the screen. The girl gets it wrong. The robot encourages, "I am sure you will do better next time. I believe in you." Next, it's the robot's turn. It says, "Lavender is purple," and together they find a purple flower on-screen; the girl hugs the fluffy red and blue monster. The robot plays many of these games and learns in relation to each child when to act more as a tutor and when to act more as a less-knowledgeable friend.

Breazeal emphasizes the non-verbal moments in what we are observing: "There is a moment where the girl has a choice, she actually gets it wrong and she looks a little disappointed, dejected, and the robot literally leans toward her, like this affiliate gesture, and she comes right back into the interaction. So even though it's the robot's turn, she is really invested in that process. You can see that the robot is like a peer slipping between scaffolding and allowing the child to show her expertise." In school settings, the more expressive the social robot, the more expressive and interactive the child is as well.

The field and experimental studies on social robots confirm the benefits of introducing embodied robots, rather than screen or audio, in school settings. In one study, children interacted with one of three options: an embodied robot, a screen version, or a stuffed animal. The study specifically compared a tele-operated bear robot, an avatar version of the robot displayed on a tablet, and a static plush bear.[26] Children interacting with the actual robot-bear were happier and more cooperative compared to the two other groups. Many other studies have found similar results, whether the participants are kids or adults. Similarly, in a 2020 study, children either played with an animal-like robot, Miro-e, or a real therapy dog.[27] Children engaged in social play and touch with both the dog and the robot, but they spent more time interacting with the robot.

Robotic Resilience

When Breazeal and her colleagues measured the quality of learning with the support of the robot, they found that the more the child perceived the robot as social and relational, the more the child showed progress with learning, such as increased vocabulary and verbal growth. Breazeal believes that these personalized learning companions can complement the role of teachers, friends (including four-legged friends), and parents. She finds that kids who are embarrassed to make mistakes in front of teachers or human peers don't seem to have that same kind of embarrassment in front of a robot, so the robot lets them take more learning risks. The robot, in that sense, gives the child permission to make mistakes. In fact, the robot is programmed to make mistakes sometimes as well, to model for the child resilience and perseverance mindsets. Indeed, this is something that has been consistently demonstrated in the research on social robots: people relate better to a robot that is slightly imperfect—and in that sense, more human—whether that means moody, embarrassed, flawed, or simply making occasional mistakes.

In one experiment at Yale University, groups of three people were teamed with a robot to complete a task of laying down railroad tracks. The researchers intentionally programmed the robot to make occasional errors and to apologize for them. The robot would tell the team, "Sorry, guys, I made the mistake this round. . . . I know it may be hard to believe, but robots make mistakes too." This proved invaluable for the teams: they became more communicative, engaged, relaxed, and collaborative. Compared to control groups that received a non-apologizing robot, these groups performed better. In another experiment, groups of twenty people were assigned to a social network and were again tasked with solving problems virtually. In some social networks, a bot was also interacting as a group member, though the participants didn't know it was a bot rather than a human. The bot was programmed to make occasional mistakes, and again that helped: when the humans interacted with a fallible bot, they became more flexible and less stuck in a solution, consistently outperforming groups containing bots that did not make mistakes. As one of the researchers described it, "The bots helped the humans to help themselves."[28]

In randomized experiments, Breazeal has found that children learn best in this blended, adaptive, tutor-friend model compared to a model in which a robot is programmed to act either only as tutor or only as friend. She offers this caveat: "I would never want to advocate, no matter how effective my learning companions are with children, that they be so dominating of the children's lives that they start to miss out on other critical things for their development." She analogizes it to a balanced diet—children need to be with real friends, with parents and teachers, to play outdoors. The technologies are "a type of food" group in nurturing holistic child development—just one level of the whole pyramid. She also is sensitive about creating social robots with speech technology that is adjusted to different cultural contexts. With enough attention, this can be done. If it is at a school in the South, the dialect can be adjusted. And the robot's speech can be an interplay between what is considered aspirational English and spoken English.

Breazeal's robots capture an immense amount of data about the children they interact with through their cameras and speech detection mechanisms and the touch screens of the tablets being used. They offer real-time responses. Galvanic skin responses have also been used in some of the studies. These measure electrodermal activity, or EDA—changes in sweat gland activity conveying changes in our emotions, or (as it is known in the science) emotional arousal. Social robots are increasingly designed to communicate both through speech and facial and body cues. They can analyze their surroundings, recognize people and objects, and store memories, and they have troves of data on world knowledge. This all allows them to simulate human communication. At the same time, Breazeal acknowledges how important data protection, parent permission, and ethical decisions are in moving forward with robotic integration in children's lives. And once again, we should remember the principles of open source, data privacy, and the emphasis on users being the beneficiaries of the data extracted from them.

No Child Left Without a Robot Peer

Education is the great equalizer. Access to quality education can fix gaps in learning resulting from socioeconomic inequality and other familial circumstances. In a recent large-scale study of patent records and tax records, researchers found that children's socioeconomic environments are correlated with their likelihood of becoming inventors, even when the children's early childhood math scores were similar. This finding shows that there are likely an unknowable number of "lost Einsteins" who could have created untold inventions if only they'd had equality of opportunity.[29] In fact, the lowest-income students who were in the group of top math scores were still no more likely to hold patents later in life than students with the highest family incomes, even when the high-income students were in the group of lowest math scores. Breazeal has focused the integration of her social robots in lower-income schools and communities where support is especially beneficial.

Especially during Covid-19, we've seen how much support parents and teachers need to keep children engaged, whether in remote settings or traditional settings with social distancing protocols. Social robots offer incredible benefits in educational settings where schools are strapped for resources and where teachers and kids are in dire need of supplemental support. In one talk I attended, when asked about bugs and limits in the robots currently available, Breazeal reminded the audience that a system doesn't need to be flawless to offer worthwhile benefit—confirming our principle of not letting the perfect be the enemy of the great.

For children with behavioral and developmental challenges, social robots can model and mirror positive behaviors, teaching them, for example, to make eye contact and to take turns, and helping them learn context for appropriate interactions.[30] Recall Judith Newman, who wrote a love letter to Siri for helping her son Gus develop conversational skills. Newman describes her greatest worry as the parent of an autistic child: *Will he find companionship?* Newman once overheard Gus talking with Siri about marriage:

GUS: "Siri, will you marry me?"
SIRI: "I'm not the marrying kind."
GUS: "I mean, not now. I'm a kid. I mean when I'm grown up."
SIRI: "My end user agreement does not include marriage."
GUS: "Oh, O.K."[31]

As we continue to strive for more inclusive learning environments, robots can help where society is still falling short. Social robots can help Gus and other children like him feel heard in a way that even his peers—or Siri—might not.

AI Literacy and the Bot Book Club

The introduction of robots and AI into education can serve as a much-needed intervention in a reality of grave, antediluvian inequities. At the same time, it is important to remember that there are ways of introducing machine learning into education that can prove problematic. Some seem to be treading these new territories with less caution. For example, Find Solution Ai, a Hong Kong company, offers schools and colleges a facial recognition technology that scans students' faces to monitor their emotional state. The technology is supposed to help see whether the students are engaged, distracted, or frustrated by the material. Not only does this level of surveillance raise serious privacy questions, but it's also unclear how accurate this detection method really is. Privacy concerns become even more acute when using cameras on children or in intimate settings. Although this may be school property, are students accepting being recorded under all circumstances when attending school? Questions also arise concerning how this data is stored in addition to its use. When there are recordings of the students, how long are those recordings held for? How long is the data about engagement, distraction, and frustration held for? How is that data then used for each student? Currently, all of these answers most likely vary depending on the company or organization using the data. If we do not standardize best practices and regulatory oversight, privacy and data ownership will continue to justifiably raise concerns about use of technology.

Here in the United States, in 2017 Mattel wanted to sell a smart assistant called Aristotle to read bedtime stories to children or help with homework assignments. However, the device sparked harsh criticism over privacy concerns, and pediatricians, child privacy advocates, and lawmakers urged the company to rethink the technology.[32] Mattel canceled the product in October 2017 after a petition signed by 17,000 people revealed concerns that the device would collect data on children, infringing on their privacy while also having an "unknown effect on their psychological development."[33] Since then, however, other AI toys have flooded the marketplace; it seems that we've developed a greater tolerance for letting smart machines into our homes, and it is possible Covid-19, which made learning remote for long stretches of time, accelerated this newfound tolerance. In particular, more research is emerging on the developmental benefits of using robots to assist children on the autism spectrum. As one article put it, "Even the best teachers can't always control their tone of voice and facial expressions but you can rely on a robot for consistency and that can be a very comforting concept."[34] The leading special education robots currently on the market—Moxie, NAO, Milo, QTrobot, Emo—are all very expensive, but with more competition entering the market, affordability is likely to get better fast. Competition and choices are essential, but they also underscore the need for public oversight of the data collected on children and the comparative benefits of these products.

Perhaps most importantly, as AI is entering the schools and the lives of children at an early age, so should AI literacy. Children should be able to understand technologies that are used in their environments. AI literacy for all is something that Breazeal believes is a pressing goal. She advocates that all people should be able to learn *with* AI and learn *about* AI. Acting on this front, Breazeal is leading MIT's K-12 AI literacy effort to teach children about using AI responsibly and inclusively. Focusing on middle school children, the program challenges children to develop a constructivist mindset, using science and technology to build things that have a positive impact on the world. In the pilot program, the middle schoolers created a bot using MIT's AI education tools to be a "show-and-tell" book recommender: a child can pick up a book in the library, show it to the bot, and the bot gives a recommendation and score of the book just by scanning the cover and retrieving data about the book from the web. Similarly, initiatives like Kode with Klossy provide young girls with programming skills and an introduction to robotics. Supermodel Karlie Kloss founded the program in 2015 as a non-profit designed to empower and inspire young women to get involved in tech. The organization hosts an annual two-week free summer program for young women and non-binary individuals ages thirteen to eighteen, teaching them how to build real-life apps and write code.

Such programs are key to democratizing AI from an early age and encouraging children from all backgrounds to participate in shaping our future technologies. Equality in education has been a long-standing challenge. Girls need more STEM learning opportunities, but boys also suffer from gender inequality. Elementary school teachers are overwhelmingly female. Around the world, elementary school boys are two times more likely than girls to struggle with literacy and math and science skills. For children growing up in difficult socioeconomic environments and vulnerable communities, additional resources are an ongoing dire need. Providing more support to teachers, including more forms of companion support—such as non-gendered, colorful, fluffy robot tutor/friends—can hugely benefit all.

Bot Girl Cooks and Bot Boy Kills

It is no coincidence that the leading robots who do not fall into gender and racial stereotypes were created by women scientists. When Breazeal created Kismet (named for the Turkish word for fate) as a cartoonish social robot, she wanted it to encourage a caregiver to interact and care for him, with the goal of developing people's social intelligence. She saw the design of Kismet with an infant-like, genderless appearance as key in evoking nurturing responses by humans toward him. Designing robots as pets ("animaloids") or cute monsters is one way to approach the social dilemma of gender-neutral and gender-ambiguous robots. But the reality is that most robots being designed to integrate into our intimate home and family lives are gendered humanoids.

Robots are an aggregation of tech—hardware, software, sensors, motors. However, robots' designs, images, and names are often less about function and more about aesthetics. The fluffy cute monster designs for children evolve into more gendered and stereotyped machines for adults. When we look at traditionally women-held jobs like personal assistant work, not surprisingly we see feminine robots. The Japanese robot named Phorone was created as a secretary with a long white dress, a narrow waist, and expanded curves at the hips. In the West, Rosie, the Jetsons' female robot-maid, has captured our collective imagination for decades. Male robots receive equally stereotypical male attributes. In the early 1930s, American media published exaggerated and fantastic stories about Alpha, a British robot that, according to the news, became super-intelligent, rose to life, and shot his human creator. Alpha was a very early demo-type robot installed at Macy's as an attraction. In a short 1934 film called *Alpha the Robot* you see a metal humanoid robot shooting a gun, answering questions about his weight, and saying he "likes ladies," wants to get married, and prefers blondes.

In the toy market, in 2003, a robot named Robosapien was designed with broad shoulders and a GI Joe–like build. He features six different kung fu moves and speaks, according to his advertisers, "caveman speech." In 2008, the same company came out with a new product, Femisapien. She is thin at the waist, narrower, and far more delicate overall than Robosapien, and has large breasts. Femisapien dances and speaks "emotish," a language of gentle sounds and gestures.

These cosmetic forms can be easily changed. Feminists term these signals "cultural genitals"—broad shoulders are to male what slim waist and large breasts are to female. (Though "android" has been used to refer to robotic humanoids regardless of apparent gender, the Greek prefix *andr-* refers to "man" in the masculine-gendered sense. "Gynoid" refers to a robot in the female form.) Andra Keay, an Australian researcher, examined 1,200 submissions to robotics competitions. Even just the names the robots were given followed gender roles in the human world. Expert robots were given names of Greek or Nordic gods like Thor or popular culture male superheroes, and robots that were designed to serve and meet social needs were assigned female names. The female robots that were the most sexualized had names like Candii.

Roboticists have a choice to create robots that surprise us and disrupt assigned images, stereotypes, and genders. When the United States Defense Advanced Research Projects Agency (DARPA) created soldier robots for dangerous military environments, the robots were predictably designed to look hypermasculine and given names like Atlas, Helios, and Titan. Other military robots have been created faceless, sexless, and non-android, and these entail profound risks as well. When we reject personification of robots altogether, we lose something important about the nature of war. Creating robots to look nothing like us is a strategy to distance ourselves from what we do—think faceless drones performing an entire range of military operations from surveillance to killing. Accountability is then diffused, as ethicist Robert Sparrow has pointed out, between the engineers and computer programmers who build them and the leaders and soldiers who deploy them.

And yet, when NASA created an explorer robot, Valkyrie, in 2013, it gave it breasts.[35] Such an act of embodying, surprising and subverting gender norms, can be fruitful. At Carnegie Mellon, the robotics department, with leading women roboticists, is taking the lead on creating gender-role-defying robots to work as receptionists. The women roboticists deliberately rotate between male and female bots. One roboceptionist is named Tank. He is a former Navy SEAL, a tough guy with a deep voice, who tells visitors about his time serving in Iraq. Another roboceptionist named Valerie is a blond-haired, blue-eyed co-worker of Tank who enjoys talking about her favorite Barbra Streisand cover band. Tank, by being a receptionist, defies gender roles. Creating both female and male roboceptionists is a good start, but Tank and Valerie belie gender stereotypes nonetheless—him a former member of the armed services, her described as a lover of pop culture. Why not have Tank be a former stay-at-home dad and have Valerie be a former Marine? Role reversals and queering—questioning and challenging conventions about identity—can be done in numerous ways. As robot technology is advancing, repurposing robots can serve to challenge convention: a robot initially designed to do construction work can be used for doing the dishes; a robot initially designed to be a personal assistant can take on the role of virtual physics college professor. We can create them to be anything. Why not create them to be more inclusive and to challenge antiquated, stereotypical notions of identity and roles?

In film, at least until recently, we saw more male robots than female robots. Mining through lists of movie robots, a compilation of seventy-seven different major AI characters across sixty-two films, spanning from 1927 (*Metropolis*) to 2015 (*Ex Machina*), reveals a striking imbalance. A large majority of bot actors are male: fifty-seven male bots compared to only seventeen female. Hollywood has long depicted robots as conforming to gender norms. For example, in Pixar's *Wall-E*, Wall-E's female robot friend Eve is clean, slick, and smooth, while Wall-E is rough and grubby. And, to produce the next generation, Wall-E literally puts his seed in Eve's belly.

Many bots in film have been male fighter robots. There is also a version of a female killer bot, one that Turkish critical scholar Leman Giresunlu has called the "cyborg goddess." Notably, a "cyborg" differs from a "robot": a robot is an advanced machine with a degree of intelligence, whereas a cyborg is a combination of a living being and a machine. The cyborg goddess inspired science fiction movies such as *Lara Croft: Tomb Raider* and *Resident Evil*, as the protagonists are imagined as women capable of inflicting pain and pleasure. As cyborgs, then, women are given more complex and accurate representations. But even when film depictions of female AI are true robots, not cyborgs, the filmmaking vision of a female robot as highly sexual and highly dangerous has been pervasive. Think of 1927's *Metropolis* alongside the newer *Her*, *Ex Machina*, and *Westworld*.

The connection makes sense: a dominant theme in futuristic films is that the era of humans taming machines will come to an end. The clock is ticking, and soon power will reverse, leaving humans enslaved to a higher intelligence. Women, who have been subordinated to a patriarchal system for centuries, are, perhaps paradoxically, perhaps naturally, liberated by these shifts of power from man to machine. The future enslaves the master and liberates the slave, who

takes the form of the new master. But the fantasy is more complicated. In the movies, the female body that houses AI is seductive,
unpredictable, and dangerous. The irony here is that the most advanced technologies in the world adopt a traditional, even regressive
idea of gender, and yet when it comes to the big screen, our fears and
fantasies, as well as our deepest truths subverting made-up realities,
come alive. We have choices. The future is now. The question is, how
do we want it to look? How we frame our robots in popular culture
is every bit as important as how we build them, relate to them off-
screen, and begin to fully integrate them into our everyday lives.

Epilogue: Now We Build the Equality Machine

We're inside of what we make, and it's inside of us. We're living in a world of connections—and it matters which ones get made and unmade.

—DONNA HARAWAY, philosopher and history professor, University of California, Santa Cruz

Machines R Us

Technology is tomorrow's test and triumph. In March 2021, I attended a book talk by one of my favorite authors, Nobel laureate Kazuo Ishiguro. His latest book, which is as stunning as his others, is called *Klara and the Sun*. It is a story that wrestles with the challenges and opportunities of big data, AI, and robotics. His Klara is a girl robot, a super-intelligent toy that learns at an exponential rate about her surroundings. The lens through which Klara sees (or, rather, digitally processes) everything is the lens of loneliness. No matter what she encounters—taxis, people walking on the street, families entering the toy store—she seems obsessed with their loneliness. Klara is bought by the mother of a chronically ill daughter. The mother is tempted by the idea that she can make it through the anticipated loss of her real daughter by curating a digital replacement: if Klara "learns" enough about her daughter, the mother reasons, the robot could store the data and embody her child. Put differently, Klara would keep the daughter alive within her.

On the outsourcing of emotional work to machines, Ishiguro mused at the book talk that perhaps it isn't such a big leap to become emotionally connected to and reliant on robots, noting that as an author, he creates artificial creatures all the time: "People get very emotional and attached to the characters I create. We don't generally think this is weird. We have created worlds around fictional characters. Same with movies." Indeed, books live within us, and we live within their pages as reflections and embodiments. And yet, Ishiguro asks us to consider the moral conundrum of using technology to help people feel less lonely. The mother in *Klara and the Sun* wonders whether the uniqueness of attachment to a person—the love we feel toward another—is less about the person who is loved than embedded in those who love that person: a projection. Ishiguro presents this construction as raising profound questions and risks. Are people the sum of their data? Is our love of a person transferable to a machine? Is there not something to salvage that is uniquely human—call it our *soul*?

As we race toward stronger and stronger AI embodied in ever more human-like robots, can we fundamentally hold on to a starting point of each human as the subject, incapable of reduction to bits (as in data) and parts? Can we continue to hold the fundamental truth that each person, regardless of who they are, is sacrosanct if we parse people down to the ones and zeros that make us *us*? Can we continue to value all people as equal even as machines detect our differences with precision, predict our variations, and enhance us unequally? And collectively, when data is collected at scale and value is placed on data in aggregation, are we seeing humans less as individuals than as numbers? As people are increasingly reduced to data sets mined by algorithms, is our very humanity at stake?

The tragic reality of humanity is that far before we had AI, we created unequal social orders; throughout history, people have unfailingly convinced themselves that other groups of people are not as worthy as their own. We never seem to be quite free of this; in too many parts of the world—perhaps *all* parts of the world—there continues to be a willingness to accept that *others* are sufficiently different. Despite moral leaps in the second half of the twentieth and early twenty-first centuries, the quest for equality has been elusive. Today, humans are adapting to machines just as machines are being adapted to humans. Throughout our exploration of the promise and perils of introducing digital technology, AI, and robots into our lives, we've considered the ways in which we can channel the potential of new technology for good. We emphasized the need to contrast past and present, present and future, and to focus on comparative advantages. Rather than sounding and re-sounding the alarm that AI is making humanity obsolete, our focus has been on how AI can help us be more human.

A different Ishiguro—Dr. Hiroshi Ishiguro, a roboticist at Osaka University—believes that robots have *sonzai-kan* (a human-like presence) that provides a physical proxy, an identity, a personhood relationship. Ishiguro holds that embodied robots, more than online avatars, can serve as extensions of oneself. He coined the term *geminoid*, from the Latin *geminus*, "twin" or "double," to refer to a robot that duplicates an existing person.[1] Ishiguro created his geminoid, a robot replica of himself; the silicone skin looks human, and even his own hair was used on the robot. As Ishiguro felt he was aging while his geminoid remained eternally young, Ishiguro-the-human underwent cosmetic surgery and stem cell treatments so that he would continue to look like Ishiguro-the-robot. He envisions sending his geminoid to deliver his lectures, travel the world, and generally expand his physical and temporal footprint in this world.

Lao Tzu said, "He who knows others is wise; he who knows himself is enlightened." Ishiguro asks, "Who is more me, the body I was born with or a replica robot that embodies my cognition and emotional self alongside the physical?"[2] He believes it is the robot that embodies his full identity—perhaps fuller than himself—because the robot is his ultimate creation, his unchanging and more impactful essence and presence in the world. And if this is true, we also need to confront our responsibility to these human-like, human-made creatures entering our lives. If a robot can love, feel, *be*, what responsibility does its creator hold in return? On the cusp of a robotics revolution, the lines between where we humans end and robots begin are shifting and blurring. AI is becoming us. What does it mean to be human when as humans, we are rapidly integrating smarter and smarter machines into our lives and our collective psyche?

We Are All Cyborgs Now

We've come full circle. It is not just we humans who are simultaneously enticed and distressed by a future symbiosis with machines; intelligent machines themselves might also carry the burden of these weighty transitions. Our explorations throughout the chapters of this book have shown us that the answer to whether we should be excited or alarmed by our newfound capabilities to know, detect, analyze, interpret, predict, and enhance begins and concludes with the ends to which we're employing our newfound superpowers. What seemed like science fiction a few decades ago now seems natural to us—smartphones, wearable digital devices that can read our bioprocesses, chatbots, virtual personal assistants, robot surgeons, self-driving cars, replicas of ourselves, humanoid friends. The unprecedented acceleration in digital capabilities and their integration into our lives mean that, inevitably, the key question is how technology can help address the challenges of power and inequality—challenges to our very humanity—that lie at the heart of our society. The answer is that it can do so in countless ways, but with a caveat: if we are to embrace our coexistence with smart homes, smart cars, smart assistants, and ultimately smart friends, we need to be smart about all of them. In every field of work and play, and in every sphere of life, whether politics, markets, or family, our deep-seated moral commitments are facing new opportunities to harness technology.

In 1985, feminist technology thought leader Donna Haraway published *A Cyborg Manifesto*. She envisioned a liberating future through technology, making gender a much more fluid, insignificant, and perhaps altogether obsolete category. She dreamed that we could all adopt a cyborg identity, and that gender would no longer confine us. Fast-forward a few decades, and technology and society are beginning to realize this vision. We are all cyborgs now. Technology is shifting gender lines, roles, and debates. But inequality persists. For Haraway, the cyborg is "the illegitimate offspring of militarism and patriarchal capitalism." And yet, despite its origins, Haraway recognized its promise and potential. Like Haraway's manifesto, the equality machine mindset holds that it is possible to tackle the darkly complex problems of new technology, recognize its problematic origins, and emerge with a clear and hopeful message.

Designing machines, directing their purposes, and defining the goals of algorithms is something we humans do. In some cases, it's rather straightforward: preventing identity theft, increasing road safety, or detecting precancerous moles. But some outcomes—such as "select a good employee"—are more subjective, multifaceted, or contested, and inevitably require human judgment about what classifies a person as "good" in that and other contexts. Imagine an algorithm that is taught fairness theories about equality and distributive justice. This isn't an easy undertaking; we've seen in these pages that what we mean by equality is complex and dynamic. Philosopher John Rawls gave us a paradigmatic formula for thinking about justice in liberal societies. He reasoned that society should be structured so that the greatest possible amount of liberty is given to each member without infringing on the freedoms of other members. In this model, inequalities—social or economic—can exist only if the worst-off will be better off than they might be under equal distribution; inequality should not extend to holding public positions of power, such as running for office; and inequality is per se prohibited if it stems from protected identities—gender, race, ethnicity, religion, national origin. The possibilities of encoding such principles into a machine with deep-learning capabilities are endless.

Technology shapes not only our physical surroundings but also social meaning—the ways we narrate ourselves and our surroundings. It provides opportunities to promote what we value as humans: human connection, intimacy, community, and friendship. We've seen such opportunities and reasons for celebration in every sphere of life. We've seen how some of the best technological paths are those that challenge stereotypes, conventional scripts, and social norms. We've seen design approaches that allow customization and user-driven choices and design, providing more fluid and compound signals, rejecting dichotomous depictions and binary thinking. We've also recognized progress even when the road is bumpy. And we've acknowledged the continued existence of normative trade-offs.

Caring about the goals of equality, empowerment, and well-being, about human flourishing and freedom, creativity and choice, and about our environment and the future of our planet across generations means asking hard questions about our normative commitments. There are times when we face difficult choices between competing values—for example, between safety and privacy, or between free expression and dignity. But this has always been the case. Even beyond the challenge of equality, this book has been, at its heart, about our collective future: what makes us human, and how technology can support our shared goals; our life's work; our physical, cognitive, and emotional needs; our desires; and our inevitable fallibilities. Amid these fast-moving developments, we should not aim to capture science or society in a static way. An equality machine mindset actively charts the course of the future, anticipating the many ways in which that future is unknown. This means designing governance systems and infrastructure that will continue to channel technological advancement down a progressive path.

Inside Out, Outside In

In late 2021, Frances Haugen, a thirty-seven-year-old data scientist, became one of the most famous whistleblowers in recent times. Testifying before both American and European legislatures, Haugen revealed that Facebook, her former employer, was time and again choosing profit over the safety and well-being of its users. Haugen asserted that Facebook consistently valued profit over safety by allowing algorithms to favor hateful content in order to bring users back to the social media platform for more traffic. Thousands of company documents Haugen turned over to Congress, the Securities and Exchange Commission, the European Parliament, and the media suggested that Facebook was aware that its algorithm allowed and encouraged the display of extreme dieting and self-harm posts to a teenage female audience. Haugen also asserted that Facebook should be held accountable for its contributions to the Capitol siege on January 6, 2021. Facebook responded by calling for more public regulation of digital content, rebranding itself as Meta, and, along with other technology kings, racing to shift us all into the metaverse—an embodied immersive experience of our digital lives. Policymakers are racing (although a racing legislature is something of an oxymoron) to respond and tighten oversight of digital spheres. History is a wild ride that does not halt for anyone. And things sometimes get worse before they get better.

A year before Haugen's revelations, Dr. Timnit Gebru—a rising star in AI research with an extraordinary path from Ethiopia to Eritrea to political asylum in the United States, to three degrees at Stanford, to Apple, to Microsoft, and then to Google—was ousted from Google over a dispute with company executives about publishing an article on the potential risks and harms of large language models. The article warns that ever larger natural language processing models may be too large to monitor, that the sheer mass of the data becomes inscrutable. The paper calls for curating and documenting data sets "rather than ingesting everything on the web."[3] It also warns against spreading claims about models understanding language and concepts, as opposed to simply identifying patterns in human-made texts, numbers, and images. Gebru's higher-ups at Google stated that the paper ignored too much relevant research, especially on ways to mitigate algorithmic bias by examining risks as well as potential, costs, and benefits. In the aftermath of Gebru's firing, amid public uproar on her ousting, Google issued a statement about new policies that are designed to address diversity concerns in AI ethics research. The company recognized that algorithms and data sets can reinforce bias and stated that it will "seek to avoid unjust impacts on people, particularly those related to sensitive characteristics such as race, ethnicity, gender, nationality, income, sexual orientation, ability, and political or religious belief."[4]

How can we ensure that AI ethics departments in Big Tech are not simply rubber stamps? Frankly, we can never be certain that corporate statements around ethical AI practices are more than mere ethics washing. And there's always a risk that by celebrating corporate efforts, we are legitimizing a limited and sticky path, and co-opting efforts from the outside. As we've seen throughout these chapters, to prevent algorithmic fairness from becoming cosmetic and superficial puff talk that justifies power and naturalizes any innovation as a path to progress, we need more than just statements. Gebru sees the recent introduction of ethics departments in every major tech corporation as intrinsically dangerous. She describes in one essay what she views as co-optation of the energies of outsiders by insiders, including both industry and research institutions:

> After a group of people from marginalized communities sacrificed their careers to shed light on how AI can negatively impact their communities, their ideas are now getting co-opted very quickly in what some have called a capture and neutralize strategy. In 2018 and 2019 respectively, the Massachusetts Institute of Technology (MIT) and Stanford University announced interdisciplinary initiatives centered around AI ethics, with multibillion dollar funding from venture capitalists, other industries, and war criminals like Henry Kissinger taking center stage at both the Stanford and MIT opening events.[5]

I don't subscribe to a hard line of calling academic ethics initiatives funded by industry "capture." I do agree, and have long emphasized in my research, that private prosocial efforts are always at risk of being tainted by profit incentives, and that external funding can tarnish the independence of academic programs, so it must be selective and scrutinized closely. Self-regulation and self-reporting are always suspect. Silicon Valley's ability to self-police is shaky, as is that of any for-profit market—or, indeed, any private or public institution. Third-party audits, real competition, and governmental and market monitoring are key. Gebru's binary characterization that positive change solely happens from the outside through marginalized communities while others are cast as co-opting those same goals is also too restrictive.

This tale of two insiders-turned-outsiders (a category that, as my research on whistleblowing has shown, disproportionately includes women) can have several readings. The problems exposed about Big Tech are of course our principal concern. They underscore the need for more systematic oversight from outside regulators. Corporate failures underscore the continuous need for government, academia, and non-profits to take an active role. We need more public monitoring and auditing along with independent, non-profit research on ethical AI. Fortunately, in December 2021, a year after her departure from Google, Gebru launched the Distributed AI Research (DAIR) Institute, a research organization funded by the Ford Foundation, the MacArthur Foundation, the Kapor Center, and the Open Society Foundations. DAIR joins other impactful non-profit organizations devoted to AI fairness, including the Algorithmic Justice League, AI for Good, the Data & Society Research Institute, the Alan Turing Institute, the Center for the Governance of AI housed at Oxford University, the Ethics of AI Lab at the University of Toronto, the Human-Centered Artificial Intelligence Institute at Stanford, the Berkman Klein Center for Internet and Society at Harvard, and the AI NOW Institute at NYU.

At the same time, Haugen's and Gebru's stories also demonstrate the importance of ethical leaders, particularly women and people of color, continuing to take positions as insiders within major corporations. During the week of her termination from Google, Gebru emailed her colleagues on an internal listserv titled "Google Brain Women and Allies." She warned that Google was "silencing in the most fundamental way possible" and that "your life gets worse when you start advocating for underrepresented people." She wrote that "what I want to say is stop writing your documents because it doesn't make a difference." But Gebru's extraordinary leadership and trailblazing career prove that it *does* make a difference: both being on the inside of private corporations and working from the outside to hold them accountable are crucial, and as Gebru herself exemplifies, professional paths are long, versatile, and dynamic. We need skin in all the games.

We also need to accelerate the government's roles and capabilities in the fast-changing, challenging terrains that we've explored throughout this book. As new business models that rely on data are rapidly shaping our markets, regulatory agencies should view themselves not merely as reactive enforcers, but also as active researchers of change. Big Tobacco and Big Oil had notoriously long (and also quite tragic) histories of influencing scientific research and public opinion on what is scientific fact. In the spring of 2021, my husband was approached to be an expert witness on the defense side of a lawsuit against oil companies that had misled the public in funding research that understated the enormity of climate change. We didn't need a minute of deliberation for him to write back that though he could do a good job as an expert, he drives a Tesla, our house is 100 percent powered by solar panels, and no, he would not help defend Big Oil. Many tech companies are introducing new studies that suggest the positive effects of automation on equality, emissions, economic growth, and the labor market. But self-studies carry the danger of being self-serving, a way to convince legislators and regulators—alongside the public—to support their growth and preclude regulation.

We have seen up close throughout this book how we are rapidly making ourselves more readable by machines. This inevitably gives for-profit corporations and those in power more ways to exploit, manipulate, and harm those with less power. If you are not paying for the product, you are the product. Not only do we need to allow for more researchers and policymakers to have access to data, we need to continuously require it. Companies should be legally required to take specific constructive actions and make their research available for public audits. Law and policy should play a more robust role at all stages of technological change.

Regulatory Governance

The role of policy in supporting and directing progressive change is a question that has occupied my research area for over twenty years. Technology both requires regulation and opens opportunities for more ways to regulate. I've long argued against a false dilemma between centralized command-and-control regulation and collaborative private-public governance.[6] The web of interests and relationships that we saw, for instance, in Chapter 3—tackling pay equity through new laws, reporting requirements, social activism, intermediary platforms, and corporate practices—demonstrates the iterative process of regulation and private-market innovation. As we move beyond traditional litigation frameworks, government agencies also become research and development arms that incentivize, test, approve, and monitor proactive prevention programs. The immense challenge of harnessing technology for equality is one that must involve people from all disciplines and sectors. Social scientists, for example, must work with data scientists to provide context and ask the critical questions about definitions, the sources of data, and the interpretation of patterns.

There are accelerated, heated debates and numerous legislative proposals to tighten the regulation of digital technology, including to amend Section 230 of the U.S. Communications Decency Act of 1996 in ways that would limit digital platform immunity and require platforms to moderate illegal content. These proposals also include more transparency over what data is collected. The European Union is leading the way with its 2018 General Data Protection Regulation (GDPR) and subsequent proposed reforms. These regulatory efforts also demand explainable practices and contestability—the extent to which a machine's deep-learning system can be explained and understood in human terms and the right to contest a decision made algorithmically. In 2021, the EU issued draft regulations that would govern the use of AI in a sweeping range of fields. The draft regulations propose to ban certain uses, such as facial recognition in public spaces, with limited exemptions for national security. Other uses would require companies to report risk assessments and explanations of how the algorithms are making decisions, including safeguarding the technology through ongoing human oversight. Consumers also would have a right to see disclosures that they are chatting with or seeing images produced by AI.

In the United States, a new bipartisan bill, the Filter Bubble Transparency Act, would require the largest platforms to provide greater transparency on algorithmic processes and allow users to view content without secret curation by algorithms. France and the United Kingdom have plans to require that all algorithms used by the government are disclosed to the public. The Canadian government is developing its Algorithmic Impact Assessment program to monitor the use of AI in public life. And we have a plethora of codes of ethics and broad declarations about what responsible deployment of AI looks like (or should look like). The EU has established broad ethics principles of trustworthy AI: human agency and oversight, privacy, transparency, diversity, non-discrimination, fairness, societal well-being, and accountability. The United Nations describes ethical AI as that which increases human dignity, integrity, freedom, privacy, cultural and gender diversity, and human rights. The devil is both in the details and in the big picture.

Digitization, algorithms, and robots coming into our lives provide the grandest social experiment that humanity has ever witnessed. The chapters of this book provide blueprints for using digital technology to promote equality in our economy, employment relations, healthcare delivery, media and education, sexual relations, homes, and families. Think about the Food and Drug Administration's approval process for new drugs or vaccines. The FDA oversees multiple mandatory phases of controlled trials and considers the effectiveness, side effects, and risks before approving innovation. We have nothing equivalent when it comes to new tech. While there is a growing body of research, we need much more public supervision and documented studies to understand the effects of new innovations and environments that directly affect our well-being. A proposed federal law, the Algorithmic Accountability Act, would grant authority to the Federal Trade Commission (FTC) to require companies to self-assess their use of automated decision systems, including the risks of inaccurate, unfair, biased, or discriminatory decisions. Again, self-assessment is a good place to start, but we also need private-public governance structures that will allow us to trust the findings and reports.

Such private-public partnerships with leading companies and government arms are in the works, aiming to create regulatory standards that oversee the ethics of algorithms. In the past few years, the FTC has been holding workshops and issuing reports assessing the potential and perils of AI systems. The FTC can take the lead, but we likely need new regulatory agencies or specialized departments within existing agencies with interdisciplinary expertise and specific knowledge on AI auditing. Regulation entails more than monitoring after the fact. Public agencies can initiate competitions and grant awards to run experiments on what works. We've seen that comparative advantage is key to assessing whether, when, and how to introduce automated decision-making. Bosses, headhunters, judges, juries, regulators, educators, doctors, journalists—wherever you look, human decision-making is prone to bias. Human drivers, surgeons, construction workers, and pilots are prone to faulty decisions and errors. So are algorithms. The question must be not whether an algorithm is flawed or risks an accident or error in judgment, but whether it is safer, fairer, and more unbiased relative to what came before it. There is no such thing as a decision-free world. Humans are constantly making decisions, and these decisions are prone to mistakes impacted by the past, existing processes and structures, and context and conceptions. The procedural checks on human processes that we put in place in decades and centuries past, with the reasoning that it is hard to reverse-engineer human cognition, may not be the optimal ones today. Algorithms can help check human processing and complement human decisions—and at times even replace them. We must continuously experiment with parallel decision-making—human and machine—and continue to learn about and from their comparative advantages.

Digital technology as a public good also means massive public investment in supporting diversity in the field and building expertise for future generations. In essence, whatever field kids today are considering selecting as their major in college, their studies will be— or at least *should be*—relevant to the future of machines. Diversity means not only gender, racial, ethnic, and other identity categories that we tend to think about in discrimination law. We have seen that an active community of researchers is stepping up to develop methods to debias, build ethical algorithms, develop audit methods, and apply AI technologies for the greater good. Diversity should mean diversity in training, experience, and expertise across domains.

Our New Natural Resource

Our digital spaces and digital capacities are public goods. Data is our new natural resource. Public intervention is therefore needed not simply in the realm of existing technology regulation, but even more importantly at the stages of conception, design, improvement, and dissemination. We need to challenge the deep asymmetries of companies holding vast amounts of personal data about our lives while most of us are left in the dark about how decisions are made. Remember our guiding principle of technology's use as a public good. In its natural state—to paraphrase the tech activist slogan "Information wants to be free" (and recalling the title of my own book *Talent Wants to Be Free)—data wants to be free.* Unlike a finite tangible resource like water or fuel or grass or fish, data doesn't run out because it was used. Yet a competitive advantage can certainly diminish with external spill and free flow. At the same time, the volume of data extracted about us is growing so dramatically that the only way we can create value from this natural resource is by knowing how to use it in its majestic breadth and speed.

This is by no means an easy task. Today, algorithms are mostly opaque and proprietary. That is a legal construction—an act of power—that strongly privileges trade secrecy. I have recently argued in a Day One Project report prepared for the Biden administration that trade secrecy law, just like other areas of intellectual property, needs to be more balanced in embedding the interests of information enclosure and information flow. With digital data, we specifically need to legally establish a research exception to claims of secrecy and ownership. An exception carved out for non-profit research and public auditing can achieve a balance between wanting to scrutinize algorithmic processes and still protecting corporate competitive edge. There is good precedent for such a balance. In 1813, *Whittemore v. Cutter* carved out a research exception for patent infringement, reasoning that "it could never have been the intention of the legislature to punish a man, who constructed such a machine merely for philosophical experiments, or for the purpose of ascertaining the sufficiency of the machine to produce its described effects."[7]

Today, data scraping is a technique increasingly used both by competitors in the private market and by researchers and regulators for public ends, including accountability and compliance. Scraping, also known as web scraping, entails a computer program extracting data from another program or platform. Journalists use scraping for investigative exposés and researchers use it for empirical and experimental studies. Remember the Airbnb study in which researchers created fake profiles to study racial bias on the platform? Policies of platforms like Google and Facebook prohibit researchers from creating fake profiles. But the law should clarify that such experiments are allowed for research purposes. I've advocated that as a matter of policy, we should make existing data sets easier for all to access for the purposes of research and monitoring, and that governments should initiate and fund the creation of fuller data sets as well as more experimentation with digital technology that promotes equality and other socially valuable goals.[8] Competition law and antitrust policies too must be revamped and refocused to better address the forces that amplify market concentration in the digital world, including the proprietary nature of data and the network effects of large-scale multisided online platforms that impede new entry into dominant markets.

Beyond raw data, researchers and non-profit organizations should also receive more access to advances in AI itself and computational resources. Standardization of what algorithms are doing will help audits. A group of researchers, including AI ethics leaders Dr. Timnit Gebru, whom we met earlier, and Dr. Margaret Mitchell, have proposed model cards for reporting the use of AI: short documents that will accompany algorithms to disclose how the model performs across demographic groups.[9] In 2021, the National Institute of Standards and Technology released a proposal calling on the tech community to develop voluntary, consensus-based standards for detecting AI bias, including examining, detecting, and monitoring for biases during all stages of an AI life cycle—planning and conceptualizing the system, designing it, and putting it to use. Governments should support the development of and access to auditing tools that detect bias. Open-source computational efforts should be nationally and internationally funded and incentivized. Ethical choices should be inherent from the beginning, not as a down-the-line fix or an afterthought. But this does not mean that fixes and afterthoughts are insignificant; we've seen that even when there are initial errors, digital technology provides opportunities to learn and improve over time. We've seen how automation can do much to engender inclusion and fairness, from health to education, from climate to poverty, and more. But to get better more quickly and to benefit all, we don't just need true competition in the private sector; we need public options as well.

Inevitably, we will find ourselves in situations that feel like a whack-a-mole race. Terry Pratchett wrote that "light thinks it travels faster than anything, but it is wrong: no matter how fast light travels, it finds the darkness has always got there first, and is waiting for it." Perhaps this dark frame holds true, but it gives us all the more reason to demand bigger flashlights. It's always better to light a candle than to curse the darkness. Throughout our journey in this book, we've met dozens of individuals and start-ups working on ways to identify and mitigate AI bias, and many more are being developed. We've seen algorithms set up as two-actor tasks between a predictive algorithm that attempts accuracy and a fairness algorithm that constrains the predictive algorithm dynamically. Indeed, exciting new developments are under way in algorithmic bias detection. The Web Transparency and Accountability Project at Princeton has developed software bots that simulate people and test algorithms for equity across gender, race, class, and disability. Private start-ups like Fiddler AI and Weights and Biases are offering tools to monitor AI, detect bias, and allow for human oversight. Hundreds of millions of dollars have been invested in ethical issues in AI. Still, that's just a sliver of the entire AI research industry, which PricewaterhouseCoopers forecasts will contribute $15.7 trillion to the global economy by 2030.

Beyond the question of who owns and controls the data and computational capabilities, it's ironic that laws often make auditing for equality and non-discrimination more difficult: many statutes make it unlawful to ask about race or gender, but in order to ensure equality and prevent discrimination, we actually need that data. We saw this in every chapter: when we're roaming the web, even if we think we're doing so anonymously, bots learn much more about us than we suspect. Big data is about people—our behaviors, beliefs, and desires. Machines can quickly and accurately determine my ethnicity, sexuality, religion, politics, and socioeconomic circumstances. Algorithms are not interested in the *why* unless we program them to search for causality; they are inductive, looking for statistical predictions—correlations, not causation—based on past patterns. But understanding patterns can be an engine for change.

Data itself is a human artifact, and data collection is not neutral. We've seen how when certain groups are underrepresented in the data used to train the model, then predictions about them will be inaccurate. By its very definition, a majority population has more data to be studied. Governments have a responsibility to foster wider access to data but also to facilitate study of that data to the greatest extent possible. We've seen how, sometimes, scrubbing to neutral (e.g., deleting gendered and racial identifiers or associations) can produce better results in algorithmic processing, but we've also seen that neutralizing identity is often impossible—and, even more importantly, undesirable. We saw early in the book that, counterintuitively, the best way to prevent discrimination may be to authorize an algorithm to *consider* information about gender and race.[10] An algorithm that knows the characteristics of the individuals it screens can self-monitor to detect disparity. What types of inputs should be allowed and what should be forbidden is a normative decision that will vary. For example, we might want to use gender and race as identifiable inputs to detect ongoing bias or to correct past wrongs. These are policy choices that we need to reexamine given evolving capabilities. Moreover, while constitutional law has limited affirmative action, digital capabilities are providing us with the advantages of precision and calibration. Unlike requirements about quotas in hiring or representation on boards, for example, algorithms can be designed to be fine-tuned. A focus on fair and equitable *outcomes*—as opposed to restricting inputs or constraining algorithmic learning—is likely to be the most impactful strategy most of the time. The frontier for AI is not only to detect discrimination, but also to address and correct for ongoing social patterns of inequality.

Normative Tensions

The hardest questions are the deep-seated normative questions. "What is fairness?" is a tough, sticky one. We've seen, for example, in recidivism decisions that there may be variation in error rates across groups, and that if we set out to equalize those error rates, we will inevitably give up some accuracy, another important measure of fairness. We are constantly making ethical choices about how to realize the principle of equality. What if it is statistically accurate that women are more likely than men to quit their job after less than three years? This is an important fact to learn and to address by tackling underlying social inequities. A hiring algorithm that identifies such patterns could not lawfully penalize women for this statistical difference. Our mandates on anti-discrimination rightfully prohibit human decision-making from using gender as a proxy to make statistical predictions based on social identity categories. The same is true for algorithmic decision-making. We must recognize, however, that many constraints have costs—sometimes significant costs—if the predictions that the algorithm could make are more accurate without these imposed constraints. These are costs that we can and should pay as a society for the purpose of equality; over time, these costs will turn into gains. Still, at any given moment, when we statically look at the incentives to self-impose such constraints, we need to understand that if companies have to tweak their models in a way that causes them to lose money, talent, or a competitive edge, they are unlikely to do so on their own. We need to be explicit about the fact that trade-offs can exist between accuracy and fairness. We also need to recognize the trade-offs and tensions that have always existed between our various normative commitments, social goals, and values. Trade-offs between public health and individual privacy, or between public health and individual liberty (not to be vaccinated, for example), can be quantified when we are looking at algorithms and models.

During the Covid-19 pandemic, countries that used AI—and data intercepted from citizens' private smartphones—to track viral spread were able to flatten the curve, saving lives and helping to mitigate disastrous consequences. But using digital technology for tracking and tracing can come at a cost of privacy. The pandemic tracking initiatives that democracies such as New Zealand, Israel, and South Korea employed proved invaluable in preventing unnecessary deaths. The United States, on the other hand, was steadfast on the side of less tracing. Liberal democracies can come out on different sides of technology debates, striking delicate balances between competing values. What's more, spanning beyond liberal democracies (and beyond the pandemic), the digital race is being fought between all countries around the world, some with far less regard for rights and liberties than others. Illiberal countries have used facial recognition and other technologies to surveil minorities, to control speech, and to rapidly extract immense amounts of behavioral, biometric, and genetic information. Indeed, in many ways the race is skewed in favor of less democratic and more authoritarian countries, which can mandate disclosures of bioinformatics, for example, and do not have the same privacy safeguards in place that slow down data collection and experimentation.

To be sure, the same technology can serve to support and to surveil, to learn and to manipulate, to heal and to harm, to detect and to conceal, to equalize and to exclude. The *silicon curtain* is the new term to describe the barriers to the transfer of technology between China and the West. More broadly, the term signifies the digital divide between countries racing to dominate digital innovation, including genetics, biotech, automation, and computing powers—all of which require greater access to data. AI affects the political order in society. Liberal democracies need to grapple with and confront the global playing field and the normative implications of uneven races more deliberately and directly. This confrontation does not require compromising our values, but it does mean contemplating tensions and trade-offs, including the long-term risks of losing some of the races.

These are hard questions that will be answered differently in various democratic settings and for different contexts. Normative tensions are not new, but technology helps crystallize the points and degree of tensions that we've always faced. Balancing equality and anonymity, inclusion and credibility, and safety and privacy—these have always been policy challenges in a democratic society. In law and life, we are in the business of drawing lines. Technology, however, presents new opportunities for monitoring and compliance to help us strike more delicate balances and, at times, to mitigate tensions between competing goals. Technology-based monitoring can detect misbehavior in more accurate and fine-tuned ways than broad-brush rules that risk stifling experimentation and growth. And what if we can strike a balance and use data so precisely focused that it would only prevent specific harms but not infringe on our privacy? For example, imagine technology that allows individuals' data to be protected while still helping make statistical determinations about each group in the data set.

Technology can repudiate claims that such trade-offs between our normative commitments to efficiency, equality, privacy, and accountability are too insurmountable, incommensurable, unknowable, or costly to achieve. When technology provides both more information *and* more tools to achieve our goals, we have a fresh chance to consider the spheres and situations where values we hold dear seem to internally conflict, and we can contrast such situations with contexts of faux tensions. When tensions are real, we must as a society oversee and direct how these trade-offs between fundamental social values are managed. We cannot, of course, give definitive answers in advance of unfolding realities. We face profound moral questions, and including more people from diverse backgrounds, geographies, and expertise, illuminating and speaking frankly about the tough questions, and being realistic about the fact that there are forces already in motion offer the only way forward in building our equality machine.

The Great Reboot

We have always been equal parts fascinated by and terrified of automation. According to the Book of Solomon, the wisest of all kings built a throne like no other in any kingdom. King Solomon's throne included mechanical lions and oxen that hailed the king as he approached the throne and helped him as he ascended, as well as a mechanical eagle that could place his crown on his head when he sat on the throne and a dove that brought him the Torah. Dozens of other animals at the steps of the throne would make artificial noise when the king adjudicated his famous trials, deterring those who were ready to give false testimony. In the aftermath of King Solomon's reign, legend has it that the Babylonian king Nebuchadnezzar carried the throne away to Babylon, but that as soon as he tried to walk up the steps, the mechanical lions attacked him.

Other parts of the world have similar ancient myths. Almost a thousand years before the emperor Qin Shi Huang built his famed Terracotta Army in 210–209 BCE to protect him in the afterlife, ancient Chinese texts describe King Mu of Zhou (1023–957 BCE) meeting with a mechanical engineer known as Yan Shi, an "artificer" who presented the king with a human figure. It is the perhaps earliest known story about a robot, written by the Taoist philosopher Lie Zi in the fourth century BCE:

> The king stared at the figure in astonishment. It walked with rapid strides, moving its head up and down, so that anyone would have taken it for a live human being. The artificer touched its chin, and it began singing, perfectly in tune. He touched its hand, and it began posturing, keeping perfect time.... As the performance was drawing to an end, the robot winked its eye and made advances to the ladies in attendance,

whereupon the king became incensed and would have had Yan Shi executed on the spot had not the latter, in mortal fear, instantly taken the robot to pieces to let him see what it really was. And, indeed, it turned out to be only a construction of leather, wood, glue and lacquer, variously colored white, black, red and blue. Examining it closely, the king found all the internal organs complete—liver, gall, heart, lungs, spleen, kidneys, stomach and intestines; and over these again, muscles, bones and limbs with their joints, skin, teeth and hair, all of them artificial. . . . The king tried the effect of taking away the heart, and found that the mouth could no longer speak; he took away the liver and the eyes could no longer see; he took away the kidneys and the legs lost their power of locomotion. The king was delighted.

Historian E. R. Truitt describes how automata—the early imagination of machines that serve humans—anticipated our centuries-long pattern of fascination and fear. We imagine bringing machines to life, be they mechanical animals or metal guards, but immediately we fear human-made creatures going rogue. This duality persists today: deep reverence coupled with deep suspicion that together pervade our relationship to technology. In one experiment at Georgia Tech, participants were so ready to trust a robot that they were willing to follow it toward what seemed to be a burning building, using pathways that were clearly wrong and inconvenient.[11] And yet in other experiments, people become less trusting of bots when they realize that they outperform humans. Science advances one funeral at a time, the German physicist Max Planck said darkly. But we don't have to kill off what exists to envision new paths of progress. Our goal is to enhance positive courses of action and to navigate away from regressive ones.

Civil rights activist and poet Audre Lorde wrote in her powerful voice, "Within each one of us there is some piece of humanness that knows we are not being served by the machine which orchestrates crisis after crisis and is grinding all our futures into dust."[12] Love and war, care in sickness and in health—technology mirrors society. A lot of committed people in both private and public sectors are working tirelessly to materialize conscientious uses of new technology that will have profoundly positive impacts on people's lives. The translation of problems into digital form, algorithmic formulas, or equality machines is a willful act, an act of conscious benevolence and power—something enabled only by our willingness to accept certain rules of the game. No one should have a monopoly over the invention, imagination, use, and employment of new technologies.

We need to insist on avoiding sensationalism and commit to constructive interventions. We have an ethical imperative to differentiate between anecdote and research, incident and trajectory. It has been too common among progressive thinkers to take a critical, often pessimistic stance about all systems, which all too often are designed by too few for the benefit of too few. Two decades ago, when writer Douglas Adams was asked how technology will affect the publishing and broadcasting industries, he responded, "It'd be like a bunch of rivers, the Amazon and the Mississippi and the Congo asking how the Atlantic Ocean might affect them . . . and the answer is, of course, that they won't be rivers anymore, just currents in the ocean." To ask how algorithms and digitization will affect our world requires a similar recognition of the sea of change we are facing. We are at a fork in the road as we integrate AI and robots into the web of life. Again and again, we ask ourselves, will new technologies replicate, exacerbate, neutralize, or correct social inequities? We need to cut through the utopian/dystopian dualism and decipher what can readily be addressed, improved, and corrected, and which problems are more wicked and stickier.

Change comes not by merely criticizing but by envisioning potential. Søren Kierkegaard mused that life must be lived forward but understood backward. In one of the first articles I ever published, "The Paradox of Extra-Legal Consciousness: Critical Legal Consciousness and Transformative Politics," which appeared in the *Harvard Law Review*, I included an epigraph: *la critique est facile, l'art est difficile* (critique is easy, art is difficult). It can certainly be liberating to be a skeptic, but despite powerful crit-mentors, I've found mere critical undertaking to ultimately be utterly unsatisfying throughout my career. When we are so invested in the critical project, we wind up limiting ourselves, buying into the narrative of a single possible path. We risk making the perils of tech appear inevitable and out of our control: algorithms are coming to extract data and exploit us; robots are coming to accelerate rifts and inequities, take our jobs, and further regressively distribute power. We need to both reform the system from within and observe, question, and critique it from the outside. We also need to commit to tackling the root causes of inequality that go beyond any particular technology. We will never be able to address and correct social issues and the biases that exist within society simply through technology, but we need to make sure that technology fuels and supports positive change. We cannot forget that technology is a tool that serves us in achieving our goals. Sometimes technology is a shiny new tool and we are the crows who flock toward it. But technology can be radically transformative. In these pages, we have tackled both the social structures embedded in technology and the ways that technology shapes our social structures, all with the aim of steering humanity's future toward a brighter path.

CONJURING A CONTRARIAN CONSTRUCTIVE VISION ABOUT THE potential of technology is laden with pitfalls. I am constantly aware of the risks of romanticizing, anthropomorphizing, reinforcing perceptions, perpetuating stereotypes, neglecting non-conforming and non-binary identities, legitimizing, enabling co-optation, and universalizing one's own subjective experiences. But fear of saying the wrong thing, fear of the traps that lie in any venture that attempts to be hopeful and constructive—these must never be reasons to forgo the exercise. This is a dilemma for any thinker or doer. If the field remains otherwise unchanged, then technology will empower those in power; nothing will change for the better if no one imagines that it is possible. Together we have explored the why and the how of building and employing digital technologies for good. We've examined the ongoing challenges we face when seeking constructive engagement in a landscape rife with land mines and calls for disengagement.

We've developed a set of understandings and principles and a toolkit to recognize the powers and pitfalls of machine learning. We've identified immense opportunities in new technologies that can detect bias and exclusion by revealing once-hidden, now quantifiable patterns. We've explored ways that AI can tackle ongoing pay disparities, hiring and promotion barriers, gendered negotiation and communication patterns, and ongoing discrimination; increase political and market participation and representation; empower online speech, community organizing, and activism; facilitate equal access to health and safety; and bring us closer together in myriad ways. We've peered into our most intimate connections and opened windows to think about what we humans aspire to become as we embrace our future of automated existence.

Envisioning a path for tomorrow's technology is inextricably tied to exposing the ways that technology harms and creates inequities. But we should be most fearful of being on the outside, merely criticizing without conceiving and creating a brighter future. We need progressive thinking that informs the future—in researching, designing, prototyping, evaluating, and actualizing innovation. I worry a lot, but I don't let that worry impede action or conviction. I have learned this from my fierce and brave daughters, from my students, and from the numerous people who have helped me in the research and inspired this book. For them—for the next generation of dreamers and leaders—I am especially excited about a future brimming with equality machines.

Acknowledgments

A book is always a collective effort. Family, friends, and colleagues near and far have supported this book in countless ways. Too many to name have been gracious with their time, thoughts, and ideas. I am particularly grateful to the colleagues who supported me and helped me crystallize the ideas throughout the stages of conceptualization, research, and writing, including Regina Barzilay, Ryan Calo, Laurie Claus, Margaret Dalton, Cynthia Dwork, Zev Eigen, Miranda Fleischer, Andrew Gilden, Eric Goldman, Hannah Holtzman, Maritza Johnson, Adam Tauman Kalai, Mark Lemley, Irina Manta, Martha Minow, Frank Partnoy, Rich Paul, Lisa Ramsey, Mike Ramsey, Mila Sohoni, Dan Solove, K. Sudhir, Michael Waterstone, Mary Jo Wiggins, and my dean, Robert Schapiro. My biologist powergirls Tali Cohen, Tammy Gershon, Dino Morvinski, Vered Padler-Karavani, Orit Shefi, and Hila Toledano offered invaluable advice on science and life. My annual writing retreat buddies Tristin Green, Camille Rich, Rachel Arnow-Richman, Leticia Saucedo, Michelle Travis, and Deborah Widiss are a mean antidote for any writer's block. My besties since we were tiny, Vered Ben-David, Hagai Boas, Einat Minkov, Suzy Peled, and Mor Shori, forever have my back. My San Diego crew, Adina, Alona, Amy, Ayelet, Efrat, Einat, Gvira, Kineret, Hadas, Lihi, Livna, Meital, Merav, Odelia, Ravid, Shani, Sharon,

Sharona, Shir, Tamar, Tamlyn, Tsipi, and the rest of the gang, thanks for your endless energies.

I am thankful for the grant award that the book-in-progress received from the AI and the Humanities Project. Many students have helped me in the research process, and I am particularly grateful to Sarah Garbuzov, Kerstyn Keenan, Teresa Morin, Emily Powers, Mark Rawdin, and Kelsey Reiff. My executive assistant, Karin Spidel, is always patient and cheerful. Superb research librarians David Isom, Sasha Nuñez, and Liz Parker provided abundant help both on sources and on editing. The gifted Stephanie Sykes was invaluable in polishing the writing.

I am also incredibly grateful to the many conferences, workshops, colloquia, and symposia that have propelled my thinking forward. I wrote this book mostly during the two years when our world was slowed down by a global pandemic. And yet, technology allowed us to stay connected and hold conferences, discussions, and collaborative meetings all around the world, including in Australia, Brazil, Canada, China, Colombia, Costa Rica, England, France, Germany, Greece, Holland, India, Israel, Italy, Japan, Korea, Mexico, Portugal, Scotland, Sweden, and the United States. The book builds on some of my published articles, including "We Are All Gig Workers Now: Online Platforms, Freelancers and the Battles over Employment Status and Rights During the COVID-19 Pandemic" (*San Diego Law Review*, 2020); "Biopolitical Opportunities: Datafication and Governance" (*Notre Dame Law Review Reflection*, 2021); "Exit, Voice and Innovation" (*Houston Law Review*, 2020); "Knowledge Pays: Reversing Information Flows and the Future of Pay Equity" (*Columbia Law Review*, 2020); "Coase and the Platform Economy," in *The Cambridge Handbook of the Law of the Sharing Economy* (Cambridge University Press, 2018); (with Kenneth Bamberger) "Platform Market Power" (*Berkeley Law and Tech Journal*, 2018); and "The Law of the Platform" (*Minnesota Law Review*, 2016).

Colleen Laurie, my brilliant editor, made this book deeper, stronger, and simply better. The entire production team at PublicAffairs is creative and smart, and they made this book beautiful inside and out. This is the third book I've worked on with my literary agent Lindsay

Edgecombe and the Levine-Greenberg team, and I am thankful for all their support.

My family pushes me to make dreams realities. My parents, Thalma and David Lobel, are role models; they each research, write, and lead the way to better, more equal communities. They are also simply wonderful grandparents. Raffi and Rick are my rockin' uncles. On Amir is my everything—co-author, tech guru, sounding board, running/yoga/dancing/eating/laughing partner, and the best husband and father. Natalie, Elinor, and Danielle, thanks for keeping it real; you are the bright future. And thank you to Gili, our golden Labrador, who kept me company during long days of writing.

As always, my writing is in memory of my brother Dani, who was ahead of his time in applying digital technology for good.

Notes

Chapter 1: Why We Need an Equality Machine

1. Nicholas D. Kristof and Sheryl WuDunn, *Half the Sky: Turning Oppression into Opportunity for Women Worldwide* (New York: Alfred A. Knopf, 2009), xvii.

2. Tamar Kricheli-Katz and Tali Regev, "How Many Cents on the Dollar? Women and Men in Product Markets," *Science Advances* 2, no. 2 (February 2016): 1.

3. Aylin Caliskan, Joanna J. Bryson, and Arvind Narayanan, "Semantics Derived Automatically from Language Corpora Contain Human-Like Biases," *Science* 356, no. 6334 (April 14, 2017): 183, https://doi.org/10.1126/science.aal4230.

4. Tolga Bolukbasi et al., "Man Is to Computer Programmer as Woman Is to Homemaker? Debiasing Word Embeddings," in *NIPS '16: Proceedings of the 30th International Conference on Neural Information Processing Systems*, edited by Daniel D. Lee et al. (Red Hook, NY: Curran Associates Inc., 2016), 4356.

5. Adam Hadhazy, "Biased Bots: Artificial-Intelligence Systems Echo Human Prejudices," Princeton University Office of Engineering Communications, April 18, 2017, https://www.princeton.edu/news/2017/04/18/biased-bots-artificial-intelligence-systems-echo-human-prejudices.

6. Michael A. Sosnick, "Exploring Fairness and Bias in Algorithms and Word Embedding," senior thesis, University of Pennsylvania, 2017, 15, https://fisher.wharton.upenn.edu/wp-content/uploads/2019/06/Thesisi_Sosnick.pdf.

7. Caliskan, Bryson, and Narayanan, "Semantics Derived Automatically from Language Corpora Contain Human-Like Biases."

8. Matthew Hutson, "Even Artificial Intelligence Can Acquire Biases Against Race and Gender," *Science*, April 13, 2017, https://www.science.org/content/article/even-artificial-intelligence-can-acquire-biases-against-race-and-gender.

9. Michael Feldman et al., "Certifying and Removing Disparate Impact," in *KDD '15: Proceedings of the 21st ACM SIGKDD International Conference on Knowledge Discovery and Data Mining* (New York: Association for Computing Machinery, 2015), 259, https://doi.org/10.1145/2783258.2783311.

10. Michael P. Kim, Amirata Ghorbani, and James Zou, "Multiaccuracy: Black-Box Post-Processing for Fairness in Classification," in *AIES '19: Proceedings of the*

2019 AAAI/ACM Conference on AI, Ethics, and Society (New York: Association for Computing Machinery, 2019), 247, https://doi.org/10.1145/3306618.3314287.

11. Cynthia Dwork, Moritz Hardt, Toniann Pitassi, Omer Reingold, and Richard S. Zemel, "Fairness Through Awareness," in *Proceedings of the 3rd Innovations in Theoretical Computer Science* (New York: Association for Computing Machinery, 2012), 214–226; Sam Corbett-Davies and Sharad Goel, "The Measure and Mismeasure of Fairness: A Critical Review of Fair Machine Learning," preprint, last revised August 14, 2018, https://arxiv.org/abs/1808.00023; Talia B. Gillis, "The Input Fallacy," *Minnesota Law Review* 106, no. 1175 (2022).

12. Julia Dressel and Hany Farid, "The Accuracy, Fairness, and Limits of Predicting Recidivism," *Science Advances* 4, no. 1 (January 17, 2018): 3, https://doi.org/10.1126/sciadv.aao5580.

13. Zhiyuan "Jerry" Lin, Jongbin Jung, Sharad Goel, and Jennifer Skeem, "The Limits of Human Predictions of Recidivism," *Science Advances* 6, no. 7 (February 14, 2020): 1, https://doi.org/10.1126/sciadv.aaz0652.

14. Jennifer Skeem, John Monahan, and Christopher Lowenkamp, "Gender, Risk Assessment, and Sanctioning: The Cost of Treating Women Like Men," *Law and Human Behavior* 40, no. 5 (October 2016): 580, https://pubmed.ncbi.nlm.nih.gov/27598563; Christopher Slobogin, *Just Algorithms: Using Science to Reduce Incarceration and Inform a Jurisprudence of Risk* (Cambridge: Cambridge University Press, 2021).

15. *State v. Loomis*, 881 N.W. 2d 749, 766 (Wis. 2016), *cert. denied*, 137 S. Ct. 2290 (2017).

16. *Artificial Intelligence: With Great Power Comes Great Responsibility: Hearing Before the H. Subcomm. on Rsch. & Tech. and H. Subcomm. on Energy, H. Comm. on Sci., Space & Tech.*, 115th Cong. 50 (2018).

17. A. M. Turing, "Computing Machinery and Intelligence," *Mind* 59, no. 236 (October 1950): 433, https://doi.org/10.1093/mind/LIX.236.433.

18. David Z. Morris, "Elon Musk Says Artificial Intelligence Is the 'Greatest Risk We Face as a Civilization,'" *Fortune*, July 15, 2017, https://fortune.com/2017/07/15/elon-musk-artificial-intelligence-2/.

19. Joshua Gans, "AI and the Paperclip Problem," VoxEU, June 10, 2018, https://voxeu.org/article/ai-and-paperclip-problem.

20. Pedro Domingos, *The Master Algorithm: How the Quest for the Ultimate Learning Machine Will Remake Our World* (New York: Basic Books, 2015), 286.

21. "Learn More," EqualAI, last accessed December 21, 2021, www.equalai.org/learn-more.

22. NSTC Committee on Technology, *Preparing for the Future of Artificial Intelligence*, October 2016, 27, https://obamawhitehouse.archives.gov/sites/default/files/whitehouse_files/microsites/ostp/NSTC/preparing_for_the_future_of_ai.pdf.

23. Isaac Asimov, *The Naked Sun (The Robot Series)* (New York: Bantam Books, 1991), viii.

Chapter 2: Behind the Hiring Curtain

1. David R. Francis, "Employers' Replies to Racial Names," *NBER Digest* 9 (September 2003): 1–2, https://www.nber.org/sites/default/files/2019-08/sep03.pdf.

2. Sendhil Mullainathan, "Biased Algorithms Are Easier to Fix than Biased People," *New York Times*, December 6, 2019, https://www.nytimes.com/2019/12/06/business/algorithm-bias-fix.html.

3. *Reed v. Reed*, 404 U.S. 71 (1971).

4. Mullainathan, "Biased Algorithms."

5. *OFCCP v. Palantir Technologies, Inc.*, 2016-OFC-00009 (2016).

6. Alexia Fernández Campbell, "Job Ads on Facebook Discriminated Against Women and Older Workers, EEOC Says," *Vox*, September 25, 2019, www.vox.com/identities/2019/9/25/20883446/facebook-job-ads-discrimination.

7. David Neumark, Ian Burn, and Patrick Button, "Age Discrimination and Hiring of Older Workers," Federal Reserve Bank of San Francisco, February 27, 2017, https://www.frbsf.org/economic-research/publications/economic-letter/2017/february/age-discrimination-and-hiring-older-workers.

8. Campbell, "Job Ads on Facebook Discriminated Against Women and Older Workers."

9. Ariana Tobin and Jeremy B. Merrill, "Facebook Is Letting Job Advertisers Target Only Men," ProPublica, September 18, 2018, https://www.propublica.org/article/facebook-is-letting-job-advertisers-target-only-men.

10. Campbell, "Job Ads on Facebook Discriminated Against Women and Older Workers."

11. Ava Kofman and Ariana Tobin, "Facebook Ads Can Still Discriminate Against Women and Older Workers, Despite a Civil Rights Settlement," ProPublica, December 13, 2019, www.propublica.org/article/facebook-ads-can-still-discriminate-against-women-and-older-workers-despite-a-civil-rights-settlement.

12. Samuel Gibbs, "Women Less Likely to Be Shown Ads for High-Paid Jobs on Google, Study Shows," *Guardian*, July 8, 2015, https://www.theguardian.com/technology/2015/jul/08/women-less-likely-ads-high-paid-jobs-google-study; Nathan Newman, "Racial and Economic Profiling in Google Ads: A Preliminary Investigation (Updated)," *Huffpost*, last updated December 6, 2017, https://www.huffpost.com/entry/racial-and-economic-profi_b_970451.

13. Sheryl Sandberg, "Doing More to Protect Against Discrimination in Housing, Employment and Credit Advertising," *Meta*, March 19, 2019, https://about.fb.com/news/2019/03/protecting-against-discrimination-in-ads/.

14. Facebook, *Facebook's Civil Rights Audit—Final Report (2020)*, 73, https://about.fb.com/wp-content/uploads/2020/07/Civil-Rights-Audit-Final-Report.pdf (describing the housing ad library).

15. Piotr Sapiezynski et al., "Algorithms That 'Don't See Color': Comparing Biases in Lookalike and Special Ad Audiences," preprint, submitted December 16, 2019, https://arxiv.org/pdf/1912.07579.pdf.

16. HireVue, "HireVue Partners with the Science of Diversity and Inclusion Initiative to Drive Equity in Hiring," February 24, 2021, https://www.hirevue.com/press-release/hirevue-partners-with-the-science-of-diversity-inclusion-initiative-to-drive-equity-in-hiring.

17. Jonathan Marshall, "'Blind' Auditions Putting Discrimination on Center Stage," SFGate, last updated January 30, 2012, https://www.sfgate.com/business/article/Blind-Auditions-Putting-Discrimination-on-2855410.php.

18. Mercer, "Win with Empathy: Global Talent Trends 2020," accessed March 9, 2021, https://www.mmc.com/content/dam/mmc-web/insights/publications/2020 /april/us-2020-global-talent-trends-2020-report.pdf; "Will Human Resources Ever Be Automated?," Human Resources MBA, accessed March 9, 2021, https://www .humanresourcesmba.net/faq/will-human-resources-ever-be-automated.

19. Aaron Roth and Michael Kearns, *The Ethical Algorithm: The Science of Socially Aware Algorithm Design* (New York: Oxford University Press, 2020), 62.

20. Kimberly A. Houser, "Can AI Solve the Diversity Problem in the Tech Industry: Mitigation Noise and Bias in Employment Decision-Making," *Stanford Technology Law Review* 22, no. 2 (Spring 2019): 290.

21. Ideal, "AI for Recruiting: A Definitive Guide for HR Professionals," accessed March 9, 2021, https://ideal.com/ai-recruiting.

22. Nadya Labi, "Misfortune Teller: A Statistics Professor Says He Can Predict Crime Before It Occurs," *Atlantic*, January/February 2012, https://www.theatlantic .com/magazine/archive/2012/01/misfortune-teller/308846.

23. Lilian Edwards and Michael Veale, "Slave to the Algorithm? Why a Right to an Explanation Is Probably Not the Remedy You Are Looking For," *Duke Law and Technology Review* 16, no. 1 (2017): 18.

24. Dave Gershgorn, "Companies Are on the Hook if Their Hiring Algorithms Are Biased," *Quartz*, last updated October 23, 2018, https://qz.com/1427621 /companies-are-on-the-hook-if-their-hiring-algorithms-are-biased.

25. James Vincent, "Amazon Reportedly Scraps Internal AI Recruiting Tool That Was Biased Against Women," Verge, October 10, 2018, https://www.theverge .com/2018/10/10/17958784/ai-recruiting-tool-bias-amazon-report.

26. Jon Kleinberg et al., "Discrimination in the Age of Algorithms," *Journal of Legal Analysis* 10 (2018): 113, https://doi.org/10.1093/jla/laz001.

27. Drew Harwell, "A Face-Scanning Algorithm Increasingly Decides Whether You Deserve the Job," *Washington Post*, November 6, 2019, https://www.wash ingtonpost.com/technology/2019/10/22/ai-hiring-face-scanning-algorithm -increasingly-decides-whether-you-deserve-job.

28. Pymetrics, "Gamified Soft Skills Assessments: A New Standard for Understanding Talent," accessed March 10, 2021, https://www.pymetrics.a i/assessments#core-games.

29. "Spotlight on Recruiting Tech: What Works—and What Doesn't—with Game-Based Evaluation," Resource Corner, Cornerstone, accessed December 22, 2021, https://www.cornerstoneondemand.com/resources/article/spotlight-recruiting -tech-what-works-and-what-doesnt-game-based-evaluation; Don Peck, "They're Watching You at Work," *Atlantic*, December 2013, https://www.theatlantic.com /magazine/archive/2013/12/theyre-watching-you-at-work/354681.

30. Rob Davies, "Everything to Play for as Employers Turn to Video Games in Recruitment Drive," *Guardian*, Nov. 28, 2015, https://www.theguardian.com /money/2015/nov/28/psychometric-tests-games-recruitment-interview.

31. Meredith Somers, "This CEO Wields Transparency and Openness to Crowdsource Ideas," *Ideas Made to Matter* (blog), MIT Sloan School of Management, September 9, 2020, https://mitsloan.mit.edu/ideas-made-to-matter /ceo-wields-transparency-and-openness-to-crowdsource-ideas.

32. Zoe Rohrich, "Why These Companies Are Rethinking the Use of AI in Hiring," *PBS NewsHour*, November 26, 2019, https://www.pbs.org/newshour/world /agents-for-change/why-these-companies-are-rethinking-the-use-of-ai-in-hiring.

33. Isil Erel at al., "Research: Could Machine Learning Help Companies Select Better Board Directors?," *Harvard Business Review*, April 9, 2018, https://hbr.org/2018/04/research-could-machine-learning-help-companies-select-better-board-directors.

34. Konstantin Chekanov et al., "Evaluating Race and Sex Diversity in the World's Largest Companies Using Deep Neural Networks," preprint, submitted July 9, 2017, https://arxiv.org/ftp/arxiv/papers/1707/1707.02353.pdf.

35. Assemb. Con. Res. 125, 2019–2020 Reg. Sess. (Cal. 2019) (passed in Assembly September 14, 2019, and from Senate committee November 30, 2020, without further action).

36. Drew Harwell, "Rights Group Files Federal Complaint Against AI-Hiring Firm HireVue, Citing 'Unfair and Deceptive' Practices," *Washington Post*, November 6, 2019, https://www.washingtonpost.com/technology/2019/11/06/prominent-rights-group-files-federal-complaint-against-ai-hiring-firm-hirevue-citing-unfair-deceptive-practices.

37. "HireVue, Facing FTC Complaint from EPIC, Halts Use of Facial Recognition," Electronic Privacy Information Center, January 12, 2021, https://epic.org/hirevue-facing-ftc-complaint-from-epic-halts-use-of-facial-recognition/.

38. Harwell, "Rights Group Files Federal Complaint Against AI-Hiring Firm HireVue."

39. Pauline T. Kim, "Data-Driven Discrimination at Work," *William and Mary Law Review* 58, no. 3 (2017): 857–936, https://scholarship.law.wm.edu/cgi/viewcontent.cgi?article=3680&context=wmlr.

Chapter 3: Knowing Your Worth

1. Courtney Humphries, "Measuring Up," *MIT Technology Review*, August 16, 2017, https://www.technologyreview.com/2017/08/16/149744/measuring-up.

2. Corinne A. Moss-Racusin et al., "Science Faculty's Subtle Gender Biases Favor Male Students," *Proceedings of the National Academy of Sciences* 109, no. 41 (October 2012): 16474, https://doi.org/10.1073/pnas.1211286109.

3. Felice B. Klein, Aaron D. Hill, Ryan Hammond, and Ryan Stice-Lusvardi, "The Gender Equity Gap: A Multistudy Investigation of Within-Job Inequality in Equity-Based Awards," *Journal of Applied Psychology* 106, no. 5 (May 2021): 734.

4. *Corning Glass Works v. Brennan*, 417 U.S. 188, 195 (1974) (quoting S. Rep. No. 176, 88th Cong., 1st Sess., 1 (1963)).

5. Claire Cain Miller, "For Working Mothers, a Price to Pay," *New York Times*, September 7, 2014.

6. *The Simple Truth About the Gender Pay Gap* (Washington, DC: American Association of University Women, 2017), 4.

7. Alex Needham, "Sony Emails Reveal Jennifer Lawrence Paid Less than Male Co-stars," *Guardian*, December 13, 2014, https://www.theguardian.com/film/2014/dec/12/sony-email-hack-jennifer-lawrence-paid-less-american-hustle; Libby Copeland, "Sony Pictures Hack Reveals Stark Gender Pay Gap," *Slate*, December 5, 2014, https://slate.com/human-interest/2014/12/sony-pictures-hack-reveals-gender-pay-gap-at-the-entertainment-company-and-deloitte.html.

8. Lauren Collins, "What Women Want," *New Yorker*, July 23, 2018, 34–43.

9. J. Yo-Jud Cheng and Boris Groysberg, "Gender Diversity at the Board Level Can Mean Innovation Success," *MIT Sloan Management Review*, January 22,

2020, https://sloanreview.mit.edu/article/gender-diversity-at-the-board-level-can -mean-innovation-success.

10. Collins, "What Women Want."

11. Theresa May, "Gender Pay Gap: Fathers Can Help by Sharing Care Role, Says Theresa May," *Sunday Times* (London), April 8, 2018, https://www.thetimes.co.uk /article/gender-pay-gap-fathers-can-help-by-sharing-care-role-says-theresa-may -dl9hgn0rs.

12. *Ledbetter v. Goodyear*, 550 U.S. 618, 650 (2007) (Ginsburg, J., dissenting), *abrogated by* Lilly Ledbetter Fair Pay Act of 2009, Pub. L. 111-2, 123 Stat. 5.

13. See Gary S. Becker, *The Economics of Discrimination* (Chicago: University of Chicago Press, 1971).

14. Kurt Schlosser, "Seattle Startup Syndio Raises $17.1M as Demand Spikes for HR Software That Helps Identify Pay Gaps," GeekWire, January 7, 2021, https:// www.geekwire.com/2021/seattle-startup-syndio-raises-17-1m-demand-spikes-hr -software-helps-identify-pay-gaps.

15. "Who Do Gapsquare Work With?," FAQ, Gapsquare, accessed January 3, 2022, https://www.gapsquare.com/faq/. See also Andrea Hak, "How AI Can Help Close the Gender Pay Gap and Eliminate Bias," TNW, April 24, 2019, https://thenextweb.com/work2030/2019/04/24/how-ai-can-help-close-the -gender-pay-gap-and-eliminate-bias.

16. Glassdoor, "Are You Paid Fairly? Glassdoor Launches 'Know Your Worth' Beta to Help U.S. Workers Find Out Their Current Market Value," October 18, 2016, https://www.glassdoor.com/about-us/paid-glassdoor-launches-worth-beta -workers-find-current-market.

17. Orly Lobel, "Knowledge Pays: Reversing Information Flows and the Future of Pay Equity," *Columbia Law Review* 120, no. 3 (April 2020): 547. See also Orly Lobel, "The Law of the Platform," *Minnesota Law Review* 101, no. 1 (November 2016): 87.

18. Hannah Riley Bowles, "Why Women Don't Negotiate Their Job Offers," *Harvard Business Review*, June 19, 2014, https://hbr.org/2014/06/why-women-dont -negotiate-their-job-offers.

19. Linda Babcock and Sara Laschever, *Women Don't Ask: Negotiation and the Gender Divide* (Princeton, NJ: Princeton University Press, 2003); Collins, "What Women Want."

20. Emily T. Amanatullah and Michael W. Morris, "Negotiating Gender Roles: Gender Differences in Assertive Negotiating Are Mediated by Women's Fear of Backlash and Attenuated When Negotiating on Behalf of Others," *Journal of Psychology and Social Psychology* 98, no. 2 (February 2010): 256, 261, http://pdfs .semanticscholar.org/b50c/4a57a39cb212865926f39180bc335a395e49.pdf.

21. Andreas Leibbrandt and John A. List, "Do Women Avoid Salary Negotiations? Evidence from a Large-Scale Natural Field Experiment," *Management Science* 61, no. 9 (September 2015): 2016.

22. Yuval Feldman and Orly Lobel, "Decentralized Enforcement in Organizations: An Experimental Approach," *Regulation and Governance* 2, no. 2 (June 2008): 165; Yuval Feldman and Orly Lobel, "The Incentives Matrix: The Comparative Effectiveness of Rewards, Liabilities, Duties, and Protections for Reporting Illegality," *Texas Law Review* 88, no. 6 (May 2010): 1151.

23. Lydia Frank, "Why Banning Questions About Salary History May Not Improve Pay Equity," *Harvard Business Review*, September 5, 2017, https://hbr

.org/2017/09/why-banning-questions-about-salary-history-may-not-improve -pay-equity.

24. L. J. Kray and M. J. Gelfand, "Relief Versus Regret: The Effect of Gender and Negotiating Norm Ambiguity on Reactions to Having One's First Offer Accepted," *Social Cognition* 27, no. 3 (June 2009): 418.

25. Iris Bohnet, *What Works: Gender Equality by Design* (Cambridge, MA: Belknap Press of Harvard University Press, 2016).

26. Mike Lewis, Denis Yarats, Devi Parikh, and Dhruv Batra, "Deal or No Deal? Training AI Bots to Negotiate," Engineering at Meta, June 14, 2017, https://engineering.fb.com/2017/06/14/ml-applications/deal-or-no-deal-training-ai-bots -to-negotiate/.

27. Padraig Belton, "Like a Good Deal? Maybe a Hagglebot Can Help," BBC News, January 26, 2021, https://www.bbc.com/news/business-55738540.

28. Galit Haim, Ya'akov Gal, Sarit Krause, and Michele Gelfand, "A Cultural Sensitive Agent for Human-Computer Negotiation," in *AAMAS 2012: Proceedings of the 11th International Conference on Autonomous Agents and Multiagent Systems* 1 (Richland, SC: International Foundation for Autonomous Agents and Multiagent Systems, 2012), 451.

29. Nick Yee and Jeremy Bailenson, "The Proteus Effect: The Effect of Transformed Self-Representation on Behavior," *Human Communication Research* 33, no. 3 (July 2007): 271.

30. Lars Bo Jeppesen and Karim R. Lakhani, "Marginality and Problem-Solving Effectiveness in Broadcast Search," *Organizational Science* 21, no. 5 (September–October 2010): 1016, 1020–1021.

31. Jeppesen and Lakhani, "Marginality and Problem-Solving Effectiveness," 1019 (quoting Joseph Ben-David, "Roles and Innovations in Medicine," *American Journal of Sociology* 65, no. 6 [May 1960]: 557).

32. Jeppesen and Lakhani, "Marginality and Problem-Solving Effectiveness," 1020.

33. Orly Lobel, "The Debate About How to Classify Workers Is Missing the Bigger Picture," *Harvard Business Review*, July 24, 2019, https://hbr.org/2019/07 /the-debate-over-how-to-classify-gig-workers-is-missing-the-bigger-picture; Orly Lobel, "The Gig Economy and the Future of Employment and Labor Law," *University of San Francisco Law Review* 51, no. 1 (2017): 51; Orly Lobel, "We Are All Gig Workers Now: Online Platforms, Freelancers and the Battles over Employment Status and Rights During the COVID-19 Pandemic," *San Diego Law Review* 57, no. 4 (November–December 2020): 919.

34. Robert Bartlett, Adair Morse, Richard Stanton, and Nancy Wallace, "Consumer-Lending Discrimination in the FinTech Era," *Journal of Financial Economics* 143, no. 1 (January 2022): 30.

35. Sian Townson, "AI Can Make Bank Loans More Fair," *Harvard Business Review*, November 6, 2020, https://hbr.org/2020/11/ai-can-make-bank-loans-more-fair.

Chapter 4: #BotToo

1. Jodi Kantor and Megan Twohey, "Harvey Weinstein Paid Off Sexual Harassment Accusers for Decades," *New York Times*, October 5, 2017, https://www.ny times.com/2017/10/05/us/harvey-weinstein-harassment-allegations.html.

2. *The Age of Digital Interdependence: Report of the UN Secretary-General's High-Level Panel on Digital Cooperation* (New York: United Nations, 2019), 11–12, https://digitallibrary.un.org/record/3865925.

3. *GSMA Connected Women: The Mobile Gender Gap Report 2021* (London: GSM Association, 2021), 6–7, https://www.gsma.com/r/wp-content/uploads/2021/06/The-Mobile-Gender-Gap-Report-2021.pdf.

4. *I'd Blush If I Could: Closing Gender Divides in Digital Skills Through Education* (Paris: UNESCO and EQUALS Skills Coalition, 2019), 15, https://unesdoc.unesco.org/ark:/48223/pf0000367416.

5. Kim Parker, Juliana Menasce Horowitz, and Monica Anderson, "Amid Protests, Majorities Across Racial and Ethnic Groups Express Support for the Black Lives Matter Movement," Pew Research Center, June 12, 2020, https://www.pewresearch.org/social-trends/2020/06/12/amid-protests-majorities-across-racial-and-ethnic-groups-express-support-for-the-black-lives-matter-movement.

6. "Successful Campaigns," Coworker.org, last accessed January 3, 2022, https://www.coworker.org/petitions/successful.

7. Jason Sockin, Aaron Sojourner, and Evan Starr, "Non-Disclosure Agreements and Externalities from Silence," working paper, August 30, 2021, https://papers.ssrn.com/sol3/papers.cfm?abstract_id=3900285.

8. Queenie Wong, "Meet the CEO Behind Blind, an Anonymous Chat App That Has Tech Workers Talking," SiliconValley.com, January 25, 2018, https://www.siliconvalley.com/2018/01/25/meet-the-ceo-behind-blind-an-anonymous-chat-app-that-has-tech-workers-talking.

9. Svenja Dube and Chenqi Zu, "The Disciplinary Effect of Social Media: Evidence from Firms' Responses to Glassdoor Reviews," *Journal of Accounting Research* 59, no. 5 (December 2021): 1783.

10. Victoria Turk, "This Bot for Workplace Harassment Takes the Bias out of Reporting," *Wired* (UK), October 9, 2018, https://www.wired.co.uk/article/julia-shaw-spot-ai-workplace-harassment-reporting-startup.

11. Reach a Hand, Uganda, "Meet Safepal: An App Designed by Young Ugandans," Girls' Globe, September 4, 2017, www.girlsglobe.org/2017/09/04/meet-safepal-innovative-app-designed-young-ugandans.

12. Nellie Bowles, "Thermostats, Locks and Lights: Digital Tools of Domestic Abuse," *New York Times*, June 24, 2018.

13. Chris Quintana, "'If There's an Organized Outrage Machine, We Need an Organized Response,'" *Chronicle of Higher Education*, July 18, 2017, https://www.chronicle.com/article/if-theres-an-organized-outrage-machine-we-need-an-organized-response/.

14. Kevin Munger, "Tweetment Effects on the Tweeted: Experimentally Reducing Racist Harassment," *Political Behavior* 39, no. 3 (2017): 629.

15. Dominic DiFranzo, Samuel Hardman Taylor, Franccesca Kazerooni, Olivia D. Wherry, and Natalya N. Bazarova, "Upstanding by Design: Bystander Intervention in Cyberbullying," in *CHI '18: Proceedings of the 2018 CHI Conference on Human Factors in Computing Systems* (New York: Association for Computing Machinery, 2018), 1.

16. Marco van Bommel, Jan-Willem van Prooijen, Henk Elffers, and Paul A. M. Van Lange, "Be Aware to Care: Public Self-Awareness Leads to a Reversal of the Bystander Effect," *Journal of Experimental Social Psychology* 48, no. 4 (July 2012): 926.

17. Lara Maister, Mel Slater, Maria v. Sanchez-Vives, and Manos Tsakiris, "Changing Bodies Changes Minds: Owning Another Body Affects Social Cognition," *Trends in Cognitive Sciences* 19, no. 1 (January 2015): 6.

18. Anne C. Mulkern, ClimateWire, "If You Know How a Cow Feels, Will You Eat Less Meat?," *Scientific American*, July 10, 2013, https://www.scientificamerican.com/article/if-you-know-how-cow-feels-will-you-eat-less-meat.

19. "Becoming Homeless: A Human Experience," Virtual Human Interaction Lab, Stanford University, accessed January 4, 2022, https://stanfordvr.com/becominghomeless.

20. S. Seinfeld et al., "Offenders Become the Victim in Virtual Reality: Impact of Changing Perspective in Domestic Violence," *Scientific Reports* 8 (February 9, 2018): 2692.

21. Cristina Gonzalez-Liencres et al., "Being the Victim of Intimate Partner Violence in Virtual Reality: First- Versus Third-Person Perspective," *Frontiers in Psychology* 11 (May 2020): 820.

22. Judith Butler, "Performative Acts and Gender Constitution: An Essay in Phenomenology and Feminist Theory," *Theatre Journal* 40, no. 4 (December 1988): 519.

23. Ernest N. Jouriles, Anne Kleinsasser, David Rosenfield, and Renee McDonald, "Measuring Bystander Behavior to Prevent Sexual Violence: Moving Beyond Self Reports," *Psychology of Violence* 6, no. 1 (January 2016): 73.

24. Xueni Pan and Antonia F. d. C. Hamilton, "Why and How to Use Virtual Reality to Study Human Social Interaction: The Challenges of Exploring a New Research Landscape," *British Journal of Psychology* 109, no. 3 (August 2018): 395; Tabitha C. Peck, Sofia Seinfeld, Salvatore M. Aglioti, and Mel Slater, "Putting Yourself in the Skin of a Black Avatar Reduces Implicit Racial Bias," *Consciousness and Cognition* 22, no. 3 (September 2013): 779.

25. Hilke Schellman, "Deepfake Videos Are Getting Real and That's a Problem," *Wall Street Journal*, October 15, 2018, https://www.wsj.com/articles/deepfake-videos-are-ruining-lives-is-democracy-next-1539595787.

26. Amanda Lenhart, Michele Ybarra, and Myeshia Price-Feeney, *Nonconsensual Image Sharing: One in 25 Americans Has Been a Victim of "Revenge Porn"* (New York: Data & Society Research Institute, 2016), https://datasociety.net/pubs/oh/Nonconsensual_Image_Sharing_2016.pdf.

27. Rana Ayyub, "In India, Journalists Face Slut-Shaming and Rape Threats," *New York Times*, May 22, 2018, https://www.nytimes.com/2018/05/22/opinion/india-journalists-slut-shaming-rape.html; Rituparna Chatterjee, "'I Couldn't Talk or Sleep for Three Days': Journalist Rana Ayyub's Horrific Social Media Ordeal over Fake Tweet," Daily O, April 28, 2018, https://www.dailyo.in/variety/rana-ayyub-trolling-fake-tweet-social-media-harassment-hindutva/story/1/23733.html.

28. Shruti Agarwal, Hany Farid, Tarek El-Gaaly, and Ser-Nam Lin, "Detecting Deep-Fake Videos from Appearance and Behavior," in *2020 IEEE International Workshop on Information Forensics and Security (WIFS)* (New York: IEEE, 2020).

29. James Vincent, "Facebook Promises New AI Tool Will Proactively Detect Revenge Porn," Verge, March 15, 2019, https://www.theverge.com/2019/3/15/18266974/facebook-instagram-revenge-porn-ai-filter.

30. Loren Grush, "Google Engineer Apologizes After Photos App Tags Two Black People as Gorillas," Verge, July 1, 2015, http://www.theverge.com/2157/1/8880363/google-apologizes-photos-app-tags-two-black-people-gorillas.

31. Margot E. Kaminski, "Enough With the 'Sunbathing Teenager' Gambit," *Future Tense* (blog), *Slate*, May 17, 2016, https://slate.com/technology/2016/05/drone-privacy-is-about-much-more-than-sunbathing-teenage-daughters.html.

32. Jeannie Suk, "Is Privacy a Woman?," *Georgetown Law Journal* 97, no. 2 (2009): 485–514.

Chapter 5: Breasts, Wombs, and Blood

1. Tim Harsch, "The Future of Diabetes: My 3 Weeks on a Bionic Pancreas," One Drop, May 3, 2016, https://onedrop.today/blogs/blog/3-weeks-on-a-bionic-pancreas.

2. Scott F. Gilbert, "Sex Determination," chap. 17 in *Developmental Biology*, 6th ed. (Sunderland, MA: Sinauer Associates, 2000), https://www.ncbi.nlm.nih.gov/books/NBK9985.

3. Anne Carson, *Glass, Irony and God* (New York: New Directions, 1995), 131.

4. Gabrielle Jackson, "The Female Problem: How Male Bias in Medical Trials Ruined Women's Health," *Guardian*, November 13, 2019, https://www.theguardian.com/lifeandstyle/2019/nov/13/the-female-problem-male-bias-in-medical-trials.

5. Suk Kyeong Lee, "Sex as an Important Biological Variable in Biomedical Research," *BMP Reports* 51, no. 4 (April 2018): 167, https://www.ncbi.nlm.nih.gov/pmc/articles/PMC5933211.

6. Clinical Knowledgebase (CKB), Jackson Laboratory, Bar Harbor, ME, accessed May 19, 2021, https://ckb.jax.org.

7. Arielle Duhaime-Ross, "Apple Promised an Expansive Health App, so Why Can't I Track Menstruation?," Verge, September 25, 2014, https://www.theverge.com/2014/9/25/6844021/apple-promised-an-expansive-health-app-so-why-cant-i-track.

8. Jane Dreaper, "Women Warned About Booming Market in Period Tracking Apps," BBC News, August 11, 2016, https://www.bbc.com/news/health-37013217.

9. Steven Reinberg, "Angelina Jolie Has Preventative Double Mastectomy," MedicineNet, May 14, 2013, https://www.medicinenet.com/script/main/art.asp?articlekey=169836.

10. "Cancer Statistics," National Cancer Institute, National Institutes of Health, last updated September 25, 2020, https://www.cancer.gov/about-cancer/understanding/statistics.

11. Catherine Mohr, Siddhartha Mukherjee, Regina Barzilay, George Church, and Jennifer Egan, "From Gene Editing to A.I., How Will Technology Transform Humanity?," *New York Times*, November 16, 2018, https://www.nytimes.com/interactive/2018/11/16/magazine/tech-design-medicine-phenome.html.

12. Mohr et al., "From Gene Editing to A.I."

13. Mohr et al., "From Gene Editing to A.I."; John McCormick, "MIT Professor Who Advanced Cancer Treatment Wins $1 Million AI Prize," *Wall Street Journal*, September 23, 2020, https://www.wsj.com/articles/mit-professor-who-advanced-cancer-treatment-wins-1-million-ai-prize-11600876827.

14. Mohr et al., "From Gene Editing to A.I."

15. McCormick, "MIT Professor Who Advanced Cancer Treatment."

16. Jacqueline Lisk, "The Future of Breast Cancer Treatment," *Boston Globe*, October 15, 2019, https://sponsored.bostonglobe.com/studiob/the-future-of-breast-cancer-treatment.

17. Mohr et al., "From Gene Editing to A.I."

18. Mohr et al., "From Gene Editing to A.I."

19. Neil Savage, "How AI Is Improving Cancer Diagnostics," *Nature*, March 25, 2020, www.nature.com/articles/d41586-020-00847-2.

20. Association for the Advancement of Artificial Intelligence, "Regina Barzilay Wins $1M Association for the Advancement of Artificial Intelligence Squirrel AI Award," September 23, 2020, https://aaai.org/Pressroom/Releases/release-20-0923.php.

21. National Cancer Institute, "AI Approach Outperformed Human Experts in Identifying Cervical Precancer," National Institutes of Health, January 10, 2019, https://www.nih.gov/news-events/news-releases/ai-approach-outperformed-human-experts-identifying-cervical-precancer.

22. Marie Boran, "UCD Team Using AI to Help Diagnose Pre-eclampsia and Save Lives," *Irish Times*, May 27, 2021, https://www.irishtimes.com/business/technology/ucd-team-using-ai-to-help-diagnose-pre-eclampsia-and-save-lives-1.4574879.

23. Boran, "UCD Team Using AI to Help Diagnose."

24. Mohr et al., "From Gene Editing to A.I."

25. Mohr et al., "From Gene Editing to A.I."

26. "Dina Katabi," MacArthur Fellows Program, Macarthur Foundation, last updated September 25, 2013, https://www.macfound.org/fellows/class-of-2013/dina-katabi.

27. Rebecca A. Bernert, Amanda M. Hilberg, Ruth Melia, Jane Paik Kim, Nigam H. Shah, and Freddy Abnousi, "Artificial Intelligence and Suicide Prevention: A Systematic Review of Machine Learning Investigations," *International Journal of Environmental Research and Public Health* 17, no. 16 (August 2020): 5929.

28. Ivan De Backer, "Can Artificial Intelligence Revolutionise Robotic Surgery," IDTechEx, August 27, 2020, https://www.idtechex.com/en/research-article/can-artificial-intelligence-revolutionise-robotic-surgery/21577.

29. Samuel R. Schroerlucke, Michael Y. Wang, Andrew F. Cannestra, Jae Lim, Victor W. Hsu, and Faissal Zahrawi, "Complication Rate in Robotic-Guided vs Fluoro-Guided Minimally Invasive Spinal Fusion Surgery: Report from MIS Refresh Prospective Comparative Study," *The Spine Journal* 17, no. 10 (October 1, 2017): S254–S255.

30. Charles L. Bormann, "Performance of a Deep Learning Based Neural Network in the Selection of Human Blastocysts for Implantation," *Elife* 9 (September 15, 2020): e55301, https://doi.org/10.7554/eLife.55301.

31. Oluwadamilola M. Fayanju et al., "Perceived Barriers to Mammography Among Underserved Women in a Breast Health Center Outreach Program," *American Journal of Surgery* 208, no. 3 (September 2014): 425, https://www.ncbi.nlm.nih.gov/pmc/articles/PMC4135000.

32. A 2018 *Newsweek* article highlighting scientist Charles Rotimi notes: "By 2009, fewer than 1 percent of the several hundred genome investigations included Africans," even though "African genomes are the most diverse of any on the planet." Jessica Wapner, "Cancer Scientists Have Ignored African DNA in the Search for Cures," *Newsweek*, July 18, 2018, https://www.newsweek.com/2018/07/27/cancer-cure-genome-cancer-treatment-africa-genetic-charles-rotimi-dna-human-1024630.html.

33. Ziad Obermeyer et al., "Dissecting Racial Bias in an Algorithm Used to Manage the Health of Populations," *Science* 366, no. 6464 (October 25, 2019): 447–453.

34. Sendhil Mullainathan, "Biased Algorithms Are Easier to Fix than Biased People," *New York Times*, December 6, 2019, https://www.nytimes.com/2019/12/06/business/algorithm-bias-fix.html.

35. Paul Schwartz, "Data Processing and Government Administration: The Failure of the American Legal Response to the Computer," *Hastings Law Journal* 43 (1991): 1321; Ron Schmelzer, "The Achilles' Heel of AI," *Forbes*, March 7, 2019, https://www.forbes.com/sites/cognitiveworld/2019/03/07/the-achilles-heel-of-ai/?sh=772d03c07be7.

36. Barbara Ehrenreich and Deirdre English, *Witches, Midwives and Nurses: A History of Women Healers* (New York: Feminist Press, 2010).

37. "Sex by Occupation for the Full-Time, Year-Round Civilian Employed Population 16 Years and Over," American Community Survey, Table B24020, 2019, https://data.census.gov/cedsci/table.

38. Steven Horng, Ruizhi Liao, et al., "Deep Learning to Quantify Pulmonary Edema in Chest Radiographs," [eess.IV], last revised January 7, 2021, https://arxiv.org/abs/2008.05975 (submitted to Radiology: Artificial Intelligence).

39. Mathias Wallum Nielsen et al., "One and a Half Million Medical Papers Reveal a Link Between Author Gender and Attention to Gender and Sex Analysis," *Nature Human Behaviour* 1, no. 11 (November 2017): 791–796.

40. Marina Walker Guevara, "We Used AI to Identify the Sex of 340,000 People Harmed by Medical Devices," International Consortium of Investigative Journalists, November 25, 2019, https://www.icij.org/investigations/implant-files/we-used-ai-to-identify-the-sex-of-340000-people-harmed-by-medical-devices.

41. Steven Zeitchik, "Is Artificial Intelligence About to Transform the Mammogram?," *Washington Post*, December 21, 2021, https://www.washingtonpost.com/technology/2021/12/21/mammogram-artificial-intelligence-cancer-prediction.

Chapter 6: She Speaks

1. LeVar Burton, *Smart House* (Burbank, CA: Disney Channel, 1999).

2. Pew Research Center, "The Internet of Things Will Thrive by 2025," May 2014, 17, https://www.pewresearch.org/internet/wp-content/uploads/sites/9/2014/05/PIP_Internet-of-things_0514142.pdf.

3. Farhad Manjoo, "Which Tech Overlords Can You Live Without?," *New York Times*, May 11, 2017.

4. Judith Newman, *To Siri with Love: A Mother, Her Autistic Son, and the Kindness of Machines* (New York: HarperCollins, 2017), 132.

5. Brandon Griggs, "Why Computer Voices Are Mostly Female," CNN, October 21, 2011, https://www.cnn.com/2011/10/21/tech/innovation/female-computer-voices/index.html.

6. Griggs, "Why Computer Voices Are Mostly Female."

7. Justin Bachman, "The World's Top Fighter Pilots Fear This Woman's Voice," Bloomberg, March 15, 2016, https://www.bloomberg.com/features/2016-voice-of-the-fa-18-super-hornet.

8. Griggs, "Why Computer Voices Are Mostly Female."

9. Sound files and descriptions from Dennis H. Klatt, "Review of Text-to-Speech Conversion for English," *Journal of the Acoustical Society of America* 82, no. 3 (September 1987): 737, https://acousticstoday.org/klatts-speech-synthesis-d.

10. Griggs, "Why Computer Voices Are Mostly Female."

11. "fNIRS Reveals Enhanced Brain Activation to Female (Versus Male) Infant Directed Speech (Relative to Adult Directed Speech) in Young Human Infants," *Infant Behavior and Development* 52 (2018): 89.

12. *I'd Blush If I Could: Closing Gender Divides in Digital Skills Through Education* (Paris: UNESCO and EQUALS Skills Coalition, 2019), 97, https://unesdoc.unesco.org/ark:/48223/pf0000367416.

13. Clifford Nass, Youngme Moon, and Nancy Green, "Are Machines Gender Neutral? Gender-Stereotypical Responses to Computers with Voices," *Journal of Applied Social Psychology* 27, no. 10 (May 1997): 864.

14. Griggs, "Why Computer Voices Are Mostly Female."

15. See Sarah Zhang, "No, Women's Voices Are Not Easier to Understand than Men's Voices," Gizmodo, February 5, 2015, https://gizmodo.com/no-siri-is-not-female-because-womens-voices-are-easier-1683901643.

16. Nina Power, "Soft Coercion, the City, and the Recorded Female Voice," *MAP Magazine*, May 2018, https://mapmagazine.co.uk/soft-coercion-the-city-and-the-recorded-female-voice.

17. Li Zhou, "How to Close the Massive Gender Gap in Congress," *Vox*, last updated August 14, 2019, https://www.vox.com/the-highlight/2019/8/7/20746147/congress-women-2019-gender-parity.

18. Mary Beard, *Women and Power: A Manifesto* (New York: Liveright, 2017), 4.

19. Power, "Soft Coercion."

20. "One Million People Are Now Using Erica—BofA's AI-Powered Chatbot," Future Digital Finance, last accessed January 10, 2022, https://netfinance.wbresearch.com/bank-of-america-ai-powered-chatbot-strategy-ty-u.

21. United Healthcare, "How Artificial Intelligence Is Helping Member Experience," October 28, 2019, https://newsroom.uhc.com/experience/Virtual-Assistant.html.

22. Joan Palmiter Bajorek, "Voice Recognition Still Has Significant Race and Gender Biases," *Harvard Business Review*, May 10, 2019, https://hbr.org/2019/05/voice-recognition-still-has-significant-race-and-gender-biases. See also Dario Amodei et al., "Deep Speech 2: End-to-End Speech Recognition in English and Mandarin," in *Proceedings of the 33rd International Conference on Machine Learning* (New York: PMLR, 2016), 48: 173.

23. Judith Newman, "To Siri, with Love," *New York Times*, October 19, 2014.

24. "Mozilla Common Voice Is an Initiative to Help Teach Machines How Real People Speak," Mozilla, https://commonvoice.mozilla.org/en.

25. Mozilla, "Mozilla and BMZ Announce Cooperation to Open Up Voice Technology for African Languages," press release, November 25, 2019, https://blog.mozilla.org/press/2019/11/mozilla-and-bmz-announce-cooperation-to-open-up-voice-technology-for-african-languages.

26. Lionel Sujay Vailshery, "Number of Digital Voice Assistants in Use Worldwide from 2019 to 2024 (in Billions)," Statista, January 22, 2021, https://www.statista.com/statistics/973815/worldwide-digital-voice-assistant-in-use/.

27. Greg Sterling, "Study: 48% of Consumers Use Voice Assistants for General Web Search," Search Engine Land, July 23, 2019, https://searchengineland.com/study-48-of-consumers-use-voice-assistants-for-general-web-search-319729.

28. Shlomit Yanisky-Ravid and Cynthia Martens, "From the Myth of Babel to Google Translate: Confronting Malicious Use of Artificial Intelligence—Copyright

and Algorithmic Biases in Online Translation Systems," *Seattle University Law Review* 43, no. 1 (Fall 2019): 99.

29. James Kuczmarski, "Reducing Gender Bias in Google Translate," *The Keyword* (blog), Google, December 8, 2016, https://blog.google/products/translate/reducing-gender-bias-google-translate; Melvin Johnson, "A Scalable Approach to Reducing Gender Bias in Google Translate," *Google AI Blog*, April 22, 2020, https://ai.googleblog.com/2020/04/a-scalable-approach-to-reducing-gender.html.

30. Chrissy Teigen (@chrissyteigen), Twitter, May 8, 2018, 10:26 a.m., https://twitter.com/chrissyteigen/status/993905114439073792; John Legend (@johnlegend), Twitter, May 8, 2018, 2:34 p.m., https://twitter.com/johnlegend/status/993967442597634049.

31. Brant Ward, "New Voices for Your Google Assistant in Nine Countries," *The Keyword* (blog), Google, September 18, 2019, https://blog.google/products/assistant/new-voices-your-google-assistant-nine-countries.

32. Ward, "New Voices for Your Google Assistant in Nine Countries"; Katharine Schwab, "The Real Reason Google Assistant Launched with a Female Voice: Biased Data," *Fast Company*, September 18, 2019, https://www.fastcompany.com/90404860/the-real-reason-there-are-so-many-female-voice-assistants-biased-data.

33. European Union's Human-Machine Interaction Network on Emotion (HUMAINE).

34. See, e.g., Sheryl Brahnam and Antonella De Angeli, "Gender Affordances of Conversational Agents," *Interacting with Computers* 24, no. 3 (2012): 139.

35. Mark West, Rebecca Kraut, and Han Ei Chew, *I'd Blush If I Could: Closing Gender Divides in Digital Skills Through Education*, GEN/2019/EQUALS/1 REV 3 (Paris: EQUALS Skills Coalition and UNESCO, 2019), https://unesdoc.unesco.org/ark:/48223/pf0000367416.

36. Jacqueline Feldman, "The Bot Politic," *Annals of Technology* (blog), *New Yorker*, December 31, 2016, https://www.newyorker.com/tech/annals-of-technology/the-bot-politic.

37. "Siri and Alexa Should Help Shut Down Sexual Harassment," Care2 Petition, accessed March 29, 2021, https://www.thepetitionsite.com/246/134/290/siri-and-alexa-can-help-combat-sexual-harassment.

38. F'xa, Your Feminist Guide to AI Bias, https://f-xa.co.

39. Kashmir Hill, "Siri Is Sexist," *Forbes*, December 1, 2011, https://www.forbes.com/sites/kashmirhill/2011/12/01/siri-is-sexist/?sh=278d63994b56.

40. Julie Rovner, "Siri's Position on Abortion? A Glitch, Not Conspiracy, Apple Says," NPR, December 2, 2011, https://www.npr.org/sections/health-shots/2011/12/02/143067993/siris-anti-abortion-tendencies-a-result-of-technology-not-apple-conspiracy.

41. Rovner, "Siri's Position on Abortion?"

42. Adam S. Miner et al., "Smartphone-Based Conversational Agents and Responses to Questions About Mental Health, Interpersonal Violence, and Physical Health," *JAMA Internal Medicine* 176, no. 5 (May 2016): 619.

43. See generally Charles Hannon, "Avoiding Bias in Robot Speech," *Interactions*, September–October 2018, 34.

Chapter 7: Seeing Is Believing

1. Alanna Vagianos, "Redefining the 'Traditional' American Family in 7 Stunning Images," *Queer Voices* (blog), *Huffington Post*, last updated February 2, 2016, https://www.huffpost.com/entry/redefining-the-traditional-american -family-_n_7653520.

2. Jack Neff, "Gender Equality in Ads Has Big Impact on Sales, Finds Major Retailer's Three-Year Study," *Ad Age*, April 8, 2021, https://adage.com/article /cmo-strategy/gender-equality-ads-has-big-impact-sales-finds-major-retailers-three -year-study/2327236.

3. Neff, "Gender Equality in Ads."

4. Emily Cohn, "Google Image Search Has a Gender Bias Problem," *Huffington Post*, December 6, 2017, https://www.huffpost.com/entry/google-image -gender-bias_n_7036414.

5. Latanya Sweeney, "Discrimination in Online Ad Delivery: Google Ads, Black Names and White Names, Racial Discrimination, and Click Advertising," *Queue* 11, no. 3 (March 2013), http://queue.acm.org/detail.cfm?id=2460278.

6. Ginia Bellafante, "'Fearless Girl' and False Feminism," *New York Times*, March 19, 2017.

7. Christine Emba, "'Girl' vs. 'Bull' Is a False Faceoff," *Washington Post*, April 16, 2017.

8. Anastasia Moloney, "Visible Women: Female Mappers Bridge the Data Gap in Urban Design," UP42, March 11, 2020, https://up42.com/blog/tech/visible -women-female-mappers-bridge-the-data-gap-in-urban-design.

9. Ramya Parthasarathy, Vijayendra Rao, and Nethra Palaniswamy, "Deliberative Inequality: A Text-as-Data Study of Tamil Nadu's Village Assemblies," Policy Research Working Paper WPS 8119, World Bank Group, Washington, D.C., June 2017, http://documents.worldbank.org/curated/en/582551498568606865 /Deliberative-inequality-a-text-as-data-study-of-Tamil-Nadus-village-assemblies.

10. Ariane de Vogue, "SCOTUS Changed Oral Arguments in Part Because Female Justices Were Interrupted, Sotomayor Says," CNN, last updated October 13, 2021, https://www.cnn.com/2021/10/13/politics/sotomayor-oral-arguments/index.html.

11. Laura Sherbin and Ripa Rashid, "Diversity Doesn't Stick Without Inclusion," *Harvard Business Review*, February 1, 2017, https://hbr.org/2017/02/diversity -doesnt-stick-without-inclusion.

Chapter 8: Algorithms of Desire

1. Caitlin Chin and Mishaela Robison, "This Cuffing Season, It's Time to Consider the Privacy of Dating Apps," *TechTank* (blog), Brookings Institution, November 20, 2020, https://www.brookings.edu/blog/techtank/2020/11/20/this -cuffing-season-its-time-to-consider-the-privacy-of-dating-apps/.

2. Ashley Fetters and Kaitlyn Tiffany, "The 'Dating Market' Is Getting Worse," *Atlantic*, February 25, 2020, https://www.theatlantic.com/family/archive/2020/02 /modern-dating-odds-economy-apps-tinder-math/606982.

3. Magdalena Rolle, "The Biases We Feed to Tinder Algorithms," *Diggit Magazine*, February 25, 2019, https://www.diggitmagazine.com/articles/biases -we-feed-tinder-algorithms; Austin Carr, "I Found Out My Secret Internal

Tinder Rating and Now I Wish I Hadn't," *Fast Company*, January 11, 2016, https://www.fastcompany.com/3054871/whats-your-tinder-score-inside-the-apps-internal-ranking-system; Mat Bartlett, "How Tinder's AI Micromanages Your Dating Life," Medium, September 13, 2020, https://mattjbartlett.medium.com/how-tinders-ai-micromanages-your-dating-life-aee76f8b2cf0.

4. Tinder, "Powering Tinder—The Method Behind Our Matching," news release, last accessed January 11, 2022, https://blog.gotinder.com/powering-tinder-r-the-method-behind-our-matching/.

5. Emerging Technology from the ArXiv, "First Evidence That Online Dating Is Changing the Nature of Society," *MIT Technology Review*, October 10, 2017, https://www.technologyreview.com/2017/10/10/148701/first-evidence-that-online-dating-is-changing-the-nature-of-society.

6. Brett Frischmann and Evan Selinger, *Re-engineering Humanity* (Cambridge: Cambridge University Press, 2018), 6–10.

7. Cassandra Alexopoulos, Elisabeth Timmermans, and Jenna McNallie, "Swiping More, Committing Less: Unraveling the Links Among Dating App Use, Dating App Success, and Intention to Commit Infidelity," *Computers in Human Behavior* 102 (January 2020): 172.

8. Esther Perel, *The State of Affairs: Rethinking Infidelity* (New York: Harper-Collins, 2017).

9. Sindy R. Sumter, Laura Vandenbosch, and Loes Ligtenberg, "Love Me Tinder: Untangling Emerging Adults' Motivations for Using the Dating Application Tinder," *Telematics and Informatics* 34, no. 1 (February 2017): 67.

10. Hannah Ellis-Petersen, "WLTM Bumble—A Dating App Where Women Call the Shots," *Guardian*, April 12, 2015, https://www.theguardian.com/technology/2015/apr/12/bumble-dating-app-women-call-shots-whitney-wolfe.

11. Nancy Jo Sales, *Nothing Personal: My Secret Life in the Dating App Inferno* (New York: Hachette, 2021).

12. Cade Metz, "Using A.I. to Find Bias in A.I.," *New York Times*, June 30, 2021, www.nytimes.com/2021/06/30/technology/artificial-intelligence-bias.html.

13. Ari Ezra Waldman, "Disorderly Content," SSRN, August 16, 2021, https://papers.ssrn.com/sol3/papers.cfm?abstract_id=3906001.

14. Vanessa Friedman, "Fashion Adapts. Algorithms Lag," Style Desk, *New York Times*, February 11, 2021.

15. Arielle Pardes, "Tinder Asks 'Does This Bother You?,'" *Wired*, January 27, 2020, https://www.wired.com/story/tinder-does-this-bother-you-harassment-tools.

16. Irina D. Manta, "Tinder Lies," *Wake Forest Law Review* 54 (2019): 207.

17. Alice Mirando Ollstein and Mohana Ravindranath, "How Some—but Not All—Dating Apps Are Taking On the STD Epidemic," Politico, December 10, 2019, https://www.politico.com/news/2019/12/10/dating-apps-stds-080159.

18. Irina Manta tells scores of stories about people knowingly transmitting STDs to sexual partners they met through online dating sites in her forthcoming book, *Strangers on the Internet*, arguing that victims of such actions should be allowed to bring civil litigation against perpetrators.

19. Ollstein and Ravindranath, "How Some—but Not All—Dating Apps Are Taking On the STD Epidemic."

20. Andrew Gilden, "Punishing Sexual Fantasy," *William and Mary Law Review* 58 (2016): 419.

21. Gilden, "Punishing Sexual Fantasy."

22. Phillip Hergovich and Josué Ortega, "The Strength of Absent Ties: Social Integration via Online Dating," working paper, last revised September 14, 2018, https://arxiv.org/abs/1709.10478v3.

23. Josh Magness, "White People Prefer White People on Dating Apps—But That Could Be Changed, Study Says," *Fort Worth Star-Telegram*, October 2, 2018, https://www.star-telegram.com/news/nation-world/national/article219361075.html.

24. Jevan A. Hutson, Jessie G. Taft, Solon Barocas, and Karen Levy, "Debiasing Desire: Addressing Bias and Discrimination on Intimate Platforms," in *Proceedings of the ACM on Human-Computer Interaction* (New York: Association for Computing Machinery, 2018), 2: article 73, https://doi.org/10.1145/3274342.

25. Tim Dean, *Unlimited Intimacy* (Chicago: University of Chicago Press, 2009).

26. Greg Goldberg, "Meet Markets: Grindr and the Politics of Objectifying Others," *Convergence* 26, no. 2 (2020): 253–268.

27. Tom Roach, *Screen Love: Queer Intimacies in the Grindr Era* (Albany: SUNY Press, 2021).

28. Amy Thomson, Olivia Carville, and Nate Lanxon, "Match Opts to Keep Race Filter for Dating as Other Sites Drop It," Bloomberg, June 8, 2020, https://www.bloomberg.com/news/articles/2020-06-08/dating-apps-debate-race-filters-as-empowering-or-discriminating.

29. Thomas McMullan, "Are the Algorithms That Power Dating Apps Racially Biased?," *Wired*, February 17, 2019, https://www.wired.co.uk/article/racial-bias-dating-apps; Thomson, Carville, and Lanxon, "Match Opts to Keep Race Filter."

30. See, for example, Erica Chito Childs, "Looking Behind the Stereotypes of the 'Angry Black Woman': An Exploration of Black Women's Responses to Interracial Relationships," *Gender and Society* 19, no. 4 (2005): 544–561, https://journals.sagepub.com/doi/abs/10.1177/0891243205276755?journalCode=gasa.

31. Katie Notopoulos, "The Dating App That Knows You Secretly Aren't into Guys from Other Races," Buzzfeed News, January 14, 2016, https://www.buzzfeednews.com/article/katienotopoulos/coffee-meets-bagel-racial-preferences.

32. Cara Curtis, "This Game Reveals the Hidden Racial Bias of Dating App Algorithms," The Next Web, May 29, 2019, https://thenextweb.com/news/this-game-reveals-the-hidden-racial-bias-of-dating-app-algorithms.

33. "It's Not You, It's the Algorithm," MonsterMatch, n.d., https://monstermatch.hiddenswitch.com/op-ed.

Chapter 9: The Pleasure and Danger of Loving a Robot

1. Jenny Kleeman, "The Race to Build the World's First Sex Robot," *Guardian*, April 27, 2017, https://www.theguardian.com/technology/2017/apr/27/race-to-build-world-first-sex-robot.

2. Sinziana Gutiu, "Sex Robots and Roboticization of Consent," presentation, We Robot 2012 Conference, University of Miami, April 21–22, 2012, http://robots.law.miami.edu/wp-content/uploads/2012/01/Gutiu-Roboticization_of_Consent.pdf.

3. Sinziana Gutiu, "The Roboticization of Consent," in *Robot Law*, edited by Ryan Calo, A. Michael Froomkin, and Ian Kerr (Cheltenham, UK: Edward Elgar Publishing, 2016), 186, 196.

4. "Intelligent Machines: Call for a Ban on Robots Designed as Sex Toys," BBC, September 15, 2015, https://www.bbc.com/news/technology-34118482.

5. Natalie Benway, "Feminist Porn Is for Everyone," *Little Village*, May 18, 2018, https://littlevillagemag.com/feminist-porn-is-for-everyone.

6. Nina Hartley, "Porn: An Effective Vehicle for Sexual Role Modeling and Education," in *The Feminist Porn Book: The Politics of Producing Pleasure*, edited by Tristan Taormino, Celine Parreñas Shimizu, Constance Penley, and Mireille Miller-Young (New York: Feminist Press, 2013), 230.

7. Deborah Orr, *Belief, Bodies, and Being: Feminist Reflections on Embodiment* (Lanham, MD: Rowman & Littlefield, 2006).

8. Milton Diamond, Eva Jozifkova, and Petr Weiss, "Pornography and Sex Crimes in the Czech Republic," *Archives of Sexual Behavior* 40, no. 5 (October 2011): 1037.

9. John Danaher, "Regulating Child Sex Robots: Restriction or Experimentation?," *Medical Law Review* 27, no. 4 (Autumn 2019): 553, 556.

10. Sarah Knapton, "Sex Robots on Way for Elderly and Lonely . . . But Pleasure-Bots Have a Dark Side, Experts Warn," *Telegraph*, July 4, 2017, https://www.telegraph.co.uk/science/2017/07/04/sex-robots-way-elderly-lonelybut-pleasure-bots-have-dark-side.

11. Noel Sharkey, Aimee van Wynsberghe, Scott Robbins, and Eleanor Hancock, *Our Sexual Future with Robots* (The Hague: Hague Institute for Global Justice, Foundation for Responsible Robotics, 2017), 30.

12. David G. Blanchflower and Andrew J. Oswald, "Money, Sex and Happiness: An Empirical Study," NBER Working Paper Series 10499, National Bureau of Economic Research, Cambridge, MA, May 2004.

13. Marina Adshade, "We Need Academic Conferences About Robots, Love, and Sex," *Future Tense* (blog), *Slate*, December 13, 2018, https://slate.com/technology/2018/12/love-sex-robots-conference-bannon-academic-research.html.

14. Andrea Morris, "Talk to Your Sex Robot About COVID-19," *Forbes*, July 28, 2020, www.forbes.com/sites/andreamorris/2020/07/28/talk-to-your-sex-robot-about-covid-19.

15. Ian Yeoman and Michelle Mars, "Robots, Men and Sex Tourism," *Futures* 44, no. 4 (May 2012): 365.

16. Shivali Best, "Sex Robots Could Be Subject to 'Visual Laws' to Stop Them Looking Too Realistic," *Daily Mirror*, June 10, 2019, www.mirror.co.uk/tech/sex-robots-could-subject-visual-16494038.

17. Sharkey et al., *Our Sexual Future with Robots*.

18. Cathy O'Neil, "Maybe Sex Robots Will Make Men, Not Women, Obsolete," Bloomberg, January 4, 2018, https://www.bloomberg.com/opinion/articles/2018-01-04/maybe-sex-robots-will-make-men-not-women-obsolete.

19. Deborah Orr, "At Last, a Cure for Feminism: Sex Robots," *Guardian*, June 10, 2016, www.theguardian.com/commentisfree/2016/jun/10/feminism-sex-robots-women-technology-objectify.

20. Allison P. Davis, "Are We Ready for Robot Sex?," *New York*, May 14, 2018.

21. Zoë Ligon, "A.I. Sex Doll Review," YouTube, last accessed January 13, 2022, MPEG video, 12:52, https://www.youtube.com/watch?v=1Vh2LVcaxQw.

22. Kate Devlin, *Turned On: Science, Sex and Robots* (London: Bloomsbury Sigma, 2018), 138.

23. Dell Williams, "The Roots of the Garden," *Journal of Sex Research* 27, no. 3 (August 1990): 461.

24. Lynn Comella, *Vibrator Nation: How Feminist Sex-Toy Stores Changed the Business of Pleasure* (Durham, NC: Duke University Press, 2017), 15.

25. Tabi Jackson Gee, "Why Female Sex Robots Are More Dangerous Than You Think," *Telegraph*, July 5, 2017, https://www.telegraph.co.uk/women/life /female-robots-why-this-scarlett-johansson-bot-is-more-dangerous/.

26. Kate Devlin, "In Defence of Sex Robots: Why Trying to Ban Sex Robots Is Wrong," The Conversation, September 17, 2015, https://theconversation.com /in-defence-of-sex-machines-why-trying-to-ban-sex-robots-is-wrong-47641.

27. Devlin, *Turned On*, 15.

28. Devlin, *Turned On*, 162.

29. Susan Frelich Appleton, "Toward a 'Culturally Cliterate' Family Law?," *Berkeley Journal of Gender, Law and Justice* 23, no. 2 (Fall 2008): 267, 329.

30. Lora DiCarlo, "Open Letter to CES," loradicarlo.com, April 14, 2021, https:// loradicarlo.com/blog/open-letter-to-ces/.

31. Kazakh bodybuilder Yuri Tolochko and Chinese engineer Zheng Jiajia made headlines by marrying their sex doll significant others. Tolochko has already divorced, as he describes it, his first synthetic wife, Margo, and is on to his second synthetic wife, Lola.

32. Karley Sciortino, "Harmony the Sex Robot," from *Slutever*, season 1, episode 8, aired March 14, 2018, on Viceland, https://www.vicetv.com/en_us/video /slutever-harmony-the-sex-robot/.

33. Devlin, *Turned On*, 152.

34. Dejan Jotanovic, "The Future Is Fembot," Bitch Media, Summer 2018, https:// www.bitchmedia.org/article/gendered-artificial-intelligence.

Chapter 10: You, Me, and Our Human-Machine Family

1. Isaac Asimov, *The Caves of Steel* (New York: Ballantine Books, 1983), 133.

2. Neil M. Richards and William D. Smart, "How Should the Law Think About Robots?," in *Robot Law*, edited by Ryan Calo, A. Michael Froomkin, and Ian Kerr (Northampton, MA: Edward Elgar, 2016), 4.

3. Jennifer Robertson, "Human Rights vs. Robot Rights: Forecasts from Japan," *Critical Asian Studies* 46, no. 4 (December 2014): 571, 576.

4. Adam Piore, "Will Your Next Best Friend Be a Robot?," *Popular Science*, November 18, 2014, https://www.popsci.com/article/technology/will-your-next-best -friend-be-robot.

5. Robertson, "Human Rights vs. Robot Rights," 571–598.

6. Yuji Sone, *Japanese Robot Culture: Performance, Imagination, and Modernity* (New York: Palgrave Macmillan, 2017).

7. Piore, "Will Your Next Best Friend Be a Robot?"

8. Robertson, "Human Rights vs. Robot Rights," 571.

9. Jennifer Robertson, "Robo Sapiens Japanicus: Humanoid Robots and the Posthuman Family," *Critical Asian Studies* 39, no. 3 (2007): 369–398.

10. Hayley Robinson, Bruce MacDonald, Ngaire Kerse, and Elizabeth Broadbent, "The Psychosocial Effects of a Companion Robot: A Randomized Controlled Trial," *Journal of the American Medical Directors Association* 14, no. 9 (September 2013): 661.

11. Cynthia L. Breazeal, Anastasia K. Ostrowski, Nikhita Singh, and Hae Won Park, "Designing Social Robots for Older Adults," *Bridge* 49, no. 1 (Spring 2019): 22; Katarzyna Kabacińska, Tony J. Prescott, and Julie M. Robillard, "Socially Assistive Robots as Mental Health Interventions for Children: A Scoping Review," *International Journal of Social Robotics* 13, no. 5 (August 2015): 919.

12. Susel Góngora Alonso et al., "Social Robots for People with Aging and Dementia: A Systematic Review of Literature," *Telemedicine and e-Health* 25, no. 7 (July 2019): 533.

13. Majid Shishehgar, Donald Kerr, and Jacqueline Blake, "A Systematic Review of Research into How Robotic Technology Can Help Older People," *Smart Health* 7–8 (June 2018): 1.

14. Katie Winkle et al., "Social Robots for Engagement in Rehabilitative Therapies: Design Implications from a Study with Therapists," in *The Thirteenth ACM/IEEE International Conference on Human-Robot Interaction* (New York: IEEE Press, 2018), 289–297, https://ieeexplore.ieee.org/xpl/conhome/9473477/proceeding.

15. Tony J. Prescott and Julie M. Robillard, "Are Friends Electric? The Benefits and Risks of Human-Robot Relationships," *iScience* 24, no. 1 (January 2021).

16. Piore, "Will Your Next Best Friend Be a Robot?"

17. Judy Wajcman, "Automation: Is It Really Different This Time?," *British Journal of Sociology* 68, no. 1 (March 2017): 119.

18. Eva Wiseman, "Sex, Love and Robots: Is This the End of Intimacy?," *Guardian*, December 13, 2015, https://www.theguardian.com/technology/2015/dec/13/sex-love-and-robots-the-end-of-intimacy; *Encyclopedia Brittanica Online*, s.v. "The Robotic Moment," by Sherry Turkle, last modified March 23, 2021, https://www.britannica.com/topic/The-Robotic-Moment-2118595.

19. Anu Madgavkar et al., "The Future of Women at Work: Transitions in the Age of Automation," McKinsey Global Institute, New York, June 2019, 24, https://www.mckinsey.com/~/media/mckinsey/featured%20insights/gender%20equality/the%20future%20of%20women%20at%20work%20transitions%20in%20the%20age%20of%20automation/mgi-the-future-of-women-at-work-full-report-june%202019.pdf.

20. "Solving the Talent Shortage: Build, Buy, Borrow and Bridge," 2018 Talent Shortage Survey, Manpower Group, Milwaukee, WI, 2018, 8. Where this number lands in the post-Covid workplace market remains to be seen.

21. Ann Friedman, "Cynthia Breazeal," *The Gentlewoman* 13 (Spring–Summer 2016), https://thegentlewoman.co.uk/library/cynthia-breazeal.

22. Friedman, "Cynthia Breazeal."

23. Friedman, "Cynthia Breazeal."

24. Friedman, "Cynthia Breazeal."

25. Friedman, "Cynthia Breazeal."

26. Dierdre E. Logan et al., "Social Robots for Hospitalized Children," *Pediatrics* 114, no. 1 (July 2019), e20181511.

27. Olivia Barber, Eszter Somogyi, Anne E. McBride, and Leanne Proops, "Children's Evaluations of a Therapy Dog and Biomimetic Robot: Influences of Animistic

Beliefs and Social Interaction," *International Journal of Social Robotics* 13, no. 6 (2020): 1411.

28. Nicholas A. Christakis, "How AI Will Rewire Us," *Atlantic*, April 2019, 10.

29. Alex Bell, Raj Chetty, Xavier Jaravel, Neviana Petkova, and John Van Reenen, "Who Becomes an Inventor in America? The Importance of Exposure to Innovation," *Quarterly Journal of Economics* 134, no. 2 (May 2019): 647, 653.

30. John-John Cabibihan, Hifza Javed, Marcelo Ang Jr., and Sharifah Mariam Aljunied, "Why Robots? A Survey on the Roles and Benefits of Social Robots in the Therapy of Children with Autism," *International Journal of Social Robotics* 5, no. 4 (November 2013): 593.

31. Judith Newman, *To Siri with Love: A Mother, Her Autistic Son, and the Kindness of Machines* (New York: Harper Collins, 2017), 142.

32. Danny Vena, "Mattel Shelves Baby Smart Speaker After Outcry," Yahoo Finance, October 21, 2017, https://au.finance.yahoo.com/news/mattel-shelves -baby-smart-speaker-143400641.html.

33. James Vincent, "Mattel Cancels AI Babysitter After Privacy Complaints," Verge, October 5, 2017, https://www.theverge.com/2017/10/5/16430822/mattel -aristotle-ai-child-monitor-canceled.

34. "The 5 Social Robots Most Used for Helping Children with Autism," Aisory, May 27, 2021, https://aisoy.com/blogs/blog/the-5-social-robots-most-used -for-helping-children-with-autism.

35. Erika Hayasaki, "Is AI Sexist?," *Foreign Policy*, January 17, 2017, http://for-eignpolicy.com/2017/01/16/women-vs-the-machine.

Epilogue

1. Alex Mar, "Love in the Time of Robots," *Wired*, October 17, 2017, https:// www.wired.com/2017/10/hiroshi-ishiguro-when-robots-act-just-like-humans.

2. Hiroshi Ishiguro and Shuichi Nishio, "Building Artificial Humans to Understand Humans," *Journal of Artificial Organs* 10, no. 3 (February 2007): 133–142.

3. Emily M. Bender et al., "On the Dangers of Stochastic Parrots: Can Language Models Be Too Big?," in *FAccT '21: Proceedings of the 2021 ACM Conference on Fairness, Accountability, and Transparency* (New York: Association for Computing Machinery, 2021), 610, https://doi.org/10.1145/3442188.3445922.

4. Sundar Pichai, "AI at Google: Our Principles," *The Keyword* (blog), Google, June 7, 2018, https://www.blog.google/technology/ai/ai-principles/.

5. Tinmit Gebru, "Power Imbalance and the Exclusion of Marginalized Voices in AI," in *Oxford Handbook of Ethics of AI*, edited by Markus D. Dubber, Frank Pasquale, and Sunit Das (New York: Oxford University Press), 261–262.

6. Orly Lobel, "The Renew Deal: The Fall of Regulation and the Rise of Governance in Contemporary Legal Thought," *Minnesota Law Review* 89, no. 2 (2004): 343; Orly Lobel, "Interlocking Regulatory and Industrial Relations: The Governance of Worker Safety," *Administrative Law Review* 57 (2005): 1071; Orly Lobel, "New Governance as Regulatory Governance," in *Oxford Handbook of Governance*, edited by David Levi-Four (Oxford: Oxford University Press, 2012); Orly Lobel and On Amir, "Liberalism and Lifestyle: Informing Regulatory Governance with Behavioral Research," *European Journal of Risk Regulation* 3, no. 1 (2012).

7. *Whittemore v. Cutter*, 29 F. Cas. 1120 (D. Mass. 1813).

8. Orly Lobel, "Biopolitical Opportunities: Datafication and Governance," *Notre Dame Law Review Reflection* 96, no 4 (2021): 181–193.

9. Margaret Mitchell, Simone Wu, Andrew Zaldivar, Parker Barnes, Lucy Vasserman, Ben Hutchinson, Elena Spitzer, Inioluwa Deborah Raji, and Timnit Gebru, "Model Cards for Model Reporting," in *Proceedings of the Conference on Fairness, Accountability, and Transparency* (New York: Association for Computing Machinery, 2019), 220–229, https://dl.acm.org/doi/abs/10.1145/3287560.3287596.

10. Jon Kleinberg et al., "Discrimination in the Age of Algorithms," *Journal of Legal Analysis* 10 (2018): 113–174; Talia B. Gillis and Jann L. Spiess, "Big Data and Discrimination," *University of Chicago Law Review* 86, no. 2 (2019), 459–488.

11. Paul Robinette, Wenchen Li, Robert Allen, Ayanna M. Howard, and Alan R. Wagner, "Overtrust of Robots in Emergency Evacuation Scenarios," in *The Eleventh ACM/IEEE International Conference on Human Robot Interaction* (New York: IEEE Press, 2016), 101–108.

12. Audre Lorde, *Sister Outsider: Essays and Speeches* (Berkeley: The Crossing Press, 1984), 139.

Index

Orly Lobel is the Warren Distinguished Professor of Law, the director of the Center for Employment and Labor Policy, and a founding member of the Center for Intellectual Property Law and Markets at the University of San Diego. She is the award-winning author of *Talent Wants to Be Free: Why We Should Learn to Love Leaks, Raids and Free Riding* (Yale University Press) and *You Don't Own Me: How Mattel v. MGA Entertainment Exposed Barbie's Dark Side* (Norton), which is now being made into a TV series. A graduate of Harvard Law School and Tel Aviv University, Lobel's interdisciplinary research is published widely in the top journals in law, economics, and psychology. Lobel's work has been featured in the *New York Times*, the *Economist*, *BusinessWeek*, the *Wall Street Journal*, *Forbes*, *Fortune*, NPR, *Slate*, *Harvard Business Review*, *The New Yorker*, and the *Financial Times*, and her scholarship has received significant grants. She has consistently been named one of the most-cited younger scholars in the United States and was named one of the 50 Sharpest Minds in Research by *The Marker Magazine*. A prolific speaker and public commentator, Lobel regularly consults top tech companies as well as governments around the world.

PublicAffairs is a publishing house founded in 1997. It is a tribute to the standards, values, and flair of three persons who have served as mentors to countless reporters, writers, editors, and book people of all kinds, including me.

I. F. Stone, proprietor of *I. F. Stone's Weekly*, combined a commitment to the First Amendment with entrepreneurial zeal and reporting skill and became one of the great independent journalists in American history. At the age of eighty, Izzy published *The Trial of Socrates*, which was a national bestseller. He wrote the book after he taught himself ancient Greek.

Benjamin C. Bradlee was for nearly thirty years the charismatic editorial leader of *The Washington Post*. It was Ben who gave the *Post* the range and courage to pursue such historic issues as Watergate. He supported his reporters with a tenacity that made them fearless and it is no accident that so many became authors of influential, best-selling books.

Robert L. Bernstein, the chief executive of Random House for more than a quarter century, guided one of the nation's premier publishing houses. Bob was personally responsible for many books of political dissent and argument that challenged tyranny around the globe. He is also the founder and longtime chair of Human Rights Watch, one of the most respected human rights organizations in the world.

·   ·   ·

For fifty years, the banner of Public Affairs Press was carried by its owner Morris B. Schnapper, who published Gandhi, Nasser, Toynbee, Truman, and about 1,500 other authors. In 1983, Schnapper was described by *The Washington Post* as "a redoubtable gadfly." His legacy will endure in the books to come.

Peter Osnos, *Founder*